From Vietnam, Laos, and Cambodia

A REFUGEE EXPERIENCE IN THE UNITED STATES

Twayne's Immigrant Heritage of America Series

Thomas J. Archdeacon, General Editor

From Vietnam, Laos, and Cambodia

A REFUGEE EXPERIENCE IN THE UNITED STATES

Jeremy Hein

TWAYNE PUBLISHERS
An Imprint of Simon & Schuster Macmillan
New York

Prentice Hall International
London   Mexico City   New Delhi   Singapore   Sydney   Toronto

From Vietnam, Laos, and Cambodia: A Refugee Experience in the United States
Jeremy Hein

Copyright © 1995 by Jeremy Hein

Twayne Publishers
An Imprint of Simon & Schuster Macmillan
866 Third Avenue
New York, New York 10022

Library of Congress Cataloging-in-Publication Data

Hein, Jeremy.
    From Vietnam, Laos, and Cambodia : a refugee experience in the
  United States / Jeremy Hein.
        p.   cm. — (Twayne's Immigrant heritage of America series)
    Includes bibliographical references (p.   ) and index.
    ISBN 0–8057–8432–2. — ISBN 0–8057–8433–0 (pbk.)
    1. Refugees—Indochina.   2. Refugees—United States.   I. Title.
  II. Series.
  HV640.5.I5H44   1995
  362.87'089'959—dc20   94–41960
                                                            CIP

The paper used in this publication meets the minimum requirements of
American National Standard for Information Sciences—Permanence of Paper
for Printed Library Materials, ANSI Z39.48-1984. ∞™

10 9 8 7 6 5 4 3 2 1 (alk. paper)
10 9 8 7 6 5 4 3 2 1 (pbk.: alk. paper)

Printed in the United States of America.

For Ronald John Hein,
who will both read and live this book

Contents

Acknowledgments

I would like to thank the many refugees who talked with me about their experiences, especially those who welcomed me into their communities and families. Their openness was personally gratifying and has allowed me to educate others about them. I also thank Carol Chin and Barbara Sutton of Twayne Publishers and Thomas J. Archdeacon, the editor of Twayne's Immigrant Heritage of America Series, for their advice and comments on how to combine firsthand experiences with the scholarly literature and to produce this book.

Map 1

Southeast Asia and Neighboring Countries

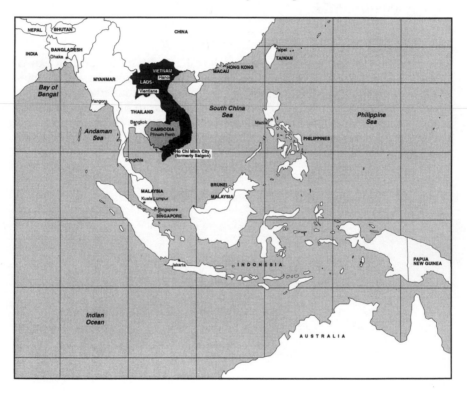

Assimilation and Ethnic-Resilience Models of Migration and Adaptation

People who flee persecution and then cannot return to their homeland for a long period of time are refugees. The refugee experience is ancient, but the number of people uprooted by political violence and warfare increased dramatically during the twentieth century. From 1900 to 1947 the largest refugee flows occurred in Europe, particularly following World Wars I and II. These European refugees resulted from ethnic persecution, the redrawing of national borders, and the creation of Communist states.

From 1947 (when the partition of India created the first contemporary Third World refugee crisis) to about 1990 refugees increasingly came from developing countries in Africa, Asia, Latin America, and the Caribbean (Zolberg et al. 1989). The immediate causes of these Third World refugees were often similar to those that produced European refugees, such as changing national borders. But the underlying causes were different. As European powers granted colonies independence, often following a war, conflicts arose within these new states and with their neighbors. Superpower conflict between the United States and the former Soviet Union became an even more serious source of refugees, as each state sought influence around the globe.

Between 1975 and 1990 more than 2 million refugees left Vietnam, Laos, and Cambodia, and about 1.5 million eventually resettled in Australia, Western Europe, and North America. Because these countries once formed the French colony of Indochina, refugees from the region are frequently called Indochinese. The term *Southeast Asian refugees* also is used to describe these people. But there are refugees from Southeast Asia other than from the former Indochina (e.g., Burma). Thus *Southeast Asian refugees* cannot be used as a synonym for refugees from Vietnam, Laos, and Cambodia. *Indochinese refugees* is the more precise term for this population provided that one is cognizant of the historical and cultural differences among people from Vietnam, Laos, and Cambodia.

The resettlement of Indochinese refugees in North America, Western Europe, and Australia was a unique solution to a contemporary refugee crisis (Hein 1993b). For most the world's 25 million refugees, resettlement in a country of permanent asylum, typically in Western Europe or North America,

1

is a much less likely solution than repatriation—the forced or voluntary return of refugees to their country of origin. Yet aside from family reunification, refugee status is now one of the primary means of gaining legal admission to Western countries. Refugees constitute approximately one in six international migrants admitted to the United States, while the ratio is one for one in France. More refugees arrive in Sweden and Germany than do immigrants. Between 1975 and 1991 more than 2.8 million refugees and asylum seekers gained permanent residence in the West (U.S. Committee on Refugees 1993). About 53 percent of them were from Vietnam, Laos, and Cambodia, and approximately two-thirds of these Indochinese refugees settled in the United States. Although Southeast Asia is not at present a major source of new refugees, the experience of Indochinese refugees in the United States is central to understanding what happens in the long run to refugees resettled abroad.

The Indochinese migration is one of the best examples of a refugee crisis owing to the cold war—the political rivalry between the United States and the former Soviet Union that began after World War II and ended with the demise of the Soviet Union in 1991. When France granted independence to Laos and Cambodia in 1953, and to Vietnam in 1954, American foreign policy sought to prevent Communist influence and support pro-American governments in the region. Despite the extensive use of American military forces in all three countries during the 1960s and early 1970s, in 1975 Communist North Vietnam conquered South Vietnam, Communist guerrillas captured the capital of Cambodia, and the Laotian government collapsed in the face of Communist opposition. The more than 1 million Indochinese refugees who subsequently resettled in the United States came not for higher wages and modern lifestyles, as do many immigrants, but because the United States has a responsibility for their fate different from that of other refugees who arrived during the cold war (Hein 1992).

While the international and foreign-policy context of their migration distinguishes Indochinese refugees from other refugees and immigrants, all share a common experience once they reach the United States: an adaptation process characterized by cultural change and social conflict, integration and pluralism. Which of these themes is the central, definitive element has always been an issue in the study of American immigration history and race and ethnic relations. But beginning in the 1980s, the debate renewed over whether the United States is a nation unified by a core civic culture (Fuchs 1990) or a multicultural society divided by racial and ethnic inequalities (Takaki 1993)—or some combination of the two (see Rose 1993 for the range of perspectives on this issue).

One does not have to look far for symbols of Indochinese refugees rapidly integrating into American society. In 1992 Eugene H. Trinh became the first Vietnamese-born space shuttle astronaut. That same year Choua Lee, a Hmong woman, was elected to the St. Paul, Minnesota, school board, marking the first electoral victory of an Indochinese refugee.

Yet events involving Indochinese refugees also reveal the worst features of American pluralism. In 1989 a white man with an assault rifle killed five Cambodian and Vietnamese children in a Stockton, California, school yard. He wounded 30 others before killing himself. Two years latter three members of a Chinese-Vietnamese gang took 40 people hostage in a Sacramento electronics store. Before being killed by sheriffs, they shot to death three of the hostages and wounded nine others. Integration and pluralism is a fundamental tension in immigrant and refugee adaptation in the United States, and the Indochinese refugee experience both illustrates this tension and suggests new ways of conceptualizing it.

The Assimilation Model: Integration through Cultural Change

The oldest perspective on immigrant and refugee adaptation is the assimilation model, which traces its roots to the works of sociologists at the University of Chicago in the first few decades of the 1900s, particularly W. I. Thomas and Florian Znaniecki (1927) and Robert E. Park (1950; 1967). For the Chicago school of sociology, migration caused uprooting and thus adjustment problems for immigrants, such as family breakdown and disorganized communities. Assimilation—replacing one's original culture with the culture of another group—solved these problems by eventually merging the newcomers with the native population. What most characterizes the writings of these sociologists is the belief in the desirability of assimilation. Writing in 1914, shortly after the peak years of European migration to the United States, Park described the liberating effect of assimilation for newcomers:

> It removes the social taboo, permits the individual to move into strange groups, and thus facilitates new and adventurous contacts. In obliterating the external signs [of cultural difference], which in secondary groups seem to be the sole basis for [inequalities based on] caste and class distinctions, it realizes, for the individual, the principle of *laissez-faire, laissez-aller*. . . . As a matter of fact, the ease and rapidity with which aliens, under existing conditions in the United States, have been able to assimilate themselves to the customs and manners of American life have enabled this country to swallow and digest every sort of normal human difference, except the purely external ones, like the color of the skin. (Park 1967, 116)

Milton Gordon's *Assimilation in American Life* (1964) broke with the Chicago school by asserting that there was no inevitable drift toward the complete assimilation of immigrants and their descendants. Instead, Gordon distinguished between changes in behavior and identification (cultural assimilation) and changes in interpersonal contacts and organizational affiliations (structural assimilation). The overall pattern of group relations in the United States, according to Gordon, was the persistence of family and associations within ethnic communities (structural pluralism) yet pervasive adoption of American culture. Seeking to advise those working with European immigrants (in an era before gender role equality), Gordon advocated recognizing the inevitability of some structural pluralism, while promoting cultural assimilation:

> The basic goal should be the adjustment of the immigrant to American culture and institutions in those areas of secondary group and

institutional contact which permit him to obtain and keep a job commensurate with his potential and training, to receive appropriate retraining and education where necessary, to perform adequately his role as a potential future citizen of both the nation and the local community, and to raise his children in ways which will neither do emotional violence to the traditions of the homeland nor subvert the family socialization process congenial to child-rearing in a basically middle-class American culture. (Gordon 1964, 243)

Herbert J. Gans's *The Urban Villagers* (1962) is the best community study to document Gordon's conception of assimilation in American life. Although the second- and third-generation Italian Americans of Boston's West End were culturally assimilated (e.g., they spoke English and felt little attachment to Italy), they were not structurally assimilated because social interaction remained confined to their Italian-American peer groups, families, and neighborhood. Some years later Gans (1979) extended this thesis by arguing that ethnicity without a basis in family and neighborhood was merely symbolic. In this interpretation the many whites who continue to label themselves with a European ancestry are nonetheless assimilated because their identity has no social or material basis (see Hirschman 1983 for a complete review of the assimilation literature).

The Ethnic-Resilience Model: Pluralism Rooted in Ethnic Conflict and Inequality

Nathan Glazer and Daniel P. Moynihan challenged the view of America as a monolithic culture in their now classic book *Beyond the Melting Pot* (1963). Ethnicity still mattered to the Irish, Italians, and other ethnic groups in New York City, they argued, because it served as the basis for many social and especially political institutions. Groups that maintained their ethnicity were better able to compete for power in America's largest city. Yet *Beyond the Melting Pot* did not entirely refute the assimilation perspective because it still used the majority group of Anglo-Protestants as the basis of comparison. According to Glazer and Moynihan, some ethnic groups had cultural skills superior to those of the majority group, such as the Irish in politics and the Jews in business. Conversely, they argued that Puerto Ricans and African Americans were handicapped by endemic social problems rooted more in their cultures than in racism, economic changes, or urban conditions at the time of arrival to the city. Thus while maintaining that religious, racial, and ethnic pluralism was central to social life, *Beyond the Melting Pot* did not develop an alternative model of immigrant adaptation because it overemphasized cultural differences as the basis for pluralism, rather than inequality and conflict.

This alternative perspective emphasizing the relationships among inequality, conflict, and pluralism developed during the 1970s and 1980s. Research on Asians and Hispanics in the United States suggested that the retention of ethnicity promoted adaptation more than did assimilation because dominant groups often exploit immigrants and ethnic minorities rather than allow them to assimilate. Edna Bonacich (1972; and Modell 1980) was one of the first researchers to move in this direction. She formulated a theory of middleman minorities to explain why ethnicity, among other factors, enabled some groups to serve as economic mediators between dominant and subordinate groups. Ivan Light (1972) presented a more encompassing notion of an ethnic economy by examining how ethnic communities support businesses through indigenous savings systems.

The greatest blow to the assimilation model came from the work of Alejandro Portes and associates (Portes 1984; Wilson and Martin 1982; Wilson and Portes 1980), particularly the publication of *Latin Journey* (Portes and Bach 1985). They developed the ethnic enclave thesis using the case of Cubans in South Florida, and have suggested its applicability to Jews, Japanese, and Koreans (Portes and Manning 1986). Enclaves are immigrant or refugee communities that support an internal economy sufficient to provide members with jobs and investment capital without recourse to the larger society. Immigrants who work in enclaves often receive better jobs and higher pay given their skills, education, and knowledge of English than if they worked for natives (see Min 1987 and Aldrich and Waldinger 1990 for reviews of the literature on enclaves and other forms of economic adaptation).

Because non-Europeans experience prejudice and discrimination even when they seek assimilation in the United States, Portes and associates argue that the economic, social, and political interests of immigrants are best served by retaining ethnicity and emphasizing pluralism. They believe assimilation is a mythology and propose an ethnic-resilience model to explain how experiences of inequality lead immigrants and refugees to use ethnicity as a means for collective advancement:

> From the ethnic-resilience viewpoint, the early function that immigrant communities play are undeniable, but the bonds of ethnic solidarity among immigrants extend beyond the early years. . . . Precisely as a consequence of socialization into the realities of American society, immigrants are made aware of the convenience of continuing their solidarity within their own communities. Having understood that theirs is a disadvantaged position and that this disadvantage is legitimized by an ideology that defines their race and ethnicity as inferior, immigrants will hold on to ethnic ties long after the early days of arrival as a logical protective strategy. (Portes and Bach 1985, 300)

The Assimilation Model Reconsidered

Despite the rise of an alternative model of immigrant adaptation emphasizing pluralism, the assimilation model remains widely used in research on immigrants and their descendants. Richard D. Alba (1990) has linked assimilation among whites to the formation of a new group in the United States, "European Americans." Mary Waters (1990) emphasizes how whites use ethnicity to give themselves a sense of social uniqueness through membership in a "costless community," although ethnicity has little impact on their lives. But the continued use of the assimilation perspective is not confined to research on Americans of European ancestry. Finding that Chinese, Japanese, and Filipino immigrants in California earn more after becoming U.S. citizens than do European immigrants in the state, Victor Nee and Jimy Sanders (1985) concluded that "our analysis supports the view that Asian Americans, as a group, are on the road to assimilation in the U.S." (89). Douglas S. Massey (1981) reviewed the literature on immigration to the United States since the reform of immigration laws in 1965 and found much evidence of a reduction of differences between immigrants and natives over time, such as in fertility rates, familial roles, intermarriage, and segregation. He concludes that most Asian and Hispanic migrants "appear to be well-launched on the path to assimilation with the core of American life" (77–78).

When shorn of the Chicago school's ethnocentrism, which presumed that immigrants should become like natives, the assimilation model remains useful for understanding immigrant adaptation. The assimilation model makes the American nation the focus of analysis and seeks to explain how immigrants change when living in this new society—a then-and-now contrast best visualized as snapshots of immigrants upon arrival and then 10 years later. The main feature of this model is integration through cultural change. Despite its continued utility, this model contains assumptions that require reconsideration.

First, the assimilation model presumes that the host society has no relationship to the sending society and that migrants end their ties with their homeland when they leave. Taking a more global view of migration, the ethnic-resilience model has shown that a host society like the United States has a range of economic, political, and cultural relationships to countries around the world (Portes 1990). These relationships influence whether a country sends migrants and the particular characteristics of these migrants, and Indochinese refugees are an ideal example. Chapter 2 of this book documents the U.S. military and political role in Southeast Asia from 1954 to 1975, which created the country's responsibility for the refugees who subsequently fled. Chapter 3 examines conditions in Vietnam, Laos, and Cambodia after the advent of new Communist regimes, which caused the first large-scale international migration in the region's history. These events from 1954 to about 1980 ultimately led to the admission to the United States of more than 1 million Indochinese refugees and also profoundly shaped these people's adaptation.

Second, the assimilation model makes an overly rigid distinction between the sending and host society. Because it focuses disproportionately on cultural change, the model inherently presents immigrants and refugees as bringing cultural values, norms, and institutions with them to a host society. The image is one of migrants transplanting their culture from one society to another, as if transported in suitcases and brought out like ethnic garb at the appropriate occasion. Reconstruction is a more accurate description of the formation of ethnic institutions within immigrant and refugee communities. The genesis of a Cambodian Buddhist temple in Chicago demonstrates the innovation required to put together a key communal institution in a new locale (Chapter 4). Indeed, the very process of rebuilding the temple inevitably led to its change as members adapted it to meet a new set of needs. While the impetus to re-create an institution like a Buddhist temple stems from homeland traditions, the resulting institution defies simple classification as part of the homeland or the host society.

A third feature of the assimilation model is its focus on the adaptation of the immigrant as an individual, particularly how he or she differs from who they were upon arrival. The individual needs to be studied when tracing the intersection of immigrant adaptation and the life course—the sequence of social experiences entailed by human development from birth to death. For example, age at arrival determines whether a refugee's primary socialization occurred in the homeland, the United States, or both locations (Chapter 7) and if the refugee is eligible to attend public school or must forgo a formal education (Chapter 8). Yet one of the most important insights of the ethnic-resilience model is the collective dimension of adaptation among international migrants (Portes and Bach 1985; Portes and Rumbaut 1990). Refugees and immigrants belong to households, families, and communities, and analysis of their adaptation should focus on these networks (Tilly 1990). Indochinese refugees' geographic settlement patterns (Chapter 4), economic cooperation in shrimp fishing (Chapter 5), formation of mutual assistance associations (Chapter 6), and renewal of kin and fictive kin relations (Chapter 7) all evidence that migrants adapt as members of groups rather than as individuals.

Fourth, implicit in the assimilation model is the premise that the United States has a core culture for migrants to integrate into—presumably that of whites of European ancestry, as they are the majority of the population. This assumption is inconsistent with the realities of contemporary urban America. Ethnic minorities account for 47 percent of the population in the country's 10 largest cities. Blacks are the majority in one of these cities and Hispanics in another. When combined, blacks, Hispanics, Asians, and Native Americans are the majority of the population in three of the other largest cities. As a result, in many urban areas international migrants most frequently come in contact with native minorities like African Americans, as well as other non-European immigrants (Lamphere 1992). Indochinese refugees' settlement in neighborhoods in New York City (Chapter 4) and Philadelphia (Chapter 5) and their work in a multiethnic warehouse in Chicago (Chapter 8) require extensive interaction with native minorities and other migrants. Each of these cases demonstrates that the presence of non-European populations was more important in shaping the refugees' adaptation than was contact with whites of European ancestry.

A final feature of the assimilation model is the image of Americanization as a voluntary process that increases the more migrants become like natives. This portrayal does not account well for the extreme intolerance that many Asian and Hispanic migrants experience. Research using the ethnic-resilience model demonstrates that migrants' perception of discrimination and conception of themselves as an ethnic minority are strongest among those who should be the most assimilated, such as migrants with more education and longer residence (Portes 1984; Hein 1994). Antipathy toward Indochinese refugees results much more from traditional racism and urban competition than from a legacy of resentment resulting from the Vietnam War (Chapter 5). Anti-Indochinese incidents became more, not less, severe from 1975 to 1990. Moreover, Indochinese refugees have used the courts to combat discrimination on the basis of race and national origin (Chapter 6). The assimilation model, while not the intellectual relic that many portray it to be, misses much in the adaptation of Indochinese refugees.

The Ethnic-Resilience Model Reconsidered

The ethnic-resilience model clearly provides many substantial advances over the assimilation model. It makes immigrants the focus of analysis and examines how inequalities among racial and ethnic groups in the United States lead immigrants to emphasize pluralism over integration. In contrast to the Old

World/New World distinction at the heart of the assimilation model, the ethnic-resilience model is based on conflict among groups in a social, political, and economic hierarchy. Yet the ethnic-resilience model also contains assumptions that require reconsideration.

First, the ethnic-resilience model exaggerates the solidarity in ethnic communities. Immigrants and refugees of the same ethnicity vary widely in their social, political, and class backgrounds. These cleavages often yield economic exploitation among community members (Sanders and Nee 1987), as well as "contentious, stratified, and segmented communities that resist unification" (Gold 1992, 230). The Vietnamese who arrived in 1975 were disproportionately government officials, military officers, and the wealthy, and they have experienced more rapid economic progress than later waves (Chapter 8). Within Vietnamese communities, conflicts over leadership roles and homeland politics have lead to acrimony and even murder (Chapter 6). Moreover, the very institutions in refugee communities that provide members with support are, paradoxically, the same ones that become sites of intense conflict over power, resources, and cultural change (such as the Cambodian Buddhist temple discussed in Chapters 4 and 6).

Second, the model conceptualizes immigrant adaptation as primarily a search for economic attainment. Very much neglected in some of the major works using the ethnic-resilience perspective is migrants' family and kin relations—an area of immigrant life no less important than the workplace (Chapter 7). Furthermore, the model's conceptualization of economic adaptation is limited to income and occupation. Jobs are important not only for their economic value but because workplaces have cultures that shape refugees' self-identity and understanding of American society and culture (Chapter 8). The social organization of work, as opposed to its remunerative value, is especially salient for migrants who previously worked in agriculture and now find themselves in factories or low-skill service jobs (Chapter 8).

Third, inherent to the ethnic-resilience model is the assumption that migrants resist assimilation while natives pressure them to do so. American culture, however, contains values and norms that many Asian and Hispanic migrants find worthy of adoption. Indochinese women experience more egalitarian gender roles in the United States than in their homeland, while youths experience greater freedom from age seniority (Chapter 7). These cultural changes entail gender and generational conflict, particularly over divorce and arranged marriages (subjects addressed in Chapter 7). Nonetheless, they evidence the liberalizing influence of American culture on immigrants. In addition, American courts have tended to take a foreign-born plaintiff and defendant's culture into consideration when making decisions, at times even undermining the legitimacy of some American norms (Chapter 6).

Related to the preceding assumption is a fourth: a conception of ethnicity as nationality rather than a common culture, a way of life embodied in values, norms, and other beliefs. Culture occupies an ambiguous place in the study of immigrant adaptation, being totally rejected by some (S. Steinberg 1989) while seen as an important factor, albeit only one of many, by others (Perlmann 1988). While the assimilation model overemphasizes cultural change as an explanation of how groups integrate into American society, the concept of culture is totally absent from the ethnic-resilience model. Values and norms do play a role in immigrant adaptation. To resurrect Buddhism in the United States, Cambodians struggle with American culture's value on materialism versus simplicity and individual choice versus tradition (Chapter 4). Vietnamese women select forms of employment consistent with their cultural roles as wives and mothers, while Cambodians seek to combine the American value of competition with their own culture's emphasis on respect for others (Chapter 8).

Finally, the ethnic-resilience model primarily describes national-level patterns, as if place of adaptation did not matter, and emphasizes the skills immigrants and refugees bring with them rather than the opportunities presented in a given locale. Urban conditions play an important role in shaping the formation of immigrant communities and economic pursuits (Waldinger 1992). In Chicago social and economic changes at the city and neighborhood levels transformed the Uptown area from a center for drugs and prostitution to a thriving home for Indochinese families and businesses (Chapter 4). Yet these same conditions also created a particular type of ethnic community: an initial place of settlement until better accommodations could be found, but a permanent, even expanding, locale for Asian American businesses as a whole.

This critique of the dominant models of immigrant and refugee adaptation leads to the key insight of this book. At least in the case of Indochinese refugees, there is not as much integration and cultural loss as the assimilation model would suggest, but there also is not as much pluralism and conflict as the ethnic-resilience model would have one believe.

Scope, Methods, and Data

While broad in scope, this book does not cover the important topic of mental health, a particular problem for refugees (see Vega and Rumbaut 1991). One reason for this omission is the highly technical nature of the subject, such as the comparability of various psychological instruments. A second reason is the questionable validity of using Western testing instruments on newly arrived Asians who have culturally specific conceptions of mental health (Dunnigan et al. 1993). The final reason is methodological. Although making extensive use of secondary sources, the data in this book are primarily derived from ethnographic and fieldwork methods. With the exception of Chapter 2 (on U.S. military intervention in Southeast Asia) and Chapter 6 (on conflict between the refugees and natives), all chapters contain information I obtained by interacting with refugees.

Some of the firsthand material came through the standard technique of open-ended questions asked during interviews with refugees selected on the basis of their experiences, such as 18 Indochinese caseworkers employed by seven resettlement agencies in San Francisco. I also used another standard data-gathering technique: taking an accepted role in order to participate in a social milieu of sociological interest—in my case a volunteer for a New York City resettlement agency who visited newly arrived refugees to familiarize them with their neighborhood and to help solve problems. The text notes information derived through these two methods.

The primary source of the firsthand material is sustained contact with individuals and families over several years, as well as participation in events in which I, too, was an actor. For this reason, most of the firsthand material is about Cambodian refugees. I was drawn to this group because of my father's experiences as a refugee from Nazi Germany and because of the parallels between the genocide of Jews in Europe during the early 1940s and the holocaust that occurred in Cambodia between 1975 and 1978. Then, in 1988, I married a Cambodian woman. Her experiences under the Khmer Rouge are the core of Chapter 3, while her work in a warehouse is a portion of the material in Chapter 8. With her, I frequently participated in events sponsored by Chicago's Cambodian community, such as weddings, funerals, and religious services at a Cambodian Buddhist temple. In this way I came to know many Cambodians in Chicago, as well as in Minnesota, Michigan, Ohio, Massachusetts, and even France. Our son was born in 1992, 10 years to the day that my wife arrived in this country. I now consider myself part of the Indochinese refugee experience in the United States.

Reliance on personal contact for data has inevitably limited the geographic scope of my qualitative material. As indicated earlier, my contacts and experiences primarily occurred in the Midwest and on the East Coast. The plurality or majority of all groups among Indochinese refugees live in California. Similarly, my contacts were mostly, but not exclusively, with Cambodians, who account for only about 15 percent of all Indochinese in the United States.

I have tried to compensate for this geographic and ethnic focus through exhaustive coverage of the social science research and newspaper reporting on the other groups and other locales. Yet what my firsthand material lacks in representativeness is made up for by access to experiences often hidden from social scientists and journalists. My personal contact with Cambodians—who knew I was studying them and whose names I have changed—has enabled me to get past the "stories" refugees develop for the numerous individuals who want to know about them, including immigration officials, caseworkers, and public aid personnel. Social scientists and journalists also receive these stories that simplify, idealize, distort, or even hide the refugees' true experiences and activities. To get behind the "official accounts" required knowing refugees as people rather than subjects. Instead of exaggerating the distinction between researcher and subject in an attempt to demonstrate scientific objectivity, this book is admittedly dedicated to bringing the two together. The result in this case, I believe, is greater insight into the experiences of Indochinese refugees in the United States.

two
   —

American Communist Containment
in Southeast Asia

Before Indochinese refugees began migrating to the United States, the American government was extensively involved with refugee migration and resettlement in Southeast Asia. In fact, America's 20-year history of intervention in Vietnam, Laos, and Cambodia began and ended with refugees. In 1954 the U.S. Navy launched Operation Exodus to help France transport 800,000 Vietnamese from Communist North Vietnam to pro-West South Vietnam following the partition of the country. In April 1975 Marine combat helicopters initiated Operation Frequent Wind to rescue American diplomats and several thousand Vietnamese employees in Saigon from the advancing North Vietnamese Army (NVA). During the preceding decade, however, the United States created refugee populations in Southeast Asia as it used migration, often forced, to achieve its military and political objectives.

France, not the United States, was the first Western power to intervene in Vietnam, Laos, and Cambodia. French colonization of Indochina began with the invasion of the southern portion of Vietnam during the 1850s, and the conquest continued for three decades. Cambodia came under French dominance during the 1860s, and Laos followed in the 1890s. France established the Union of Indochina in 1887, creating a single, colonial government for all three regions.

Before World War I, Indochina was primarily of geopolitical value to the French empire—a presence in the orient comparable to that of Hong Kong for the British. After World War I France sought, however, to rebuild its war-shattered economy through exploitation of its colonies. During the 1920s plantations, industries, and taxation increased dramatically. After defeat by Germany in 1940, France ceded the colonies to Japan but then temporarily returned to power in 1945. French and Vietnamese troops fought against a predominately Communist national independence movement for nine years before conceding defeat in 1954.

American intervention in Indochina began with support for Vietnamese guerrillas fighting Japanese occupation during World War II. But when France resumed control of its colony after 1945, the United States provided financial and military aid for France's war against Vietnamese nationalists. Political developments in Asia following World War II heightened American interests in Vietnam and its neighbors. The Chinese Revolution in 1949, which brought a Communist government to power, led to accusations within the American government over "losing China." Then, in 1950, North Korea invaded South Korea, leading the United States into its first war against communism. Containing communism emerged as the leading goal of U.S. foreign policy, particularly after the partition of Vietnam in 1954. Fears that the fall of South Vietnam would inevitably result in more Communist states in Southeast Asia—the so-called domino effect—led the United States to replace France as the dominant Western power in the region.

Refugees and the Partition of Vietnam, 1954

The deterioration of the French military position in Tonkin, soon to become North Vietnam, provided the first opportunity for U.S. foreign policy makers to use migration to attain military and political goals. In March 1954 French troops relocated 50,000 villagers from sensitive combat zones. Since the United States already funded 80 percent of the French war effort in Indochina, this costly resettlement project fell within the domain of American foreign service officials. The American consul in Hanoi wrote the State Department that "the situation appeared to offer the opportunity for U.S. aid to make a timely and effective contribution. . . . Embassy reported that the country team had decided that FOA [Foreign Operations Administration Mission to Vietnam] should provide aid but that the U.S. should avoid identification with the relocation program" (U.S. Department of State 1982a, 1127n1).

American diplomats perceived refugee relocation as a chance for the country to do something at which it was good. Aid to displaced persons in post–World War II Europe had begun rebuilding war-torn economies and cementing ties among the new allies (Barnet 1983). Refugee aid in Vietnam also might demonstrate American beneficence. The FOA proceeded to fund six American voluntary agencies to provide relief programs in Vietnam, including two that would assist Vietnamese civilians during the 1960s and then resettle refugees in the United States after 1975. With the partition of Vietnam in July 1954, U.S. foreign-policy makers seized the chance to undertake relocation and relief efforts on a national scale.

At the insistence of Secretary of State John Foster Dulles, the Geneva Accords that ended the French Indochina War contained a provision providing "for the peaceful and humane transfer, under international supervision, of those people desiring to be moved from one zone to another of Vietnam" (U.S. Department of State 1982b, 1758). Article 14-d allowed 300 days for the withdrawal of French troops from the North and the relocation of civilians to the South. But the agreement required France, and not the United States, to meet this provision. The day the American choice for prime minister of South Vietnam, Ngo Dinh Diem, took office, French forces withdrew from the predominately Catholic northern provinces of Nam Dinh and Phat Diem, thus exposing the villagers to the Communist Vietminh. In mid-July, Diem (himself a Catholic) reported that the French Army was obstructing northerners from reaching relocation points on the coast, and he appealed for American intervention to ensure the resettlement provisions (U.S. Department of State 1982a, 1783). Ambassador Donald Heath in Saigon relayed that Diem "feared the French could not handle refugee problem of such magnitude, but US with its experience in human relief and its organizing ability could" (U.S. Department of State 1982a, 1873). After Diem officially requested President Eisenhower's assistance in August, refugee specialists from the State Department's European, Middle East, and Far East operations flew to Saigon. Between July 1954 and May 1955 ships of the U.S. Seventh Fleet carried 150,000 refugees south.

Although the United States transported less than 20 percent of the 800,000 Vietnamese who migrated to South Vietnam, Operation Exodus snowballed into resettlement aid to all the refugees: "The United States is also prepared to provide as far as possible material help needed to enable refugees from Viet Minh domination to resume existence under their chosen government with maximum opportunity to add to the strength of that government through their own efforts" (U.S. Department of State 1954, 241). The skilled workers among the refugees generally made their own resettlement arrangements in or around Saigon, while military and government personnel found jobs with the new South Vietnamese administration. Eighty-five percent of the refugees, however, were farmers and fishers (Luong 1959, 52). Using its own criteria of need, including the date the refugee arrived in the South, the FOA estimated that "660,000 refugees were eligible for assistance" (Cardinaux 1959, 87). More than 20 years before the resettlement of Vietnamese refugees in the United States, the American government was already managing Vietnamese migration and selectively providing assistance to some of the migrants.

Between 1954 and 1956, 80 percent of U.S. nonmilitary aid to Vietnam was spent on the transportation and resettlement of these refugees (Lindholm 1959, 317). But this aid quickly came to be seen as economic development, thus making refugee resettlement the first step in what would become two decades of nation building. In February 1955 State Department representatives from several Vietnam operations concluded that the "usual type U.S. escapee program with emphasis on 'American impact' form of relief, care, and transfer of escapees is unsuitable to this situation" (U.S. Department of State 1982b, 88). This oblique reference—"usual type"—is to the escapee quotas allocated for Eastern European refugees under the Immigration and Nationality Act of 1952. Rather than encouraging a continuing flow of refugees, which was the U.S. policy toward new Communist countries in Eastern Europe, State Department officials would pursue economic development for those Vietnamese refugees who had already escaped and nation-building efforts for South Vietnam as a whole. By the summer of 1956, 91 percent of the "recognized refugees" were participating in more than 150 development projects (U.S. Senate 1965, 46). One year later 319 resettlement villages had been established under U.S. auspices for 500,000 refugees (Luong 1959, 52).

The Cai San project was the largest and most symbolic of America's nation-building agenda in South Vietnam. A miniature "green revolution" (a 1960s buzzword for Third World development projects), this agricultural community on 150,000 acres in the Mekong Delta eventually numbered nearly 100,000 refugees. "Whole villages sent a representative to Saigon to volunteer their names" for the project. Refugees from 13 provinces were eventually included, although the majority came from the Saigon area (U.S. Senate 1965, 38–39). U.S. agencies provided seed, fertilizer, and 100 tractors to clear 90,000 acres of rice land. According to the director of the refugee program, "The Cai San project presented an entirely new approach to the integration problem. Increasing attention was given to technical matters, to economic aspects of the program: The relief provisions still in existence moved more and more into the background" (Cardinaux 1959, 90).

American assistance to the refugees, while fulfilling humanitarian goals, deepened U.S. alignment with the increasingly authoritarian government of South Vietnam. Project sites included "uncultivated" land that could be requisitioned by the government and land that had "formerly" been under Vietminh control. By resettling refugees in the highlands, the Government of Vietnam (GVN) hoped to bring this strategic but sparsely populated region under its control (Jackson 1969). Between 1957 and 1961 the GVN sent 200,000 persons, including many northern refugees, to remote settlements "to build a 'living wall' between lowland centers of population and the jungle and mountain redoubts of dissidents" (*Pentagon Papers* 1971, 1: 255). In aiding refugees from North Vietnam, the United States contributed to the political machinations of the GVN.

The resettlement villages for the refugees also were located in regions inhabited by the Hoa Hao and the Cao Dai religious sects, which had fought the central government for greater autonomy, and in areas with Chinese and Cambodian minorities. Not only were the refugees predominately Catholic and resettled in groups that kept former villages and parishes intact, but they received substantial government assistance while "old settlers" in the resettlement regions did not (U.S. Senate 1965, 26). In 1962 a U.S. Marine intelligence officer noted that in a western province "helicopters were sent almost everyday to several fortified Catholic communities in the area, laden with a shopping list ranging from barbed wire to beer. These were militantly anti-Communist refugees from the North, in a surrounding sea of antagonized Buddhists, Hoa Hao and ethnic Cambodians, and their only reliable means of supply were our U.S. helicopters" (Marr 1972, 203–204). Even a Vietnamese government report concluded that the northern refugees formed "a distinct group" in South Vietnam (U.S. Senate 1965, 398). The resettlement of northern refugees in South Vietnam thus increased the polarization of Saigon from the rest of the country and allied the United States with one faction, as Catholics comprised only about 10 percent of the Vietnamese population.

The settlement of northern refugees under American auspices had profound political consequences for South Vietnam and the United States. Those refugees from the middle and upper class formed the core of Diem's political machine, both in Saigon (Karnow 1983) and as replacements for local leaders in the hinterlands who were unsympathetic to his policies (Jumper 1957). In time, the northern refugees constituted the political core of South Vietnam, and "under cover of the Diem regime the U.S. first forged its alliance with this isolated elite" (Fitzgerald 1973b, 552). The link between U.S. foreign policy and a Westernized elite from central and northern Vietnam was established in the 1954–56 period, but it continued in the Vietnamese governments that followed Diem's assassination in 1963 (Wurfel 1967).

The demographic, fiscal, and political scope of the North-Vietnamese refugee program inevitably meant that U.S. government officials concerned with Vietnam would link it with military policy. In April 1955 debate increased in Washington over the extent of American commitment to the GVN. The Defense Department saw Diem as a poor political ally and Vietnam as a military risk, yet General J. Lawton Collins, President Eisenhower's special ambassador to Vietnam, acknowledged "that the U.S. has a moral obligation in relation to the 500,000 Vietnamese refugees and that it would be difficult for the U.S. to withdraw from Viet-Nam" (U.S. Department of State 1982b, 286). President John F. Kennedy took the same position to explain the "why" of U.S. involvement in Vietnam at a July 1963 news conference: "You may want to think of our support to Viet-Nam as American help to the nearly 1 million Vietnamese refugees who fled North Viet-Nam in 1954 and 1955 to avoid living under a communist regime" (*Pentagon Papers* 1971, 2: 827). Aid to Vietnamese refugees in the 1950s created the path for American military intervention in Vietnam in the 1960s.

Following Operation Exodus, U.S. intervention in Vietnamese migration worked through the GVN policies that were concentrating the Vietnamese population into *agrovilles* (1959–61) and strategic hamlets (1962–63). Both programs created fortified settlements to better combat Communist guerrillas, and they entailed tremendous internal migration to achieve this goal. The GVN claimed that 4,322,000 people had been relocated by late 1962 (*Pentagon Papers* 1971, 2: 157). This strategy was hatched by Diem and his brother Nhu to control political activity in the country. Although the United States did not initiate the programs, senior officials in the State and Defense departments supported them (Karnow 1983). The U.S. Operations Mission (1962) also noted that "resettlement of families from areas of overpopulation to areas of agricultural promise is an integral part of the development plan" (18). Even into the early 1960s American diplomats continued to view migration as a nation-building tool and, as had the French before them, a means to distribute the Vietnamese population concentrated along the coast. With the escalation of the war, however, American military and civilian leaders began to take their own initiatives regarding the migration of Indochinese peoples. The United States both created refugee flows in South Vietnam, Laos, and Cambodia and, to varying degrees, sought to relieve them.

Pacification in South Vietnam, 1965–1968

Actual U.S. direction of migration movements in South Vietnam hinged on the readiness of the American government to send people there, not simply money and memoranda. In the fall of 1961 President Kennedy made the fateful decision to increase U.S. advisors to South Vietnam in the hopes of propping up the Diem regime. He followed the advice of General Maxwell Taylor, who favored a "limited partnership" with South Vietnam, and ignored those in the State Department, such as Chester Bowles, who argued for a negotiated solution to conflict with North Vietnam. U.S. advisory staff in South Vietnam rose from 3,205 in 1961 to 9,000 in 1962, and 1,600 Vietnamese officers came to the United States for training (Herring 1986, 85–86).

Diem's inability to generate public support for his administration, and his persecution of those non-Communists who opposed him, led Kennedy to support an army coup against him in 1963. To Kennedy's dismay, the coup resulted in Diem's assassination, which was one of the great ironies of the period, as Kennedy would meet his own death by an assassin three weeks later. The South Vietnamese regimes that followed the coup proved equally incompetent and corrupt, and the increasing political instability led President Lyndon B. Johnson to the "Americanization" policy: using the American military not just as advisors but as combatants. In 1965 Johnson sent troops as independent battle units alongside the Army of the Republic of Vietnam (ARVN). Troop strength peaked at 540,000 in 1968, and more than 16,000 civilian and military advisors were still deployed in 1969 (Komer 1986, 125). By then a third American president, Richard M. Nixon, was consumed by the war. Under pressure to reduce American casualties and prove that South Vietnam could win the war by itself, Nixon ordered the Defense and State departments to begin the "Vietnamization" of operations.

It was between 1965 and 1969 that the number of refugees rose substantially. Before 1965 peasants moved from rural to urban areas under GVN control largely owing to Vietcong (VC) kidnapping and murder of village leaders, teachers, and other residents loyal to the government. In 1962, 120,000 of the highland people called Montagnards were driven out by VC attacks and confiscation of food. In a July 1962 memorandum the CIA voiced a theme that was to dominate America's approach to Indochinese refugees during the 1960s—the political value of civilian flight. The memorandum stated that it was "becoming increasingly apparent . . . that GVN and US faced with long term problem looking after uprooted Montagnards. . . . Whatever inspiration their movement toward GVN-controlled centers, GVN faced with opportunity and challenge forge new and better relations with tribal people" (*Pentagon Papers* 1971, 2: 687–88).

After 1965 American military intervention vastly increased the numbers of displaced villagers. Workers for the U.S. Agency for International Development (AID) reported a doubling of refugees between April 1966 and May 1968 and acknowledged the inadequate preparation of GVN and U.S. relief organizations (U.S. Senate 1968). In May 1967 there were 667,600 refugees; two years later the number reached 1,212,000 (U.S. Senate 1967, 286). Almost 60 percent were concentrated in five provinces along the northern coast of South Vietnam. Altogether, between 1965 and 1973, some 5,809,700 Vietnamese, excluding 2,350,000 displaced by Communist offensives in 1968 and 1972, registered as refugees with the GVN (U.S. Senate 1973a, 8). While many factors contributed to the refugee crisis, U.S. military strategy and diplomatic initiatives in this period directly displaced large numbers of Vietnamese civilians.

Hearts, Minds, and Feet: The Ideological Need for Migration   American officials had long claimed an interest in "the hearts and minds" of the Vietnamese people—a euphemism for political loyalty. It was this concern for the ideological dimensions of the war that eventually led to the policy of forced migration of Vietnamese civilians away from areas of VC activity. *Nation building* was the term in the 1950s for efforts to win the loyalty of Vietnamese peasants through economic development. It was replaced by the military term *pacification* in the early 1960s. In February 1966 President Johnson held a conference in Honolulu with South Vietnamese officials and decided to pursue the war through a strategy of pacification—a combination of military tactics and social programs. The movement of peasants to GVN-controlled areas was central to this new strategy.

At the Honolulu conference Johnson emphasized rural South Vietnam's need for local administration, agricultural modernization, and health and educational services (Kinnard 1977). Johnson's military policy often showed a reckless disregard for the Vietnamese people. But his social policy toward them reflected the president's New Deal background, and rural development represented an effort to transplant the social-welfare ideology behind the War on Poverty program in the United States to South Vietnam (Miller 1980). In the memorandum that followed the conference President Johnson reiterated his commitment to social change. He borrowed ideas from American antipoverty legislation and named Robert Komer as the senior official in charge of pacification: "Before the Honolulu conference and since, I have stressed repeatedly that the war on human misery and want is as fundamental to the successful resolution of the Vietnam conflict, as our military operations to ward off aggression. . . . In my view it is essential to designate a specific focal point for the direction, coordination and supervision in Washington of U.S. nonmilitary programs relating to Vietnam" (*Pentagon Papers* 1971, 2: 568; ellipses in text).

Johnson's reformist vision initiated the pacification program, but in actual application under Komer and others it became closely tied to military strategy. The social-welfare approach to political problems in Southeast Asia remained, however, a persistent theme in Washington, even as it was thwarted in practice in Vietnam. Foreign policy makers believed that portions of the American welfare state could be exported to benefit the Vietnamese people. In 1969 the chief administrator of the AID programs in Vietnam invoked the language of the Economic Opportunity Act of 1964 to define his organization's role in the struggle for the hearts and minds of the Vietnamese: "The kind of war that is significant is what we do to encourage the local people to have aspirations to develop what they have in human resources so that they may utilize whatever the nation may have in other resources for the improvement of their own people. Thereby that [sic] may have the maximum opportunity in determining the course and pattern of their own society" (U.S. Senate 1969, 37). Although the aid provided was primarily for agricultural development rather than for job training, as it was in the United States, in aiding civilians uprooted by the war America rehearsed the provision of social welfare to the refugees who arrived after 1975.

In 1971 a U.S. General Accounting Office report on assistance to war victims discussed the variety of U.S.-sponsored social welfare and medical programs in South Vietnam (U.S. Senate 1972b, 46). Among these were community centers that bore a remarkable resemblance to the community action programs for urban minorities in the United States: "Emphasis was on local determination and participation in community center activities including job training, child day care, credit services, legal services, and job-referral services." Although construction of five centers began in 1966, the GVN backed them with reluctance and, five years later, only 17 were in operation. The United States might have sought to transplant domestic social-welfare policy to Indochina, but in the context of war and a national government with little interest in coping with human problems, such efforts proved futile.

Indeed, until 1966 the GVN did not even have a special program for assisting refugees (U.S. Senate 1968, 51). And in June 1970 President Nguyen Van Thieu "decreed that Province Chiefs may no longer receive new refugees" (U.S. Senate 1970b, 9). Between 1967 and 1971 the United States provided approximately 80 percent of the budget for the South Vietnamese Ministry of Social Welfare, which assisted refugees (U.S. Senate 1972b, 17). After five years of investigation into the problems of war victims in Indochina, the Senate Refugee Subcommittee concluded, "With very few exceptions, then, the competence, the interest, and the initiative for refugee aid and resettlement remains today, as it has from the very beginning, in American hands" (U.S. Senate 1970b, 6).

The U.S. predominance over refugee relief opened the way for the managing of migration for military purposes: "The Americans were the prime movers in the series of events which led to the reemphasis of pacification" (*Pentagon Papers* 1971, 2:515). Early in 1966 refugee relief and counterinsurgency tactics began to converge. Propelling this synthesis were unresolved questions of which U.S. agency should control pacification and the extent of U.S. intervention in what the GVN termed "revolutionary development" or psychological warfare (*Pentagon Papers* 1971, 2:484). Until December 1966 AID handled American contributions to GVN refugee assistance. Then the Office of Civil Operations in the U.S. embassy managed refugee problems for a brief period in 1967. But in May 1967 the Civil Operations and Revolutionary Development Support (CORDS) was created, placed under Military Assistance Command, Vietnam (MACV), and assumed the funding, staff, and functions of the civilian agencies aiding refugees.

MACV's organizational flow chart for CORDS listed Purpose 8 as "Provides MACV focal point for economic warfare to include population and resource control, and for civic action by US forces" (*Pentagon Papers* 1971, 2:489). The only Vietnamese participation depicted in the flow chart was a "provincial representative" at the bottom of the hierarchy. AID, the original sponsor of relief programs, increasingly emphasized economic development as the long-range solution to refugee problems. In 1969 AID eliminated its social-welfare projects, leaving CORDS to supply humanitarian assistance to meet the "human problems" (U.S. Senate 1972b, 18–19). These organizational changes made Vietnamese refugees significant for the American military operations. In the MACV flow chart, refugees were listed next to "psychological operations" and the defector program.

Refugee Flight as a Military Option   In formulating plans for 1967 General William Westmoreland hoped to spread "security radially from the bases to protect more of the population. . . . We intend to employ all forces to get the best results measured among other things, in terms of population secured; territory cleared of enemy influence; VC/NVA bases eliminated; and enemy guerrillas, local forces, and main forces destroyed" (*Pentagon Papers* 1971, 2:493). The result of this strategy was a large flow of refugees owing to free-fire zones; the use of defoliants like Agent Orange, which ruined crops; and a policy of relocating villagers to deprive the VC of their supply and support bases (Lewy 1978). The free-fire zones—areas presumed to be continuously occupied by Communist forces and thus eligible for artillery barrages or bombing at any time—were drawn with little regard to the presence of civilians, because U.S. military commanders assumed that those who had not fled a contested area must have VC sympathies. Defoliants were primarily used to remove vegetation that might hide VC forces. Yet the vegetation-destroying chemicals also ruined peasants' crops, often ending their only reason for remaining in their village. These tactics appeared to produce refugees unintentionally, but they were actually part of a campaign. Speaking in 1965 of his plans to force Vietnamese peasants to choose between bombardment in their villages and security in GVN-controlled areas, Westmoreland concluded, "I expect a tremendous increase in the number of refugees" (Fitzgerald 1973a, 459).

The most direct cause of refugees was the forced migration of Vietnamese civilians by American troops. In 1967 alone some 100,000 Vietnamese were relocated by military sweeps (Lewy 1978, 65). Entire villages were often moved, as in the case of Ban Tach near the border with North Vietnam, a hamlet of 850 northern refugees. The villagers were moved to "Cam Ranh Bay, some 80 miles down the coast, where they would find sanctuary and employment near the huge and growing U.S. military supply depot" (Angeloff 1967, 17). Operation Cedar Falls, in which 6,000 civilians were relocated in a week, was one of the most thorough. Helicopters transported villagers, possessions, and livestock while gigantic plows scoured the earth for underground tunnels where the VC hid, leaving the village in ruins (Schell 1988). One Marine officer recalled that by the mid-1960s "the original Eisenhower phrase, 'winning hearts and minds,' had been reduced in the field to an acronym—WHAM—and ironically this brought out the true content of counterinsurgency" (Marr 1972, 205).

High-ranking nonmilitary officials approved of the U.S. military's uprooting of Vietnamese civilians. In 1966 Ambassador Henry Cabot Lodge responded to MACV's pacification strategy by writing, "Our forces will vigorously support and participate in the program in such areas as logistics, sanitation, medical care, construction, and resources and population control" (*Pentagon Papers* 1971, 4: 329). In the context of military conflict, "population control" meant the movement of civilians for strategic purposes.

The policies of Robert Komer, the director of U.S. pacification and refugee programs, provide the most compelling evidence that forced migration of Vietnamese civilians was a standard operating procedure. In 1966 Komer advocated to Deputy Ambassador William Porter in Saigon that "increased flow of refugees is a plus. It helps deprive VC of recruiting potential and rice growers, and is partly indicative of growing peasant desire to seek security on our side" (*Pentagon Papers* 1971, 2:569). As the pace of the war increased, Komer's counsel regarding Vietnamese refugees became more blunt. In April 1967 he sent a memo to President Johnson with this advice for military operations: "Step up refugee programs deliberately aimed at depriving VC of a recruiting base" (*Pentagon Papers* 1971, 4:439–40).

This memo came at a time when U.S. military strategy on Vietnam was being hotly debated in Washington. Should the VC or the NVA be the central targets for attack? Should more American advisors be added and bombing raids on North Vietnam escalated? Komer advocated decreasing the bombings and ground fighting and increasing pacification and the U.S. advisory role to the ARVN. This view was not shared by Under Secretary of State Nicholas Katzenbach. He wanted the Department of Defense to "use the great bulk of US forces for search and destroy, rather than pacification" (*Pentagon Papers* 1971, 4: 508). Katzenbach agreed, however, with Komer on one point: "We should stimulate a greater refugee flow through psychological inducements to further decrease the enemy's manpower base. Improve our ability to handle the flow and win refugees' loyalty." Clearly, American policy makers considered the relocation of Vietnamese civilians an important aspect of the war effort.

The director of an American voluntary agency working in South Vietnam reported in mid-1967 that even after villagers were uprooted, they were often relocated for purposes other than effective relief (U.S. Senate 1968, 66–67). Vietnamese province officials settled them in areas where they might serve as buffers against Communist attacks. Others were housed near American military bases with demand for labor. After nine years of experience in Vietnamese relief and development projects, starting with agricultural projects for the northern refugees in 1958, the director concluded, "I believe in trying to destroy the infrastructure of the Vietcong we are actually destroying the infrastructure of the Vietnamese village itself or of the Vietnamese community itself." The effort to win the loyalty of Vietnamese peasants by spurring their migration to GVN areas actually contributed to the fall of South Vietnam.

When questioned by the Senate Refugee Subcommittee in June 1969 about such social destruction, representatives from AID and the Department of Defense reported a change in policy. Their testimony suggests that the counterinsurgency work of CORDS—for example, the Phoenix program to capture or assassinate suspected VC—had eventually led to more selective U.S. military activities at the village level: "An intensive effort has gone into the campaign to identify members of the Vietcong political infrastructure . . . when they are believed to be in a particular village for organizational activities. . . . This differs a great deal from the tactics of the intensive reconnaissance into an area and then a full sweep through, or a full search with large scale deployment of troops, which was the original kind of tactic used in large areas" (U.S. Senate 1969, 27).

While Senator Edward Kennedy's Refugee Subcommittee continued to link virtually all U.S. military activities to mounting refugee flows, by 1969 these were no longer part of a policy, although forced migration continued to occur (U.S. Senate 1970b). Between 1969 and 1973, however, the United States expanded the war into Laos and Cambodia, turning a large proportion of their civilian populations into refugees.

Secret Armies in Laos, 1969–1970

The refugee problems in Laos began with the use of mountain-dwelling ethnic groups, particularly the Hmong, as special forces during the 1960s. The problem worsened following the massive bombing of the country in 1969–70 as the Hmong army proved unable to meet a sustained Communist offensive. The Hmong first received U.S. military overtures in the late 1950s from Special Forces teams (Blaufarb 1977; U.S. Senate 1970b). In return for their military assistance, the Hmong believed they would be given greater political and economic autonomy within Laos, perhaps even an independent state (Scott 1990). By 1961 there were 100,000 Hmong refugees, largely the dependents of soldiers who had been forced to flee their bases. For several years after the Geneva Peace Accords of 1962, which temporarily halted the war in Laos, the Hmong remained marginal to U.S. foreign policy, although contact was maintained through the CIA. By 1964 the number of refugees had dropped to 30,000.

But renewed offensives by NVA units and the Communist guerrillas called the Pathet Lao brought the Hmong back into the war. Between 1965 and 1967 some 100,000 Hmong were on AID's rice distribution list, and many were resettled to other parts of Laos as the intensity of the war increased. Schools and hospitals, mail service and transportation, and programs to improve agricultural techniques accompanied these relocation efforts. The result was the concentration of the Hmong population in several settlements under the auspices of the AID and the CIA.

In 1968 the give-and-take cycle of the war was broken when the NVA launched an offensive that eventually spilled into the strategic Plain of Jars. Despite repeated efforts to hold off the NVA, the Hmong and the Laotian army were unable to stop the advance, and the United States intervened with massive bombings. The years 1969 and 1970 account for 47 percent of the total bomb tonnages for Laos during the nine years of U.S. military involvement, and 60 percent of total bomb tonnages in the Indochina theater of operations in those two years. More important, the percent of bomb tonnage from B-52s (the most powerful bomber in the air force) rose from 31 to 50 percent (U.S. Senate 1973a, 24). Reliance on the B-52 signaled a far more indiscriminate use of force and thus a perception that all populations below were hostile (Marr 1972, 205). Given that this massive bombing was regulated by a single person at the U.S. embassy in Vientiane, the Senate Refugee Subcommittee concluded that much of Laos had become a free-fire zone where aerial warfare was conducted with little attention to its consequences on civilians (U.S. Senate 1970b, 30).

The number of refugees in Laos rose from 128,000 in 1968 to 246,000 in 1970. Of those, 40 percent were military personnel and their dependents from the Hmong, Mien, Lao-theung, and other highland ethnic groups (U.S. Senate 1970b, 63). The extent to which hardships experienced under the Pathet Lao, U.S. bombing, or the inducement of U.S. relief organizations caused the refugee flight was much debated at the time. While the mountain armies clearly fled under U.S. auspices and because of their role in the war, lowland Laotians were more likely to flee from the war itself. A voluntary agency worker in Laos attributed the larger number of refugees in 1969 to American planes increasingly attacking populated areas with more indiscriminate types of explosives (U.S. Senate 1970b, 119). A survey of 200 refugees from the Plain of Jars found that 97 percent had witnessed a bombing attack—one-third on their own village (Chapelier and Malderghem 1971, 75). While such evidence indicates the role of the U.S. military in creating refugees, civilian agencies also managed refugee flight in Laos.

According to the State Department, the evacuation of refugees from the Plain of Jars was a decision made by the Laotian government (U.S. Senate 1970b, 68–74). AID costs in Laos, however, rose from $8.4 to $15.8 million between 1969 and 1970, and in 1971, 55 percent of the AID expenditures in the country were for refugee relief and "air technical support," which meant evacuations (U.S. Senate 1972a, 116, 126). Americans were clearly organizing Laotian refugee migrations. The General Accounting Office examined the Laotian Refugee Program and found that "although this is a joint program, the United States has assumed virtually all operational and funding responsibility for it. The Royal Lao Government's support of the refugee program is mostly in the form of providing land and personnel" (U.S. Senate 1972a, 122).

Lao refugees in the period 1969–70 were thus evacuated under U.S. auspices and because the United States had raised the intensity of the war to the point that villagers had to choose between certain attack, if they remained in areas controlled by Communist forces, and the relative safety of AID resettlement camps. The State Department explicitly supported this strategy: "Most Lao civilians learn quickly that bombing necessarily follows the North Vietnamese. But they also know that life under the NVA is difficult in any event. It is therefore not surprising that the Lao move to Government areas to avoid the Vietnamese" (U.S. Senate 1970a, 73). The bombings in Laos served a function similar to the displacement of Vietnamese villagers. An AID review listed one of the benefits of "strategic evacuations" as: "It will deny the enemy control over a considerable population of villagers and their services under Communist forces" (U.S. Senate 1970a, 25). Hmong and Laotian refugees arriving in the United States after 1975 took their place in a much older American policy of regulating refugee migration in Southeast Asia.

Bombings in Cambodia, 1971–1973

Cambodia was drawn into the war as the VC and NVA established base camps and supply routes along the Vietnam-Cambodia border. The United States believed these activities had great military significance, although subsequent investigation proved they were of only minor value (Karnow 1983). President Nixon proceeded to secretly attack the bases and routes by land and air, without congressional approval, for 13 months in 1969 and 1970. Prince Norodom Sihanouk had ruled Cambodia since independence from France (Sihanouk had been king since 1941, even though his title was merely titular until 1953) and kept the country neutral during most of the Vietnam War. In 1970, however, General Lon Nol took power in a coup widely believed to have been sponsored by the CIA, which wanted a pro-American government in Phnom Penh. The Lon Nol government quickly escalated military conflict with the NVA and the Communist guerrillas known as the Khmer Rouge (*Khmer* is the term for the Cambodian people in their own language; *rouge* is French for "red"). The guerrillas were led by Pol Pot, the son of a low-level Cambodian civil servant. He had joined the French Communist party while a university student in Paris and returned to Cambodia in 1953 with the goal of leading a peasant revolution like that in China.

The 1970 bombings of Communist sanctuaries in southern Cambodia displaced few civilians because the area was relatively unpopulated (Shawcross 1977). But between 1971 and 1973, when the United States flew sorties in support of the Cambodian army, the bombings hit populated areas. Although bomb tonnage declined from 63,646 in 1971 to 54,206 in 1972, the percentage from B-52s rose from 53 to 69 percent. When the Paris Peace Agreement ended U.S. participation in the Vietnam War in January 1973, the NVA violated Article 20 calling for the withdrawal of all foreign troops from Cambodia. The United States then concentrated all aerial warfare on Cambodia until August (Shawcross 1977, 266–67). In the first three months of 1973, 41,424 tons of bombs were dropped, 70 percent from B-52s (U.S. Senate 1973a, 24). In April and May 1973, B-52s dropped 71,000 tons of bombs (Shawcross 1977, 272). One off-course B-52 killed 125 civilians and wounded more than 250 in a government-held town (Shawcross 1977, 400).

The creation of a virtual free-fire zone in the eastern one-third of Cambodia dramatically increased the flow of refugees (U.S. Senate 1973a). Called "Freedom Deal," most air strikes in this area did not require the standard clearance process: a request by the Cambodian military, mediation by the U.S.

embassy, examination by U.S. spotter planes, and final referral to U.S. air bases in Thailand. After much investigation Sydney Schanberg (a reporter for the *New York Times*) concluded that the intense bombing in 1973 was "an American operation that has been modeled to give the appearance that the Cambodians are playing a significant role in coordinating and directing it" (U.S. Senate 1973a, 85). The U.S. Senate agreed that air strikes "are not cleared individually with the Cambodian General Staff, and the Embassy plays no coordinating role" (U.S. Senate 1973b, 50–51). A voluntary agency director returning from a fact-finding mission for the Senate Refugee Subcommittee reported the human results of the bombing: "Bombing is the most pervasive reason for refugee movement. Our interviews with refugees . . . largely confirm the findings of the GAO interviewers in 1971. The GAO found that some 60 percent of the refugees interviewed cited bombardment as the principal reason for moving" (U.S. Senate 1973a, 7).

Given that the U.S. military considered war victims an inevitable part of the campaign in Cambodia, the U.S. experience with refugees in South Vietnam and Laos would have suggested a major relief effort. But from the beginning of hostilities in 1970, the American government persistently ruled against such aid: "According to the U.S. Ambassador to Cambodia, it has been the policy of the United States to not become involved with the problem of civilian war victims in Cambodia" (U.S. Senate 1972a, 89). The rationale for this inaction was to keep a low profile in the country. Despite heavy bombing in 1970 and 1971, an AID official asserted that "during this period, it was the policy of our Government, reinforced by action of the Congress, to keep US involvement in Cambodia to an absolute minimum" (U.S. Senate 1973a, 32).

Cambodian officials also were reluctant to address the refugee problem. One relief worker voiced a protest against social-welfare policies in general, explaining that "the Government did not want to make beggars out of the people" (U.S. Senate 1972a, 90). Others cited the strength of the Cambodian family, the self-reliance of the Khmer people, and their distrust of the government as reasons that refugee relief was not a high priority. By 1973 only 10,000 refugees were receiving aid in government camps (U.S. Senate 1973a, 12). In what amounted to a debate over social-welfare philosophy, U.S. officials cited this figure as evidence that Cambodian refugees were able to provide for themselves (U.S. Senate 1973a). To assist Cambodian refugees, proponents had to start with the argument, first raised during the industrial revolution, that national governments had a responsibility for the welfare of their citizens.

By August 1972 the war had displaced 700,000 Cambodians, and nearly 60 percent were clustered in and around the capital of Phnom Penh (U.S. Senate 1973a, 64). That month Lon Nol finally requested assistance from the United States. An AID team then in Cambodia to investigate the refugee problem modestly concluded, "The requirements of the refugees for assistance . . . are not being fully met by help currently being provided by the GKR [Cambodian government] and other donors. There is room for the USG [U.S. government] to augment such help. . . . USG assistance should be portrayed as a response to the GKR's August 10, 1972, formal appeal to the US" (U.S. Senate 1973a, 69). The report recommended, however, that the United States neither provide funds to the GKR directly nor to an outside voluntary agency. Either approach, it argued, would lead to an uncoordinated and inadequately supervised program or a further internationalization of the situation.

What was to be the only U.S. aid to Cambodian refugees came hesitantly. AID, the organization with the most experience in such relief efforts, argued that economic assistance was sufficient. On the topic of relief for Cambodian refugees one official stated: "In dealing with problems of housing and resettlement of people back in their own homes, bringing rice production back to peacetime levels . . . one finds that those are national problems and have to be dealt with not as refugee problems as such" (U.S. Senate 1973a, 43). Between July 1972 and July 1973 only $1.5 million was delivered to two voluntary agencies. By then there were more than 1 million refugees and an additional 500,000 dependents of Cambodian soldiers in flight (U.S. Senate 1973a, 4). In 1974 the United States finally provided another $1 million. These figures contrast with $517 million in military aid since the beginning of the war (Shawcross 1977, 319). In Cambodia the United States showed the most disregard for the plight of the war victims its military policies generated.

Conclusion

The U.S. government had a long history of managing the migration and resettlement of Vietnamese, Laotians, and Cambodians before the first Indochinese refugees arrived in the United States. Not only did U.S. policy on refugees in Southeast Asia during the 1960s and early 1970s mirror the country's larger objectives in the region, but refugee migration itself was often a key tactic to further these objectives. Beginning with Operation Exodus in 1954, U.S. aid to refugees from North Vietnam established the organizations and ideologies used in later nation-building policies. The U.S. commitment to the refugees augmented arguments in favor of continued involvement in South Vietnam. In addition, these predominately Catholic refugees became actors significant beyond their numbers, particularly as supporters of South Vietnam's first president from 1954 to 1963. Following Operation Frequent Wind in April 1975, President Gerald Ford used nearly $100 million in AID money for South Vietnam (now under Communist rule) to resettle this first wave of government officials and army officers, 40 percent of whom were Catholic (Taft et al. 1980).

In the years between Operation Exodus and Operation Frequent Wind, the United States sponsored even more profound refugee migrations in Vietnam, Laos, and Cambodia. From 1965 to 1968 the American military gained control of relief operations for Vietnamese villagers displaced by the war. As civilian agencies increasingly left refugee aid to organizations engaged in counterinsurgency and pacification, the inevitable result was the forced migration of Vietnamese peasants to further military objectives. These objectives included depriving the Vietcong of a support population but also providing evidence that Vietnamese peasants were "voting with their feet" for the government in Saigon by migrating to areas it controlled.

In terms of the proportion of the population uprooted, American military policy in Laos and Cambodia led to even greater migration. Recruitment of the Hmong and other highland populations in Laos to serve as a "secret army" meant that the fate of entire ethnic groups now depended on military victory. As Hmong troops were forced to withdraw against overwhelming North Vietnamese forces in 1969 and 1970, the retreat turned into a mass migration of extended families and communities. When the U.S. military attempted to stop the retreat through intensive bombing in the Plain of Jars, the result was an even greater flow as Laotian civilians became the targets of indiscriminate attacks. A similar fate awaited many civilians in Cambodia between 1971 and 1973. A large portion of the country was opened to almost unrestricted bombing by the U.S. Air Force, with little or no regulation by the Cambodian government. The bombings created more than 1 million refugees in a population of 7 million, and the United States provided only the most limited aid to these refugees under the pretext of not intervening in Cambodian affairs.

The United States risked all during its military intervention in Southeast Asia, including the uprooting of civilian populations without their consent. Achievement of U.S. political objectives in Southeast Asia might have provided some justification for the destruction, since the new Communist regimes proved more brutal than their pro-American predecessors. But the collapse of allied governments in the spring of 1975 meant that the United States had failed in its mission despite making the populations of Vietnam, Laos, and Cambodia pay a heavy price in lives lost and ruined. As a result, the United States bore a special responsibility for Vietnamese, Laotian, and Cambodian refugees who fled to neighboring countries in the 1970s and 1980s.

three

The New Communist Regimes in Southeast Asia

The Communist forces that assumed power in South Vietnam, Laos, and Cambodia in April and May of 1975 confronted devastation resulting from a decade of intense military conflict. Warfare had driven rural populations to the cities, thus curtailing agricultural production. The land itself had often been ruined through mining, bombing, and use of herbicides, and many cities lay in ruins. Foreign aid ended with the demise of pro-American governments. Large populations of demobilized soldiers had no jobs to return to, and thousands were disabled as a result of combat. Such conditions would have presented any government with daunting problems.

These postwar hardships, however, did not lead to the first mass international migration in the history of mainland Southeast Asia. Instead, it was the new governments in Vietnam, Laos, and Cambodia that created one of Asia's largest refugee crisis. These Communist regimes began transforming society along socialist lines, rigidly enforcing political control, and testing their military strength against neighbors. The result was the exodus of more than 2 million Indochinese refugees.

Postwar Conditions in Vietnam, Laos, and Cambodia

During the 10 years following the fall of South Vietnam, between 90,000 and 500,000 people were sent to "reeducation camps" because of their association with the former South Vietnamese government (U.S. Committee for Refugees 1988). Hard labor, lack of food, absence of medical care, and indoctrination sessions were both punishment and a means to coerce obedience to the new regime (Nguyen 1983). Despite this political repression, for several years it appeared that the Vietnamese government would not pursue draconian policies to achieve a socialist society.

But then in 1978 new economic policies began rapidly transforming the South, historically the most prosperous region of the country (Ngo 1991; Osborne 1980). Businesses and private property were confiscated—actions that disproportionately affected the country's ethnic Chinese population concentrated in the commercial sector. China's invasion of Vietnam in 1979, in response to Vietnam's invasion of Cambodia and alliance with the Soviet Union, further jeopardized the ethnic Chinese (Chanda 1986). The government also created "new economic zones" on land that was abandoned during the war or never brought into cultivation. To boost agricultural production, the government relocated people to these areas but often failed to provide the needed supplies (Nguyen 1983).

In Laos, a close ally of Vietnam, a similar pattern prevailed (Sutter 1990). Camps to punish and indoctrinate those associated with the former regime were called "seminars." After several years of comparatively open economic policies, agricultural collectivization and camps in "new liberated zones" led to the uprooting of peasants and food shortages (Chanda 1982). The teaching and practice of Buddhism, which had been central to Lao culture for centuries, became increasingly regulated by the government so that it would conform to Marxist principles (Lafont 1982).

The Hmong and other highland ethnic groups that had been recruited by the American military for its "secret army" in Laos were particularly vulnerable (Lee 1982). The Laotian government's attempts to change Hmong agricultural practices, draft men and women for heavy labor, and send some to the "seminars" provoked Hmong resistance. From their mountain strongholds, the Hmong fought with success until Vietnamese military intervention overwhelmed them. In 1977 the Hmong alleged that they had been the victims of chemical attacks (Nichols 1988).

The hardships imposed by the new Communist regimes in Vietnam and Laos were vastly exceeded by those in Cambodia. Following the collapse of the pro-American government, the victorious Khmer Rouge embarked on a revolution to level Cambodian society in order to rebuild it along principles derived from Mao Tse-tung, the leader of the Chinese Revolution (Jackson 1989). To start, they moved urban populations into rural areas. Most Cambodians had been farmers before 1975, but now all were required to work the land with little food and severe punishment for disobedience.

The Khmer Rouge revolution aimed to reshape an entire way of life, not merely the country's economy (Becker 1986; Ponchaud 1989). Literacy, occupational skills, and symbols of modernity as trivial as eyeglasses became grounds for execution. The Khmer Rouge particularly targeted the approximately 65,000 monks who served in the Buddhist temples that were the core of Khmer culture. Only about 3,000 survived. With religious institutions dismantled, the Khmer Rouge assaulted the family in order to indoctrinate youth to switch their loyalty from parents and relatives to the Angka, the name for the Khmer Rouge organization that was both government and purportedly the collective will of the people. From starvation, disease, and execution, about 2 million Cambodians died between 1975 and 1978, or one-quarter of the country's prerevolution population. The story of life under the Khmer Rouge is one of the most tragic episodes of the twentieth century.

Coming of Age under the Khmer Rouge

Phea's mother ran away from home the day the Khmer Rouge arrived in Battambang, Cambodia's third largest city in one of the country's more prosperous provinces bordering Thailand. The Khmer Rouge planned to take the city's inhabitants to rural areas and make them work as agricultural laborers. Phea's mother, Roun, had finally decide to leave her abusive husband, Ron.

As a teenager, Roun's parents had forced her to marry Ron, a tall, slim, and light-skinned man—physical traits valued by Cambodians. Roun, on the other hand, looked more typically Cambodian: short, stocky, muscular from hard farmwork as a child, and dark skinned. Her parents had found Ron sleeping next to Roun. Although he claimed that he had just snuck in for the night—indeed, the room was occupied by other sisters—the parents forced them into marriage. The marriage was unhappy from the beginning and continued that way after Phea was born. Roun's husband had girlfriends, often neglected his family, and occasionally beat Roun. That day in April 1975, when the Khmer Rouge finally overran Battambang, Roun had decided once and for all to leave her husband. She moved across town to the house of a relative. But the start of a cruel revolution changed her plans. Although none could foresee the horrors that would occur, Roun sensed that it was better to return to her family during this turmoil. She found Ron and Phea four days later, and spent the next three years with Ron until the Khmer Rouge executed him in 1978.

Phea's first encounters with the Khmer Rouge came well before 1975, when she was only 10 years old. Her father bought land in the countryside and the family moved there to grow peanuts, potatoes, and other crops with the aid of a few families they employed as laborers. At this time the Khmer Rouge were not yet the powerful force they would become by 1975. Some nights a few guerrillas would sneak into the village to steal food. They lived deep in the jungle and were so poor that they made their sandals from old tires. (In the morning, Phea and her friends would search for traces of these night visitors: footprints with the texture of tire tracks.) But the Khmer Rouge's power grew steadily. Soon the villagers locked their doors at night, and the town's leaders were particularly fearful.

Phea's father took the precaution of having a loaded rifle in their house, and he provided Phea and Roun with sharpened sticks. One night there was a knock on the door. Phea's father woke and told his family: "If the Khmer Rouge come in I will fight them. Run away if you can. If you can't run, then fight them with your sticks." But it was only one of Ron's best friends. He asked Ron to come out and talk. Phea's father refused, citing the late hour. The next day the villagers discovered the dead bodies of this friend, the village chief, and a few other men. The Khmer Rouge had come to each of their houses, forced an acquaintance to get the man to come out, and then killed them all. Soon after this incident, Phea's family returned to Battambang.

The Khmer Rouge began attacking urban areas as part of their strategy to destabilize the government. About one year after Phea's family returned to Battambang, the Khmer Rouge planted a bomb in a crowded movie theater; the blast killed and wounded many. Phea's parents rushed to the scene when they heard the news knowing that Phea and some relatives had gone to the movies that evening. Frantically searching among the bodies on the sidewalk, they then went to the hospital, finally returning home when they could find no trace of Phea. Several hours later, Phea and her relatives returned home with this story. They had tried to enter the theater, the only air-conditioned one in the city, which was playing the most popular movie of the time. But the show had been sold-out, forcing them to go elsewhere.

When the Khmer Rouge emptied Battambang in April 1975, they warned the people to hurry, saying, "You must leave quickly. The Americans planes are coming to bomb the city." Twelve-year-old Phea, accompanied by her father, grandmother, and a cousin, left holding a kitten named Riches and leading on a string a pig named Spot. Long lines of families pushing carts and carrying belongings moved outward from the city into the surrounding farmlands. Phea's father carried their possessions in two bundles attached to opposite ends of a long pole. The weight was great, and he frequently stopped to rest. When the line of refugees finally camped for the night, Phea's father discovered what had made the baggage so heavy. Phea's grandmother had packed a stone mortar and pestle used to prepare spice mixtures, hardly a necessity on a forced march.

Phea and the other children were at first thrilled with the move. Indeed, the Khmer Rouge said it would be temporary, and many inhabitants were not aware that selective executions had already begun. Phea had positive memories of the country: holidays, visiting relatives, and her time in the small village. But the disintegration of life that would leave Phea an emaciated stick figure by 1979 proceeded quickly during the first year under the Khmer Rouge regime. One of the earliest changes was the requirement that everyone wear black clothing. The Khmer Rouge deemed even ordinary but colorful clothing a sign of status distinctions. Phea and her family were instructed to soak their clothes in water mixed with a fruit that produced a dark stain. This treatment obliterated the colors and designs from Phea's clothing. Yet she could still detect a flower pattern in one skirt, a sad reminder of happier times now submerged in a sea of blackness.

After living a few months at a spot near Battambang, Phea's family was among those picked to move to a more remote location. Their lives became harder as the backbreaking agricultural work that would consume Phea's life for the next four years began. Her father and other men did the heavy labor, while Phea and other children did smaller but nonetheless demanding tasks. She learned how to harvest rice with a sickle, but only after cutting herself so often that she permanently scarred her hands.

Her grandmother was sent back with other old women to live near Battambang. Phea visited once before her grandmother died and found the old woman ill and unhappy. The grandmother told Phea about a horrible sight she had seen. The Khmer Rouge were bent on destroying all institutions in Khmer society and culture, and they took particular aim at the Buddhist religion. Phea's grandmother recounted how she had seen statues of the Buddha dumped into a pond, with a pole stuck in the hand of one to give the appearance it was fishing. This desecration was unimaginable prior to the revolution, since even the least devout Buddhist would have feared an eternity of bad luck for such an act. But the fishing pole was an even worse affront because it violated the Buddhist ethic against taking life. For Phea's grandmother, such sacrilege truly meant that Cambodia was at "the year zero," the Khmer Rouge term signifying that they would undo society in order to remake it.

The Khmer Rouge took a special interest in Roun. Because she was illiterate and from a poor peasant family, local Khmer Rouge leaders asked her to run the kitchen. This was a highly privileged position, because cooks had no shortage of food for themselves and their family. Indeed, some cooks were corrupted by their new power, using the distribution of food to reward friends and punish enemies. Roun refused the offer out of shyness rather than principle. As a leading figure she would be expected to contribute to the nightly speeches on hard work and loyalty that the Khmer Rouge used to indoctrinate their captives.

Then, toward the end of 1976, the Khmer Rouge began rounding up children and sending them away from their parents. The first to go were the oldest teenagers; later, those of about 16 years of age. Finally, even boys and girls as young as 13 were sent to remote locales. Phea was among this last group. Perhaps because she had entered the rebellious teenage years, which even life under the Khmer Rouge did not entirely extinguish, Phea welcomed the move. In fact, she knew many of the children in her group before the revolution. Since April 1975 Phea had become very close to Nang, a girl her age who came from a poor family that once worked on her grandfather's land.

Nang and Phea became inseparable friends for the year they spent together, an unintended but nonetheless real consequence of the mixing of social classes that was central to Khmer Rouge ideology. For several weeks after the move, Phea, Nang, and the other children slept in hammocks high up in the trees. But one morning they smelled a foul odor. Climbing down, they discovered the remains of a body at the foot of the tree, identifiable only by a pair of legs with expensive women's shoes on the feet. That night they moved to a new tree. Some nights the Khmer Rouge required Phea and Nang to stand guard. What they were guarding or who they were guarding against they did not know, but leaders would sneak up on them to check if they were sleeping. Phea and Nang were required to hold sticks and had been instructed how to strike at a person's temple for greatest effect. When the girls finally moved into a crudely constructed longhouse, they slept next to each other. After a morning fight over who had wet the bed, the Khmer Rouge threatened to send them apart. Grasping each other tightly, they pleaded to be allowed to remain in the same bunk. Several months later this friendship was tested when Nang jumped into a river to save Phea from drowning, only to be nearly pulled under herself. Both were saved by a young Khmer Rouge soldier.

Despite the company of other children and much-appreciated freedom from parents, the move to the children's camp brought hardships. Phea had her first glimpse of "the killing fields": bodies of Khmer Rouge victims decomposing in partially flooded paddies. For the first time, food was in short supply, and Phea permanently chipped her front teeth by biting the hulls from stray pieces of rice, which she then hoarded until there was a sufficient amount to cook. One night a woman in charge of cooking for the children took pity on Phea and told her where a bag of freshly caught fish could be found. Sneaking over to the location, Phea was about to open the bag when she was startled by the sound of someone approaching. The Khmer Rouge severely punished theft of food. It was only a woman who proceeded to urinate, but in her hasty retreat Phea stumbled against the bag; a sharp stick of bamboo run through the gills of the fish pierced her foot. The next morning, instead of being sent to work, leaders brought the children to witness an execution. Normally, asking to be excused from such events brought punishment. But the Khmer Rouge deemed Phea's injury sufficiently serious to grant her a visit to her parents. She stayed with them for about a year, unable to walk because of her wounded foot.

Returning to the girls' camp, Phea found that conditions had become even worse. The Khmer Rouge ideology of a classless society had reached new extremes, and workers were allowed fewer possessions in order to make them more equal. Pots and other utensils were the first to go, ending workers' ability to cook their own food and making their survival more dependent on the Khmer Rouge. Then a long meeting was held at which the simple food bowl was described as materialistic. With their bowls confiscated, the girls were left only a spoon with which to eat from large communal bowls placed on the ground. Of course, a group of 10 girls (the basic work and sleeping unit in the camp) could not all eat from a bowl at the same time. Mealtimes thus became a contest. When the leader signaled that workers could eat, the girls raced to their group's bowl. The fastest and strongest girls would get there first, but all would have to eat the thin rice soup very hot or risk not having any left when it cooled. On some occasions, Phea made her way to the bowl only to find it empty.

Under these circumstances, the loss of a spoon was one of the most disastrous events that could befall a girl, since she would then have to grab hot soup with her hands or soak it up with a piece of cloth. Phea guarded her spoon closely. Tied with a piece of string around her neck, this spoon necklace symbolized how the Khmer Rouge's attack on materialism only made the few remaining possessions even more valuable. Toward the end of 1977 even the spoons were confiscated.

Life was also made harder by long treks to distance work sites or in search of food. On one occasion Phea and three other girls were sent to a distant lake for fish. Nets, baskets, and other fishing equipment no longer existed. Instead, the girls waded through the water, scaring the fish in the direction of the shore, quickly pushing mud and weeds into low walls to prevent the fish from escaping, and then repeating this process all over again to narrow the area confining the fish. After working for hours, they decide to rest on a small island that was within wading distance. Climbing the slope, Phea was astonished to find a small hut. The girls called out and a middle-aged man slowly hobbled out the door. He beckoned the girls to come forward and for the next hour he recounted the sad tale that led him to live this isolated existence, abandoned even by the Khmer Rouge. He had accidentally cut his leg with a saw about one year ago. But his neighbors and the Khmer Rouge attributed the resulting inflammation to leprosy rather than infection. Lepers are shunned by Cambodians, who believe the disease is infectious even though it is not. Now he lived alone on this small island, visited occasionally by a relative who brought him food. The girls left him some of their catch, amazed to find someone in an even more pitiful state than themselves.

One day the leaders announced that some of the girls would be visiting Battambang for a parade. A truck would come sometime during the next week and take a select few to the city, where they would join representatives from other work groups. The leaders selected only the prettiest girls and told them to wear their best clothes or borrow some from friends. One of Phea's friends borrowed a pair of stylish shoes. To protect this rare possession, the girl looped the shoes' straps around her arm while she slept. One night, the girl felt someone brush against her. She jumped up struggling and yelling for the thief to leave her possessions alone. But it was only the leader making her rounds. Such a display of materialistic attachment could have meant severe punishment. Yet Phea learned that instead the leader put the girl's name down on a list of people to be given new shoes. Phea thought that the upcoming event in Battambang surely must be extraordinary for the leader to react with such uncharacteristic kindness.

When the truck suddenly arrived a few days later, the girls bundled into it and were driven to Battambang. The silence stunned Phea. The city was deserted except for a few Khmer Rouge families who had taken their pick of the abandoned houses. Where once children played and merchants sang praise for their food and produce, there was now an eerie silence. But Phea quickly lost interest in the city because the Khmer Rouge celebrated the upcoming event by allowing the children to eat rice (not hot water with a few grains floating in it), meat, and vegetable dishes, and even to pick oranges. Phea enjoyed the meal, yet she thought of her hungry mother and father. Deprivation tested Cambodians. Some became selfish. Husbands and wives concealed scraps of food from each other; parents withheld a morsel from their children; and children quickly consumed a chance finding. Phea hid an orange and some dried hot peppers to bring to her parents on their next meeting. She imagined their surprise at these rare commodities, although they had once been as common as water. Several nights after returning to the camp, Phea discovered that her gifts had disappeared, the victims of someone with less control over their hunger.

The great event in Battambang was marred by an act of defiance. Whether a spontaneous or planned disruption, a man waiting near Phea suddenly grabbed a stick from a stack of firewood, struck a Khmer Rouge soldier in the head, and attempted to take his rifle. Other soldiers immediately shot him to death. Attention quickly returned to the main spectacle: a parade. As cars approached, leaders shouted the names of each camp, and the teams of workers waved and cheered. When the cars reached her group, Phea realized that the parade was for visiting dignitaries from China, an ally of the Khmer Rouge, come to observe Cambodia's progress toward a socialist society.

Phea identified the visitors' nationality from their clothing. But what struck her most was their skin and faces. These people did not work out-of-doors under the hot sun and incessant rain with no change of clothing and little food when they returned home. In contrast to Phea's skin, which had become scarred, rough, and darkened, the dignitaries' skin was cared for. They could tend to cuts and wash away dirt. Their faces expressed emotions and interest in the surroundings, rather than the dull look that comes from focusing on a growling, unfed stomach. Phea had forgotten normalcy, and the visitors were a shocking reminder of how accustomed she had become to life as a slave.

Conditions deteriorated within months of the parade. New leaders with strange, regional accents came from the South. Soon the old leaders disappeared, and at the nightly meetings Phea learned that they had been disloyal. The Khmer Rouge revolution was consuming itself as the most radical factions began purging the moderates. This period in 1978 proved one of the most deadly. As Khmer Rouge factions vied with one another, leaders, cadres, and common soldiers sought to prove their loyalty to the revolution by betraying others. After surviving hard labor and starvation for more than three years, Phea's father became one of the victims. Phea pieced together the events leading to his death from her mother, who spoke with him once before the execution and then talked with an old man who guarded the jail. Information also came from a cousin who was gathering vegetables at dusk and witnessed Ron's death.

Phea's father was betrayed by Khorn, his best friend. They had attended school together, entered the same temple for the several months of Buddhist training customary for teenage boys, and married and had children at about the same time. Such bonds formed the basis of life before 1975, but after nearly four years under the Khmer Rouge they counted for little. Khorn had become a mid-level leader and, in the context of the 1978 purges, sought to maintain his position by accusing others of betrayal. His testimony that Ron was disloyal and a former landowner led to Ron's arrest and confinement in a house that served as a local jail. But Khorn initially recoiled at killing Ron himself. For two weeks, Ron waited alone in the small hut. Then he heard Khorn whispering to two soldiers, telling them to kill Ron. Ron responded, "Just give me rice and some fish so I won't be hungry when I die. Then you can kill me. I'm not afraid to die, but make my death quick. If you give me a slow death, my ghost will see that you are punished." The meal came the next day, and, when dusk approached, Khorn and the two soldiers brought Ron from the hut and into the fields. His death was not quick. When blows with sticks and then partial burial failed to kill him, Khorn and the soldiers used their knives.

Phea was initially ignorant of Ron's death. The first repercussion was that a shadow of suspicion fell on her, since the execution of one family member jeopardized other relatives. Friends now were reluctant to associate with her, and Khmer Rouge cadres seemed to single her out for observation. The initial hint of something wrong came when a soldier said to Phea, "How's everything going?" and with a leer he drew his finger across his neck to signify decapitation. Phea turned to a companion and asked, "Was he talking to me?" "I don't know, maybe or maybe not, you should know," came the evasive reply, since word had spread quickly that Phea might soon follow her father's fate. Disturbed by the sudden change in her treatment, Phea went to her grandfather's hut and asked for her father. Her grandfather would not look at her but said, "Go back to your camp." Instead, Phea asked to stay the night and return the next day. Soon after falling asleep, she was awakened by a strong, burning smell. "Grandfather, are you smoking tobacco?" she asked. "No, go back to sleep," came his reply. But when she awoke to the same smell a second time, her grandfather told her, "It's your father. Just say to him, I'm staying here but I'm leaving tomorrow." According to Cambodian beliefs, a ghost seeking contact with a person will create a strong smell that, even in a crowded room, is only perceptible to the intended individual. The visitation was final proof for Phea that her father had been killed.

Phea returned to her camp, unable to cry openly for her deceased father. A display of grief would only further heighten her isolation from former friends. Worse, it would incite the Khmer Rouge, who expected individuals to have greater loyalty to them than to parents, especially when they had judged that one merited death. Under these circumstances, where even emotional expressions were politicized, Phea was forced to allocate her tears. She allowed herself to cry only while stooped at work in the rice paddies so that her face would not be exposed.

Marching with her group toward a work assignment about two months later, Phea passed a man in a bamboo cage, his clothes shredded and his body covered in mud. He called out to her, and Phea had great difficulty determining his identity. After a moment she realized it was Khorn. For reasons unknown, he too was now a victim of the Khmer Rouge. Surely headed for execution, Khorn spent his last days pulling a heavy plow through the fields like a water buffalo. A young boy was his taskmaster. When not laboring, Khorn was placed in the cage. Although Phea was too shocked to take any pleasure in the torment of the man who had ordered her father's death, Khorn's fate confirmed for her the power of her father's threat to seek revenge if tortured.

Soon after witnessing Khorn's demise, Ron's ghost visited Phea again, giving instructions that she credits with saving her life. In a dream she heard his voice repeating, "Go west, go west." For two days Phea pondered the meaning of these words, finally concluding that they were instructions to flee. A minor eye injury gave her an excuse to ask her leaders to be allowed to visit an aunt living nearby, who could heal the injury. When the leaders consented she headed straight for her mother.

She found Roun cutting rice with other women and immediately told her, "We have to go. We're going west." Phea's mother was stunned but quietly placed her rice bundle on the stack, went to her leader, and said, "I'm going away." It was inconceivable that a worker would report her impending flight, and the leader gave no objection. Roun and Phea began walking westward across the dikes that separated the flooded rice paddies. Eventually they passed Phea's work group in the fields. The girls and the leaders looked up at them but said nothing. Farther along they passed a group of soldiers passing the time by playing a game with balls. They, too, saw Phea and Roun but did not stop them. The same thing happened at another checkpoint. Now it was nightfall, and Phea and her mother were in the wilderness. Suddenly they heard something approaching, and called out. It might have been a Khmer Rouge patrol or a wild animal. Instead it was a distant uncle who greeted them with astonishment. He explained that he had been taking two cows to a nearby farm when he had suddenly become lost, although he had made the trip on numerous occasions and the distance could be covered in about half an hour. On this evening he had inexplicably become disoriented and found himself walking in circles, returning to the same spot where he now discovered Phea and Roun.

Phea and Roun returned with the uncle to his house, and he listened incredulously as they recounted their escape. He was especially surprised that they had not been stopped at the last checkpoint, where the soldiers were infamous for their rough treatment of people caught without travel authorization. Fortunately, communication among the Khmer Rouge was quite limited, and local leaders allowed Phea and Roun to stay with Phea's uncle. They even permitted Phea to live with the adults instead of being sent to the local children's camp. But soon the uncle learned that the Khmer Rouge in Phea and Roun's camps had begun searching for them.

Phea and Roun lived in fear that their whereabouts would be discovered. Ron's execution, their escape, and rivalry among Khmer Rouge factions led them to believe that they faced death should they be located. Several weeks passed, and their apprehension grew. One day the children who watched over the cattle came running into the village, breathlessly explaining that they had seen a large group of men approaching who did not speak Cambodian and were wearing green uniforms and round hats. Adults told the children to shut up lest the Khmer Rouge accuse them of being spies. Several of the children received blows to make them understand the seriousness of spreading rumors. But soon Phea, Roun, and the others heard gunfire. Then Khmer Rouge leaders and soldiers came running by with their families and belongings. "Hurry! Come with us. The Vietnamese are here," they shouted. "If you stay they'll bury you with just your heads sticking out and use them to support their cooking pots." Phea had heard this tale before—an old piece of Cambodian folklore about the brutality of the Vietnamese who conquered portions Cambodia in the early nineteenth century. She begged her mother to leave, but Roun said, "No, if we have to die, it's better to die here." The arrival of Vietnamese troops did not signal their deaths, only the end of the Khmer Rouge regime.

Flight, Camp Life, and Migration to the United States

The Vietnamese invasion of Cambodia in December 1978 pushed the Khmer Rouge forces into Thailand within a few months. The ensuing chaos enabled tens of thousands of Cambodians to flee, although the intent of the invasion was colonization rather than rescue. Thailand initially attempted to bar the refugees from entry (Lawyers Committee for Human Rights 1989). One of the most horrendous acts of *refoulement* (forced repatriation) occurred in June 1979, when Thai troops moved about 40,000 Cambodians back across the border. The chosen route was a mined mountain slope and thousands were killed and wounded as a result. International pressure eventually persuaded Thailand to open its border to some 250,000 refugees. Another 250,000 refugees arrived in the mid-1980s following offensives by the Vietnamese army against Cambodian guerrilla forces along the Thailand-Cambodia border. Altogether, about 8 percent of Cambodia's population fled to Thailand in search of refuge. Some 60,000 Cambodians died during their escape (Wain 1981).

In the two years following the formation of a Communist government in Laos, more than 100,000 refugees fled the country (Wain 1981). The escape of the Hmong was particularly harrowing. Harassed by government troops as they fled toward Thailand, many Hmong died crossing the Mekong River, the principal waterway in mainland Southeast Asia. One Hmong group numbered 8,000 when it began the trek to Thailand. Incapacity and death reduced it to 2,500 by the time the last of the band crossed the border (Lee 1982). Within 10 years of the revolution, more than 350,000 refugees, or 10 percent of the total population, had fled the country. At least 15,000 Hmong and 5,000 lowland Laotians perished during their flight (Wain 1981).

The fall of South Vietnam led to the evacuation to the United States of about 125,000 refugees, most of whom were associated with the American or Vietnamese government. Subsequent persecution of ethnic Chinese led some 250,000 to cross into China, and more sought to escape by boat. The number of these "boat people," who often had to bribe government officials before departure, was estimated at 300,000 by the middle of 1979.

Flight from Vietnam by boat was fraught with peril. The overcrowded boats were in poor condition and, on reaching Thailand, Malaysia, and other adjacent countries, government vessels might refuse them landing and tow the leaking vessels out to sea. Thai fishermen and pirates roamed the South China Sea preying on the boat people. About three-quarters of all refugee boats that left Vietnam for Thailand during the early 1980s were attacked two or more times. Between 1980 and 1983 more than 2,200 women were raped and another 500 of them abducted, presumably to work in Thai brothels (Sutter 1990). Cases of cannibalism were reported on some boats when provisions ran out, and a U.S. Navy captain was courtmartialed for failing to adequately aid refugees on one

Map 2

Country of First Asylum for Indochinese Refugees, 1975–82

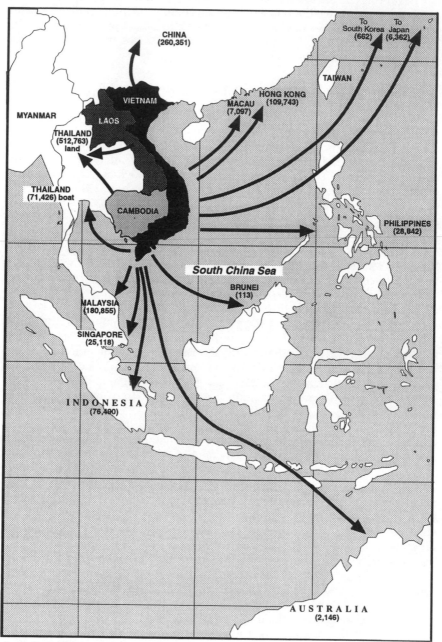

CHINA
(260,351)

To
South Korea
(662)

To
Japan
(6,362)

TAIWAN

VIETNAM

LAOS

MYANMAR

MACAU
(7,097)

HONG KONG
(109,743)

THAILAND
(512,763)
land

THAILAND
(71,426) boat

CAMBODIA

PHILIPPINES
(28,842)

South China Sea

BRUNEI
(113)

MALAYSIA
(180,855)

SINGAPORE
(25,118)

INDONESIA
(76,490)

AUSTRALIA
(2,146)

Source: Rogge 1985

such boat (*Refugee Reports* 1989). Altogether, more than 600,000 boat people arrived in other Asian countries, primarily Malaysia, Hong Kong, and Indonesia. Some boats landed as far away as Australia, while merchant ships that rescued the refugees dropped them off in ports as distant as Saudi Arabia and the Ivory Coast (Wain 1981). Estimates of the deaths among Vietnamese boat people range up to 142,000 (Banister 1985).

In response to the flow of refugees from Vietnam, Laos, and Cambodia, the United Nations established camps in Thailand, Malaysia, and other countries in Southeast Asia to shelter the refugees and permit Western countries to select some for admission. It also created a route for legal emigration from Vietnam. More than 125,000 refugees have left via this Orderly Departure Program since it was established in 1979. In Thailand there were nine camps for refugees from Laos, seven for Cambodian refugees, and two for Vietnamese refugees. Malaysia and Indonesia contained 13 camps for Vietnamese boat people. Special transit camps in Indonesia and the Philippines provided several months of language and cultural training for those refugees selected for admission to the United States (Tollefson 1989).

While the refugees from Vietnam, Laos, and Cambodia shared a general reason for leaving their homeland—repression by new Communist regimes—they differed in the motives that prompted their flight (see Table 3.1). The Hmong and Laotians were much more likely to feel that their physical safety was threatened. Cambodians were the only group for whom famine was a leading motive. The chaos produced by the Vietnamese invasion of Cambodia in 1978 and military offensives in the mid-1980s disrupted agricultural production. In addition, food distribution by international relief agencies in Cambodia was at times confiscated by the new Vietnamese government and sent to Vietnam. Only a significant proportion of Vietnamese refugees migrated for the purpose of resettling abroad. This aspiration stemmed in part from their greater contact and knowledge of the United States, but also from their hope for economic advancement

Table 3.1

Motives for Migration from Homeland among Indochinese Refugees in Thai Camps
(in percent)

	Hmong	Laotian	Cambodian	Vietnamese
Political situation	52	41	51	55
Afraid of being killed	23	41	3	2
Famine	3	10	34	6
Resettlement in West	1	0	8	20
Other	21	8	4	17

N = approximately 150 for each ethnic group (number varies slightly with "no response" on each question)
Source: Institute for Asian Studies 1988

Table 3.2

Major Fears If Returned to Homeland among Indochinese Refugees in Thai Camps
(in percent)

Hmong	Laotian	Cambodian	Vietnamese
Jailed, killed 30	Jailed, killed 37	Vietnamese hurt 20	No freedom 25
Seminar 23	Accused enemy 19	Jailed, killed 19	Jailed, killed 19
Ex-official 13	Seminar 14	Communism 14	Forced work 16
Communism 9	Ex-official 9	Forced work 11	Ex-official 13
No freedom 6	No freedom 9	Forced army 9	Communism 12

N = approximately 150 for each ethnic group (number varies slightly with "no response" on each question)
Source: Institute for Asian Studies 1988

owing to their higher job skills and educational levels compared with the other refugees. Indochinese refugees were as much different as alike in their motives for fleeing to Thailand.

The differences between refugees from Laos and Cambodia, and those from Vietnam, are even more apparent when considering what life would be like should they return to their homeland (see Table 3.2). Direct threats to personal safety was the greatest concern of the Hmong, Laotians, and Cambodians. The Hmong were especially worried about being forced to attend a "seminar," the Laotian regime's euphemistic term for indoctrination camps where noncooperation meant punishment or even death. Laotians had the greatest fear of direct persecution based on accusations of disloyalty, forced attendance at a seminar, and association with the prerevolutionary government (42 percent combined). The Vietnamese occupation of Cambodia was the primary reason Cambodian refugees felt they could not go home. Many feared personal harm from the Vietnamese authorities. Others expected coercion in the form of labor or conscription to fight the Cambodian guerrilla armies on the Thailand-Cambodia border. The plurality of the Vietnamese, however, gave only a very general objection to the lack of freedom as the primary reason they could not return to their homeland, although 35 percent had specific fears of persecution. Overall, between one-fifth and two-fifths of the refugees feared for their personal safety should they repatriate, and another one-third to two-fifths feared some lesser form of persecution, often because of their association with the pro-American government in power prior to 1975.

Although the common image of refugees is one of panicked, spontaneous flight, there was a degree of social organization to the refugee movements in Southeast Asia (see Table 3.3). Only Laotian and Cambodian refugees migrated with almost no counsel or advice from relatives, friends, and others in their homeland. But about one-third of Hmong refugees joined the migration because

Table 3.3

Decision and Information about Migration to Thailand among Indochinese Refugees in Thai Camps (in percent)

	Hmong	Laotian	Cambodian	Vietnamese
Who persuaded to migrate				
No one	67	92	90	65
Friends	8	2	5	15
Family and kin	21	6	3	15
Other	4	0	2	5
Source of information about Thai camps				
No one	80	87	84	68
Friends	6	3	6	21
Family and kin	8	8	*	7
Other	6	2	9	4

* less than 1 percent
N = approximately 150 for each ethnic group (number varies slightly with "no response" on each question)
Source: Institute for Asian Studies 1988

someone, usually a relative, persuaded them to, although most knew nothing about the Thai camps that were their destination. Vietnamese refugees were as likely to be convinced to migrate by a relative as they were by a nonrelative. Moreover, one in four Vietnamese refugees had received information about the Thai camps from friends or people with whom they had even less acquaintance. This pattern indicates how kin and friendship networks can form the basis for migration even among refugees, particularly when flight requires locating and paying for scarce transportation on a fishing boat (Allen and Hiller 1985).

Not only did about one in five of the refugees have information about the camps or migrate because of someone else's decision, but the refugees made the migration as members of different types of groups (see Table 3.4). Vietnamese traveled largely in nonkin groups consisting of unknown individuals and friends, usually accompanied by a child although infrequently with a spouse. Conversely, the Hmong made the trek in very large groups that typically included not only a spouse and children but parents and other relatives. The very large proportion of nonrelatives in the Hmong migration reflects the movement of clans and bands of soldiers and their dependents. Most Laotians traveled in small groups of nine persons or fewer, and most came only with their spouse and children. Cambodian migration also occurred within the nuclear family but

Table 3.4

Number and Type of Persons Accompanying Migration among Indochinese Refugees in Thai Camps
(in percent, unless otherwise noted)

	Hmong	Laotian	Cambodian	Vietnamese
Number starting				
1–4	11	49	43	20
5–9	27	38	23	17
10–14	7	7	7	8
15+	55	6	27	55
Mean	47	6	24	18
Type*				
Spouse	60	58	55	35
Children	96	81	68	60
Parent	41	6	12	5
Other relative	18	8	12	7
Friends	16	16	17	40
Nonrelatives	50	26	20	59

* multiple answers accepted
N = approximately 150 for each ethnic group (number varies slightly with "no response" on each question)
Source: Institute for Asian Studies 1988

included a wider range of other kin than among Laotians. Thus the social organization of the Indochinese refugee migration ranged from groups comprised largely of friends and nonrelatives to nuclear and extended families up to entire communities and clans.

Most Indochinese refugees left their homeland with some relatives, typically a spouse and children. But the vast majority also left relatives behind (see Table 3.5). The one exception are the Hmong: almost two-thirds report no relatives remaining in Laos—another indicator of the extensive kin groups involved in their migration to Thailand. Siblings are the most common relatives residing in the refugees' homelands. A large proportion of Laotians also have parents in Laos. Cambodians have kin ties to their homeland through aunts and uncles, while the Vietnamese have both parents and parents' relatives in Vietnam. Despite migrating with kin, most Indochinese refugees still have kin ties to their homeland.

Living in refugee camps granted the refugees protection from the hardships in their homeland, but the camps had hardships of their own (Mayotte 1992).

Table 3.5

Relatives Still in Homeland among Indochinese Refugees in Thai Camps (in percent)

	Hmong	Laotian	Cambodian	Vietnamese
Relatives still in homeland				
Yes	37	92	77	92
No	63	8	23	8
If yes, type				
Spouse	2	*	0	0
Children	2	*	*	*
Parent	2	17	3	3
Sibling	48	30	40	17
Parent and sibling	2	21	6	21
Parents' relatives	7	17	33	37
Distant relative, friend	38	8	12	4
Close relative and in-law**	2	6	5	17

* less than 1 percent
** includes spouse, children, parent, and sibling
N = approximately 150 for each ethnic group (number varies slightly with "no response" on each question)
Source: Institute for Asian Studies 1988

Food and water were rationed and sometimes in short supply. Health facilities were rudimentary. Security could be a problem, whether the threat came from the Thai military and police or bandits and gangs of compatriots. Social services and recreation were also limited. Many refugees, particularly the Hmong and Cambodians, lived for many years in these conditions because they were neither accepted for resettlement abroad nor willing to voluntarily return to their homeland (see Table 3.6). Indeed, the majority of refugees other than the Laotians had lived in at least one other camp, many of the Vietnamese more than one. Most Vietnamese used their time to prepare for eventual resettlement, again confirming the mix of economic and political motives to their migration. But only about one-third of Laotians and Cambodians used their time to study, while the Hmong found very little to do. Except for the Vietnamese in Thailand, life in the refugee camps was bleak and prolonged for most Indochinese refugees.

With the exception of the Hmong, almost all Indochinese refugees hoped to resettle in a third country, with the United States being their overwhelming first choice, followed by Australia (see Table 3.7). Unlike most other Indochinese refugees waiting in anguish for their names to appear on a list of refugees

Table 3.6

Years since Migration, Previous Camps, and Time Use among Indochinese Refugees in Thai Camps (in percent)

	Hmong	Laotian	Cambodian	Vietnamese
Years since migration				
< 1	0	*	0	34
1–2	*	53	0	63
3–4	*	9	0	2
5–6	18	10	2	0
7–8	12	7	97	0
9–10	19	8	*	0
≥ 11	49	12	0	*
Previous camps				
None	3	61	24	1
One	81	34	55	25
Two or more	16	5	21	74
Time use in present camp				
Nothing	52	22	12	17
Study	8	22	20	69
Work	19	18	43	4
Work and study	4	10	16	4
Household tasks	14	8	4	3
Other	3	20	5	3

* less than 1 percent
N = approximately 150 for each ethnic group (number varies slightly with "no response" on each question)
Source: Institute for Asian Studies 1988

accepted for resettlement, the Hmong were actually refusing resettlement offers (Long 1993). Led on by political leaders, some still expected to return to Laos following a military victory by Hmong guerrilla forces operating from the Thai camps. Others had received negative reports about life in America from Hmong refugees resettled there. Despite a widespread reluctance to leave Southeast Asia, most of the Hmong were unsure if they would ever return to their homeland. Only among Cambodians did a substantial proportion of refugees believe that they would eventually return, and they cited the ending of war and

Table 3.7

Desire to Resettle in Third Country and Return to Homeland among Indochinese Refugees in Thai Camps (in percent)

	Hmong	Laotian	Cambodian	Vietnamese
Wish to resettle				
Yes	47	80	99	100
No	53	20	1	0
If yes, where				
United States	84	64	53	53
France	5	5	3	*
Canada	1	7	8	9
Australia	1	14	18	19
Other, depends	8	11	17	19
Job expected if resettled				
Never thought about it	83	32	32	11
Any	8	11	4	0
Depends	2	25	29	31
Specific job cited	7	32	35	58
Return to homeland in future				
Yes	8	6	32	6
No	8	24	17	45
Depends	84	70	51	49

*less than 1 percent
N = approximately 150 for each ethnic group (number varies slightly with "no response" on each question)
Source: Institute for Asian Studies 1988

Vietnamese occupation as the conditions that would precipitate repatriation. With these conditions met by 1993, the last of the 320,000 Cambodian refugees returned to their homeland under U.N. auspices. Conversely, nearly one-half of the Vietnamese believed they would never return to their homeland, most citing their dislike of communism as the main reason.

The majority of the refugees were unable to name a job they expected to get should they be resettled. Even the Vietnamese, the group with the strongest preference for resettlement, had little knowledge of labor market conditions in the major resettlement countries. The leading jobs expected by the Vietnamese were work and study (11 percent), sewing (11 percent), and fishing (10 percent).

Cambodians and Laotians listed mechanic, laborer, and sewing. Most Indo-chinese refugees in Thailand wished to resettle in a third country yet were reluctant to permanently sever ties with their homeland and had little knowledge of the country where they hoped to start their new lives.

Although the vast majority of refugees did not leave their homeland with the purpose of eventually resettling in the West, officials from the United States, Canada, and other countries conducted interviews in the camps to select refugees for admission. U.S. criteria for admission were, in order of priority:

P-1. National interest or imminent danger.
P-2. Former U.S. government employee.
P-3. Close relative in the United States.
P-4a. Former employee of U.S. business or agency.
P-4b. Civil or armed forces service for former governments in Vietnam, Laos, and Cambodia.
P-5. Married sibling or grandchildren in the United States.
P-6. Special humanitarian interest.

The interviews determined which, if any, of these criteria applied to the refugees, and the refugees needed documentation and credible stories to be accepted. The following excerpt is from an interview between a U.S. official, a Hmong interpreter, and a Hmong woman and her four children in the Thai camp of Ban Vinai (Long 1993, 160–63). It illustrates the difficulty of creating a linear life history for a people with a non-Western conception of time, complex kin relations, and lives disrupted by war:

Interviewer: How many brothers and sisters do you have in the United States?
Response: [interpreter holds up fingers in response]
Interviewer: It really is her sister? Same mother, same father?
Response: Yes.
Interviewer: Does she have any information about American prisoners of war or Americans missing in action?
Response: No.
Interviewer: Does she know any of the months of date of birth of her children?
Response: No.
Interviewer: All right. . . . I'm going to assign a day and a month—2/2, 3/3, 4/4, 5/5 [pointing to each child as he assigns a birth date for future immigration, school, hospital, and refugee assistance forms]. Does she have an address for her former husband?
Response: No.
Interviewer: How old was she when her father died?
Response: Six years ago.
Interviewer: Laos or Ban Vinai?
Response: Laos.
Interviewer: Occupation before?
Response: Soldier.
Interviewer: Did she live in her home village until she got married?
Response: No.

Interviewer: Where did she move to when they moved, where did she grow up before she was married?
Response: She moved from [village in Laos] and she married her first husband in Chua Long.
Interviewer: Did she stay there with her family after her husband died?
Response: Yes.

By the mid-1980s the prospects for resettlement abroad were growing more remote. Western nations that offered permanent settlement, and the Southeast Asian countries that provided temporary asylum, began focusing on changing political conditions in the homeland and repatriation as the means to solving the refugee crisis. Approximately two-thirds of the refugees already had relatives resettled in third countries (see Table 3.8). But only

Table 3.8

Possibilities for Resettlement among Indochinese Refugees in Thai camps (in percent)

	Hmong	Laotian	Cambodian	Vietnamese
Relatives resettled				
Yes	77	81	52	61
No	23	19	48	39
Sponsor abroad				
Yes	20	50	36	33
No	80	50	64	67
Ever interviewed				
Yes	43	70	90	15
No	57	30	10	85
If yes, number interviews				
One	89	77	56	82
Two	7	12	24	12
Three or More	4	11	19	6
Certain of resettlement				
Yes	2	11	3	10
No	98	89	97	90

N = approximately 150 for each ethnic group (number varies slightly with "no response" on each question)
Source: Institute for Asian Studies 1988

about one-third of the refugees reported that these relatives would act as sponsors for them, probably because they were not close relatives or the refugees in Thailand did not know their exact location and thus could not contact them. Most Laotians and Cambodians, and about two in five Hmong, had already been interviewed once. A substantial proportion of Laotians and Cambodians had been interviewed more than once, and yet few had firm resettlement offers.

Ultimately the U.S. government admitted more than 1 million Indochinese refugees (see Table 3.9). The Intergovernmental Committee for European Migration (ICEM) coordinated flights to the United States. It had been formed in 1952 to assist with population movements resulting from World War II. Working with refugees from the Third World during the 1970s and 1980s eventually forced the ICEM to drop the adjective in its name indicating its regional origins. ICEM paid for the refugees' airfare and then sought repayment sometime after the refugees reached their destination. Once the refugee landed in the United States, immigration officials gave him or her residence documents, which the refugee placed in a large white plastic bag with the blue ICEM emblem and his or her visa number written in black marker. Newly arrived refugees were identifiable for days after their landing because they carried their ICEM bags everywhere they went, having been instructed never to leave beyond their reach the precious documents granting them refuge.

Because of the large number of refugees fleeing Vietnam and the intensive American presence that created political ties to the United States, Vietnamese comprise three-fifths of the Indochinese refugee population in the United States. About one in five Vietnamese arrived in the first wave to flee the fall of Saigon. Another one in three came during the peak of the boat-people crisis between 1979 and 1981. By the late 1980s and early 1990s a large proportion of arriving Vietnamese were detainees released from the reeducation camps established by the Socialist Republic of Vietnam to punish and indoctrinate citizens with ties to the pro-American regime. The Amerasian Homecoming Act of 1987 added another stream of migrants from Vietnam. The migration of Cambodians had all but ended by the early 1990s. Indeed, two-thirds of the Cambodians arrived in a six-year period following the collapse of the Khmer Rouge and the resulting military conflict with the subsequent Vietnamese-backed government. The admission of refugees from Laos was more prolonged than that of Cambodian refugees, in part reflecting the reluctance of the Hmong to accept permanent resettlement in the West as a solution to their exile. Indeed, the Hmong and other highland groups arrived during the late 1980s and early 1990s in numbers higher than at any other time except the peak years of 1979–80.

U.S. government officials expect that the admission of Indochinese refugees will end during 1995, with the arrival of the last Vietnamese political prisoners, Amerasians, and their families (*Refugee Reports* 1993b). If these projections prove correct, it will have taken the United States 20 years to solve through refugee admissions what it could not solve through military intervention and diplomatic pressure: political stability in Vietnam, Laos, and Cambodia. Symbolic of the longevity of the American impact on the region was the arrival in 1992 of some Montagnards, an ethnic group from the Vietnam highlands who were staunch military allies of the United States (Ruiz 1993). This group of

Table 3.9

Admission of Highland Laotian, Lowland Laotian, Cambodian, Vietnamese and Amerasians to the United States, 1975–1992

	Highland Laotian*	Lowland Laotian**	Cambodian	Vietnamese	Amerasian***
1975	300	500	4,600	125,000	0
1976	3,000	7,100	1,100	3,200	0
1977	1,700	400	300	1,900	0
1978	3,900	4,100	1,300	11,100	0
1979	11,300	18,900	6,000	44,500	0
1980	27,200	28,300	16,000	95,200	0
1981	3,700	15,600	27,100	86,100	0
1982	2,600	6,800	20,100	42,600	0
1983	700	2,100	13,200	23,000	0
1984	2,800	4,500	19,900	24,900	0
1985	1,900	3,500	19,200	25,400	0
1986	3,700	9,200	9,800	22,800	0
1987	8,300	7,300	1,500	23,000	0
1988	10,400	4,200	2,800	17,300	400
1989	8,500	4,000	1,900	22,600	8,700
1990	5,200	3,600	2,200	27,300	13,400
1991	6,400	2,900	50	27,700	16,500
1992	6,800	500	100	27,200	17,100

* primarily the Hmong but also Mien, Tai Dam, and Lao-theung
** ethnic Lao
*** American-Vietnamese children born in Vietnam and accompanying relatives
N = approximately 150 for each ethnic group (number varies slightly with "no response" on each question)
Sources: Gordon 1987; Olney 1986; Refugee Reports 1986a, 1993a; U.S. Office of Refugee Resettlement 1993

nearly 400 men, women, and children had been fighting the Socialist Republic of Vietnam for the entire 17 years following the fall of Saigon. Pushed into the Cambodian jungle, they were finally discovered by U.N. personnel and convinced to end their war.

Conclusion

U.S. military and political intervention in Southeast Asia during the 1960s and early 1970s set the stage for the flight of refugees from Vietnam, Laos, and Cambodia once pro-American regimes fell to Communist forces. Over the next two and one-half years, 130,000 Vietnamese arrived in the United States, along with 8,000 Laotians, 6,000 Cambodians, and 5,000 Hmong and other ethnic groups from the Laotian highlands. American immigration and foreign policy officials expected the migration to end there, a brief dénouement of the Vietnam War. These approximately 150,000 Indochinese refugees might have remained an obscure footnote in American immigration history but for the actions of the new Communist regimes in Southeast Asia. They pursued brutal totalitarian policies against their own people and war against their neighbors. By the late 1970s a long-run refugee crisis had developed in Southeast Asia.

The underlying causes of the crisis were political and economic, but they took different forms in each of the refugee-sending countries. Discrimination against the ethnic Chinese in Vietnam and the persecution of the Hmong in Laos created two refugee flows. Retribution against officials in the former pro-American regimes added more Vietnamese and Laotian refugees. Agricultural collectivization and forced labor created further incentives for flight in both countries, but especially in Cambodia, where the entire population was transformed into slaves for four years. Vietnam's invasion of Cambodia in 1978, the subsequent border war with China in 1979, and then efforts to colonize Cambodia during the 1980s added to the military and political turmoil. By 1980 camps for Vietnamese, Laotians, and Cambodians dotted Thailand's inland and coastal borders, while large camps for Vietnamese boat people extended from Malaysia and Indonesia to the Philippines and Hong Kong. To get to a refugee camp in an adjacent country, Indochinese refugees had to evade armed patrols, cross mined borders and combat zones, or make land on unseaworthy boats after eluding pirates. The death toll from this trek will never be known, but the total number may be as high as 220,000.

Those refugees who did arrive to the comparative safety of the refugee camps, principally in Thailand, migrated for the common reason of political repression in their homelands. Some were more motivated by famine, others by direct threats to their personal safety, and still others by the desire to resettle in the West. Vietnamese tended to flee in groups comprised of one or two close relatives, some friends, and many nonrelatives. Laotians migrated in small groups based on the nuclear family, Cambodians in larger groups comprised of nuclear and extended family members. The Hmong crossed into Thailand in very large groups averaging 50 people and including not only spouse, children, and parents but other relatives and clan members. Despite the presence of kin among all the refugee flight groups, the vast majority of Vietnamese, Laotians, and Cambodians, and more than one-third of the Hmong left relatives behind in their homeland, typically a sibling. One-half of the Hmong, and almost all of the other refugees, eventually hoped to resettle abroad, usually in the United States. Yet most were also unwilling to admit that they would never return to their homeland, with the proportion indicating some likelihood of repatriation ranging from slightly more than one-half of Vietnamese to more than nine in ten of the Hmong. But the slow pace of political change in the new Communist regimes of former Indochina meant that many years would elapse before the refugees felt safe enough to return.

The impatience of Thailand and other Southeast Asian hosts to be rid of the refugees, and a sense of responsibility for the refugees' plight, prompted the United States to initiate the largest refugee admissions program in the country's history. The one-millionth Indochinese refugee arrived in America during 1991. Given the characteristics of the refugees admitted that year, this individual was probably a Vietnamese political prisoner who had been punished for ties to the old pro-American government, or an Amerasian child of an American soldier and a Vietnamese woman.

four

Settlement and Community
in the United States

Beginning in 1975 and continuing through the 1980s, the officials managing the U.S. refugee resettlement program sought to disperse arriving Indochinese refugees across the country. The refugees, however, increasingly concentrated in a few states as they sought job opportunities, social-welfare programs, warmer climates, and especially reunification with kin, friends, and compatriots. Despite the refugees' largely successful resistance to this dispersal policy, urban conditions determine in which neighborhoods they form communities.

In Chicago the social and economic history of the community area known as Uptown explains why the Indochinese initially settled there. Over time, however, a community that began with residential concentration and few businesses has shifted to a business district comprised of several Asian-American groups, although the area is losing its refugee population. Local conditions profoundly shape community formation among international migrants—a factor largely missing from the ethnic-resilience model despite the centrality of the ethnic community for its conception of the adaptation process.

Ethnic stores and dwellings are only the outward symbols of refugee communities. A case study of a Cambodian Buddhist temple in Uptown demonstrates how the refugees reconstruct communal institutions that were central in their homelands. This rebuilding process, which inevitably changes these institutions, does not fit within the assimilation model's exaggerated distinction between homeland and host society. From the assimilation perspective, homeland institutions are transplanted, as if immigrants and refugees brought them ready-made. Yet institutions like Buddhism were changing before the migrants even left their homeland. Refugees' efforts to reproduce them in the United States contribute to this change because the refugee communities themselves are evolving rather than being little pieces of the homeland relocated to a new land.

Urban areas are the sites at which refugees reconstruct communities, but they contain inhabitants who preceded the refugees' arrival. A chronicle of a rent strike in a New York City building containing Indochinese and African-American households reveals how newcomers and established residents come to terms with each other's presence. The increasing proportion of foreign-born and native ethnic minorities in American cities calls into question the assimilation model's depiction of the adaptation process. In this model, integration proceeds as non-European newcomers interact with a single, uniform culture and society, presumably that of the majority of the population. The new urban pluralism suggests that the adjustment of immigrants and refugees is influenced as much by African Americans, among other minorities and immigrants, as it is by the whites of European ancestry who the assimilation model implicitly takes as the core of the United States.

Resisting Dispersal

Since 1975 the federal government has funded 14 voluntary agencies to resettle Indochinese refugees. The agencies vary in their orientation and historical mission to assist newcomers (see Table 4.1). The Hebrew Immigrant Aid Society originated during the early 1900s in response to the settlement needs of Russian

Table 4.1

Characteristics of American Voluntary Agencies

	Affiliation	Year of origin	Years working with Indochinese	% of all Indochinese resettled*
ACNS	Nonsectarian	1930	Since 1975	11
AFCR	Nonsectarian	1948	Since 1975	3
BCRRR	Buddhist	1979	1979–86	1
CWS	Protestant	1946	Since 1975	9
HIAS	Jewish	1902	Since 1975	3
Idaho	Nonsectarian	1980	1980–85	1
Iowa	Nonsectarian	1975	Since 1975	1
IRC	Nonsectarian	1933	Since 1975	12
LIRS	Lutheran	1948	Since 1975	5
EMM	Episcopalian	1939	Since 1982	1
TF	Nonsectarian	1939	Since 1975	2
USCC	Catholic	1936	Since 1975	43
WR	Evangelical	1945	Since 1975	5
YMCA	Christian	1844	1980–83	2

* For fiscal year 1981, the year with the second largest number of Indochinese refugee arrivals (131,000) and when all but one agency were in operation. The figure for EMM is for 1982.
Source: Hein 1993a

Jews, although it began work in Europe several decades earlier. The arrival of European refugees before World War II and then displaced persons after the war produced seven other agencies. Three agencies developed in response to the Indochinese refugee crisis.

Agencies vary not only by their seniority but also by the degree to which they have an ethnic or religious affiliation. Three agencies (the American Fund for Czechoslovak Refugees, the International Rescue Committee, and the Tolstoy Foundation) began by assisting ethnic groups from Central Europe (Czechs, German Jews, and White Russians, respectively). When the Indochinese arrived, refugees from these earlier cohorts were still represented among top executives and members of the boards of trustees. The American Council for Nationalities Service, which originated during the settlement-house movement for European immigrants, is the only agency that did not have an ethnic or religious affiliation. The Idaho State Voluntary Agency and the Iowa Bureau of Refugee Services are state governments that legally could not have a religious orientation. Although eight agencies identify with a religion, religious philosophy and institutions are present in their work to different degrees. Those utilizing church groups (such as the Church World Service and World Relief) carry much of their religious background into their contact with refugees. Agencies that provide services through caseworkers (such as HIAS and the U.S. Catholic Conference) bring comparatively little theology to their work.

The Refugee Act of 1980 codified the provision of income support and social services to recognized political migrants (Hein 1992). It created the Office of Refugee Resettlement in the Department of Health and Human Services. Between 1980 and 1990 this office provided state governments with $710 million for refugee social services and $3.315 billion for the refugees' medical costs and use of public assistance. The act also established the Bureau for Refugee Programs in the Department of State, which provides a per capita grant of about $500 to voluntary agencies for each refugee sponsored.

When the first Vietnamese refugees arrived in April 1975 the federal government stipulated to the voluntary agencies that no more than 3,000 of the refugees be resettled in any one state (Kelly 1977). When the last refugees left the mainland reception camps used to process them into the United States, however, 11 states were above the quota. Together these states accounted for 58 percent of all the refugees resettled. Furthermore, the Vietnamese concentrated in key urban areas within each state, a residential pattern reflecting the availability of sponsors, housing, and jobs.

Nonetheless, public and private officials continued their efforts to disperse arriving refugees (Hein 1992). Their goal was not to assimilate the refugees and prevent the formation of ethnic communities but to limit the cost in social, health, and educational services incurred by counties with large numbers of refugees, and to avoid the potential of job competition between the refugees and natives. In 1981 the State Department's Bureau for Refugee Programs formulated a new dispersal policy (U.S. ORR 1984). The bureau requested that the voluntary agencies make a list of "impacted areas" in which further refugee resettlement was undesirable owing to lack of jobs and affordable housing, long-term welfare dependency, and high rates of secondary migration by refugees already settled in the United States. Refugees "impacted" an area when their presence led to "a drain on community resources of sufficient mag-

Table 4.2

Areas of the United States Restricted to Arriving Indochinese Refugees by 1982

State	County	Principal city	County inhabitants per refugee
California	San Diego	San Diego	159
California	Orange	Santa Ana	132
California	Los Angeles	Long Beach	217
California	Sacramento	Sacramento	171
California	San Francisco	San Francisco	53
California	Alameda	Oakland	216
California	San Joaquin	Stockton	129
California	Stanislaus	Modesto	n.a.
Illinois	Cook	Elgin	717
Minnesota	Ramsey	St. Paul	74
Oregon	Multnomah	Portland	70
Rhode Island	Providence	Providence	n.a.
Texas	All counties on the Gulf Coast		n.a.
Virginia	Arlington	Arlington	62
Virginia	Fairfax	Arlington	987

Note: U.S. inhabitants per refugee equals 671
Source: ACVA 1982

nitude to materially affect the quality of services to the general community" (U.S. DHHS 1983, 55,301). This dispersal policy meant that arriving refugees without immediate relatives in the United States would not be resettled in areas already containing a large number of refugees (see Table 4.2).

There were two impediments to the dispersal policy. First, the refugees often moved within the United States after initial placement. This secondary migration reinforced existing settlement patterns rather than more evenly distributing the refugees (Desbarats 1985). The refugees concentrated on the West Coast, Gulf Coast, and in the Midwest. Once approximately 1,700 Indochinese refugees live in a state, more will follow, while states that never reach this threshold have stable or even declining numbers of refugees. California in particular is the destination for many refugees leaving their initial resettlement site. A survey of refugees who had moved to the state found that the climate (76 percent) and the presence of relatives and friends (67 percent) were the leading motives (Nguyen 1993). But about one-third of the refugees also cited employment and training opportunities, while about one-fifth cited public assistance.

The second stumbling block to the dispersal policy was that by 1981 many Indochinese refugees were admitted to the United States as family reunion cases. A survey of sponsorship patterns among Indochinese refugees found 33 percent with close relatives already in the United States, such as siblings, parents, and children; 34 percent with more distant relatives, such as cousins; 8 percent with friends; and only 25 percent with no contacts who could act as sponsors (U.S. GAO 1983). These strong kin ties meant that the dispersal policy could only be applied to about one-third of arriving refugees, since the voluntary agencies could choose the resettlement site only for arriving refugees not sponsored by relatives.

Despite the dispersal policy, Indochinese refugees had already established their settlement patterns by the time the last Vietnamese left the mainland reception camps in December of 1975 (see Table 4.3). Eight of the ten states in which the first wave settled continued to be the main sites into the 1990s. Like other Asian Americans, Indochinese refugees are disproportionately concentrated in California. But excepting that state, the settlement of the refugees bears a greater resemblance to that of the total U.S. population than to the Asian-American population. Florida and Oklahoma received comparatively large contingents of refugees in 1975 because of two military bases used as reception centers. Massachusetts and Oregon replaced these states owing to secondary migration. A willingness to move within an unfamiliar country soon after arrival, and the kin networks between refugees in Southeast Asia and their sponsoring relatives in the United States, enabled Indochinese refugees to determine their own settlement over the objections of officials in the public and private sectors. Although the refugees chose the states and cities in which to start their new lives, urban conditions greatly determined which neighborhoods they entered.

An Indochinese Neighborhood Grows in Chicago

Uptown is the home for many Indochinese refugees in Chicago. The refugees attend the adjacent community college and also work in administrative and teaching positions there. About 50 Southeast Asian, primarily Vietnamese, businesses crowd a three-block strip—restaurants, boutiques, grocery stores, beauty salons, jewelry shops, and a bank among them. The neighborhood is so symbolic of Southeast Asia that a Vietnam veterans' organization opened up a small, privately funded museum there. Annual street fairs occur in August, to promote business, and in January, to celebrate the Vietnamese New Year. Mutual-assistance associations (MAAs) representing Cambodians, the Hmong, Laotions, ethnic Chinese, and Vietnamese have offices in the area, and there is a Cambodian Buddhist temple. The formation of this community in a neighborhood that previously was "a ghost town after dark . . . dominated by pimps, prostitutes and drug pushers who assembled on unlit, crumbling sidewalks" (*New York Times* 1985, 1) symbolizes the successful urban settlement of Indochinese refugees. It also reveals how local urban conditions create different types of refugee communities.

Following its incorporation into the city of Chicago in 1889, Uptown experienced improved conditions until about 1920 (*Chicago Local Community Fact Book*

Table 4.3

States with the 10 Largest Indochinese Refugee Populations (in percent)*

1975	Indochinese refugees	1990	Indochinese refugees	Asian Americans	U.S. population
California	20.9	California	39.6	39.1	12.0
Texas	7.0	Texas	7.5	4.3	6.8
Pennsylvania	5.5	Washington	4.7	2.9	1.9
Florida	4.1	Minnesota	3.7	1.0	1.7
Washington	3.2	New York	3.6	9.5	7.2
Minnesota	2.9	Pennsylvania	3.2	1.8	4.7
New York	2.9	Massachusetts	3.1	1.9	2.4
Virginia	2.9	Illinois	3.1	3.9	4.5
Illinois	2.8	Virginia	2.5	2.1	2.4
Oklahoma	2.8	Oregon	2.2	0.9	1.1

* ranked by actual number of refugees when percentages are equal
Sources: Kelly 1977; U.S. ORR 1991

1963). The extension of the elevated train line first to Wilson Avenue in 1900 and then to Howard Street in 1907 (the present-day limit of Chicago) brought the area within travel distance for many Chicago residents. The city drained swamps along Lake Michigan and created several beaches. Developers built housing for young singles and married couples who found the area's location desirable. Older ethnic groups, such as Germans, Swedes, and Irish, moved into the area as more recent immigrants from Southern and Eastern Europe occupied their neighborhoods—a process known as ethnic succession.

Development subsided during the 1920s, and between 1930 and 1950 Uptown experienced two decades of stability (*Chicago Local Community Fact Book* 1963). During this period the area was home to a Jewish community, whose past residence is attested to by an abandoned synagogue and a still-functioning kosher butcher sandwiched between a Vietnamese restaurant and grocery. The Uptown population began declining beginning in 1950. By 1980 Uptown was synonymous with American urban problems.

Uptown's demise resulted from municipal and regional developments that its residents could not control themselves or pressure the city to confront. Some developments involved new and unstable populations entering the area. The in-migration of poor whites from Appalachia began in the 1950s and peaked in the mid-1960s (De Meth 1976; Stark 1972). The development of alcohol rehabilitation centers commenced during the 1960s. By 1965 the Uptown population had the highest rate of alcoholism in the nation (Miner and Washington 1971).

Map 3

Indochinese Settlement in Chicago

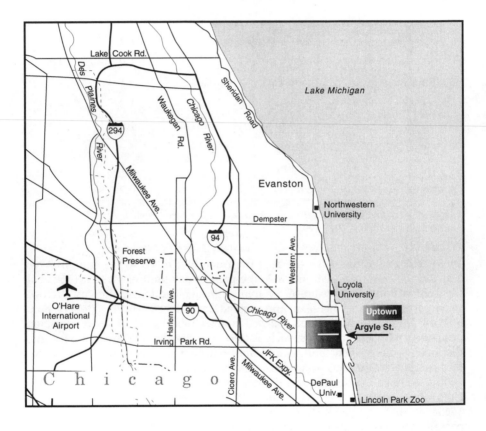

Finally, mentally ill individuals moved in during the late 1960s as a result of federal and state deinstitutionalization policies (Jacobson 1975).

Other developments involved changing economic conditions and property values. To create a community college in the early 1970s, the city destroyed more than 1,200 housing units and displaced 4,000 residents (*Chicago Reader* 1977). Real estate speculation undercut property values and left many buildings abandoned in the mid-1970s (Aronson 1973). Then failed development projects produced shuttered storefronts (De Meth 1976; Washburn 1973).

In 1974 an investment association from the South Side Chinatown made elaborate plans to remodel a three-block section of Argyle Street and then purchased nearly 60 percent of the commercial and mixed commercial-residential buildings on the street (Carlos 1984). Immigration from Hong Kong and Taiwan to Chinatown, and consequent population pressures, motivated this entrepreneurial drive. Other contributing factors included the declining profitability of businesses in Chinatown owing to city population shifts and the rise of take-out Chinese restaurants in more accessible locations (Cutler 1982). The investment group abruptly ended its support, however, and by 1976 the buildings along Argyle Street were rapidly being sold or abandoned (De Meth 1976) and 28 percent of apartments in Uptown were vacant (*Refugee Reports* 1986c).

About the time when Chinese Americans were attempting to transform Argyle Street into a Chinatown North, an adjacent area known as Newtown was experiencing a middle-class influx and an escalation of property values. There were optimistic predictions that gentrification would eventually make its way to Uptown (Jacobson 1975; Washburn 1973). But property values plummeted when the middle-class migration failed to materialize. Termination of a plan to construct a major shopping center in the southern section of Uptown further doomed prospects for an economic revival (Aronson 1973).

By 1980 Uptown had reached its nadir. Between 1970 and 1980 the proportion of Uptown residents below the poverty line increased 48 percent compared with an increase of only 37 percent in the city as a whole. Uptown had the sixteenth highest poverty increase of Chicago's 77 community areas. Median family income in 1980 was $14,455, well below the city's level of $18,776 (Brune and Comacho 1983).

Yet Uptown retained one positive feature that set it apart from other Chicago areas: it was racially and ethnically diverse in a city known for segregation. In 1980, 59 percent of Chicago's 847 census tracts were virtually all white or all black. Only 7 percent remained racially mixed between 1970 and 1980, when white flight to the suburbs reduced the city's white population by 33 percent (Brune and Comacho 1983). Of the city's 77 community areas, only nine had a significant population of both whites and blacks by 1980, and Uptown was one of them.

But Uptown was not a stable, integrated area. Rather, it lagged behind the social changes transforming the city. Between 1970 and 1980 the white population declined by almost half, while the black population tripled. But it was the arrival of populations that were neither black nor white that began to give Uptown its multicultural ambience. In 1980 whites comprised 34 percent of its population, blacks 15 percent, Asians and American Indians 28 percent, and Hispanics 23 percent.

By 1980 Uptown was an "open niche": an urban area with conditions suitable for a very particular group of people. It was lightly inhabited and ready for a population willing to live with a bad reputation and visible signs of decay in order to obtain comparatively low rents, good transportation facilities, access to Lake Michigan, and the educational opportunities of the nearby community college. Two international events coincided to bring such a population to Uptown.

The first event was the defeat of pro-American governments in Vietnam, Laos, and Cambodia by Communist forces. Between 1975 and 1978, about 5,400 Indo-chinese refugees settled in Illinois, of which approximately one-half went to Chicago. Then, in 1979, Vietnam invaded Cambodia and defeated the Khmer Rouge, thus permitting tens of thousands of Cambodians to flee to Thailand and eventually migrate to the United States. That same year Vietnam expelled tens of thousands of ethnic Chinese, and these refugees too found asylum in adjacent Southeast Asian countries and later in the United States By the mid-1980s about 10,000 Indochinese refugees lived in Uptown, and newspaper headlines pro-claimed, "Argyle Strip Sees New Life" and "Vietnamese Reviving Chicago Slum."

Over time many refugees have moved from Uptown to neighborhoods closer to their workplace or to other states in search of job opportunities. Others have moved to better neighborhoods or the suburbs, where they have purchased homes. Some families have even purchased three-story apartment buildings, where they live with relatives and rent an apartment or two to other refugees. Those refugees remaining in Uptown tend be the poorer families with many children.

At the same time as Uptown has become less of the residential core of the Indochinese population in Chicago, the number of Asian businesses on and near Argyle Street has increased dramatically. Working with the city, local merchants and Indochinese MAAs transformed a vacant lot into a parking area to accom-modate the heavy traffic on weekends. A new mini-mall containing 10 stores has replaced an ailing car dealer. Indicative of this economic expansion even as the refugee population moves elsewhere is the presence of businesses other than restaurants, grocery stores, and boutiques—for example, photography, hardware, mortgage, tax prepartion, real estate, and even an Asian bank. Local urban condi-tions create different types of refugee communities. Significantly, many of these businesses are owned by Chinese and other Asian Americans. Uptown was an entry point for Indochinese refugees but not a permanent place of settlement for most of them. The refugees' initial residence, however, created a lasting symbol-ism for the neighborhood. Coupled with the right social and economic conditions prior to their arrival—which made Uptown a vacant niche—Indochinese refugees' settlement fostered an Asian business district.

Community Life around a Buddhist Temple

For Cambodians in Uptown, the center of community life is their Buddhist tem-ple: a house with a prayer room containing a life-sized statue of the Buddha, rooms where several Buddhist monks live, and two kitchens for preparing com-munal meals. In a typical year the temple is the site of seven services for Buddhist holidays or special ceremonies held at the request of Cambodians, such as offerings for deceased relatives. About 40 people donate money at each event. Contributions range from $5 to $10 at temple-sponsored events, and from $10 to $15 at the personal ceremonies. The hosts of the personal ceremonies usually donate a substantial portion of the proceeds to the temple to earn merit for themselves and their ancestors. Altogether, these seven events yield about $3,000 for the temple. The monks also receive donations from performing 10 to 15 weddings each year and 20 to 25 other rituals outside of the temple, like blessing a new house or accepting gifts on behalf of a deceased relative. The temple also hosts two annual events at a local high school: the New Year celebration and a ceremony to commemorate ancestors. Approximately 400 people attend each event, and their donations total about $3,000. These donations have enabled the temple to build up a sizable bank account—a testament to Cambodians' interest in supporting Buddhism in the United States despite the fact that low-paying jobs, public assistance, and other forms of aid account for most of the income in the community.

The temple loans cooking utensils, mats, and other gear Cambodians need when hosting rituals in their home, such as a wedding. It also distributes small amounts of clothing and food to needy refugees. Several elderly widows live at the temple and cook for the monks, but the temple also is a temporary home to older men and women who do not live with relatives. One such man is slightly deranged. Cambodians explain that he was a monk in Cambodia but left the temple without the appropriate exit ritual and never fully adjusted to life as a layman.

The vitality of the Cambodian Buddhist temple gives the appearance of cultural transmission uninterrupted by war, migration, and adaptation pressures. In fact, the temple is a creation of the refugees in the United States rather than an institution transplanted from Cambodia. From the laymen who officiate at ceremonies to the most senior monk, each has entered a new role that he did not perform in his homeland. The senior monk was ordained about 10 years before "the war between France and Japan" (i.e., during the 1930s). Following the war, Cambodia was so poor that he left the temple to help support his parents and eventually married, which is traditionally forbidden to Buddhist monks. He returned to being a monk after fleeing from Cambodia to Thailand in 1979. Another monk was a very devout layman but became a monk in Chicago to help maintain the temple. A third monk, while living his entire adult life within a temple, is a Burmese immigrant. He communicates with the Cambodian monks through a specialized dialect used in Buddhist texts and prayers, but he does not speak Khmer, the language in Cambodia.

The laymen who operate the temple and handle its finances (monks are forbidden to handle money) also come from diverse backgrounds. Several were knowledgeable about Buddhist customs in Cambodia yet did not have their present status nor perform their current roles. Once in Chicago, they were among the few Cambodians with any knowledge of the chants, rituals, and other components of Buddhism and thus assumed positions of importance. One layman was a police chief in Cambodia. He now uses his skills organizing the temple's finances. Through their eclectic backgrounds, these men support the most important institution in the Cambodian community.

Despite the patchwork character of the temple, it is the site for collectively defining events affecting community life, such as the death of respected community members. Less than 5 percent of the Indochinese refugee population in the United States is over age 65, but this generation has special significance for the refugees. These senior citizens embody customs and traditions as they were practiced in the refugees' homelands rather than as they are remembered by the younger generation. Yet their advanced age also means that these seniors will be the first of the refugees to die in the United States. The death of these grandparents and great-grandparents symbolizes the passing of the refugee generation and its replacement by Indochinese born in the United States. Death is especially symbolic for Cambodian refugees because to settle in America they had to first survive starvation, illness, and violence under the Khmer Rouge.

When a much respected older woman named Neang died suddenly, the grieving community members came to the Buddhist temple to reflect on the meaning of her passing. For three consecutive days they held funeral rituals as an indication of respect for this woman who regularly prepared food for the monks and supervised cooking for weddings and funerals. She was a widow who had lost her husband and two of three children to the Khmer Rouge. Living with her one remaining son, his wife, and two grandchildren, Neang's household was like the last remaining branch on a withered tree. Some saw in her swift death a sign that she had accumulated very little sin during her life. For Buddhists, good actions produce merit, while bad actions will cause distress later in life.

But Neang died while gambling at cards, raising an alternative interpretation of her death. One older refugee commented, "The women she was playing cards with should have put a deck of cards in her coffin [prior to cremation, when mourners put flowers, incense, and candles with the corpse]. But it's really her fault that she died. A 70-year-old woman shouldn't play cards all night." Others joked (with black humor) that she had been killed by an elephant or tiger, since the Chinese cards in the game portray wild animals. Many older Cambodians play cards to relieve boredom, homesickness, and loss of status. The fact that this respected woman who had participated in so many religious rituals should die while engaged in a profane activity sadly symbolized the degradation of Cambodian culture that accompanies settlement in the United States.

During the three-day funeral other refugees added to the collective interpretation of her death. The senior monk at the temple is over 70 and in poor health. His view of this pious woman expressed the survivor guilt among the elderly when a younger person dies: "I'm the one who is sick. I have trouble walking. I don't know why Neang died and not me." A former soldier who regularly attends temple services said her death brought back feelings he had on the battlefields in Cambodia: "It's like when I was in the army. You never knew which soldier would die. Maybe it would be you. One day you'd see them and the next day they would be gone. Last week Neang was telling me stories about Cambodia. Now she's dead. In army slang we said, 'Born to kill. Kill to die.'" A board member of the Cambodian Buddhist association had a cultural interpretation of Neang's death: "The Cambodians really miss Neang because she always cooked for the monks. She also helped people organize and cook for celebrations, like honoring ancestors. Young people don't know how to do that type of cooking anymore. When she died a part of Cambodian culture died."

Although the temple is the most important institution in the Cambodian community, aspects of American culture pose a threat to the continuation of Buddhism among Cambodian refugees, as illustrated by the following exchange between two monks:

Senior Monk: In Cambodia, everyone went to the temple and many boys stayed there for a few months or a year to learn Buddhist traditions. In the United States only 10 out of every 100 Cambodians still follow these traditions.
Author: Why have things changed so much?
Senior Monk: Cambodians are more individualistic now. People don't do things together anymore.
Junior Monk [interjecting]: Let's get to the truth. The truth is that under the Communists the Cambodian people had nothing. Many were very poor before that. Here it is easy to get money and buy things. They're more materialistic here. They were also brainwashed by the Communists. The Communists told the people that religion didn't matter and not to believe what the monks had said. A lot of Cambodians still think that way.

As the junior monk suggests, the erosion of religious belief among Cambodians began in their homeland. Thus it would be a mistake to view secularization as solely the result of a conflict between the homeland and the host society. Both monks, however, point to central values in American culture—individualism and materialism—that are anathema to Buddhism.

The preservation of religious institutions is also jeopardized by the very process of attempting to re-create them. For example, Buddhism prohibits taking life yet accepts eating meat. Killing an animal is sinful for Buddhists. But eating meat is permitted provided one did not order the killing. As one of the temple monks explained, "When you travel by car you kill countless insects by mistake. But it's not sinful because you didn't intend to kill them. When you buy meat in a store, that meat is dead, it's not alive. So you haven't sinned." One of the more Americanized members of the Cambodian community offers a different interpretation of this belief: "I asked a monk why eating meat wasn't wrong. If there are a hundred people who eat meat, but only one who kills animals, then all those people depend on that one person, even the monks." This view emphasizes the social context of religious practices rather than the intent behind an individual action. Yet although critical of one Buddhist belief, this man is active in the Cambodian Buddhist Association. His role in re-creating communal institutions and yet questioning them at the same time reveals how homeland traditions become vulnerable in the United States because they depend for their existence less on custom than on the initiative of community members.

Indeed, reconstructing religious institutions can foster communal conflict, since it is much easier in the United States than in the homeland for disaffected members to establish a rival organization. A few years after the founding of the Cambodian Buddhist temple, a senior monk accused a young monk of an impropriety. But three young monks felt that in the United States his transgression of a rule was not a serious offense. The four older monks stood their ground, however, and the younger monk was forced to leave, taking the other young monks with him. To minimize the resulting schism, the Cambodian Buddhist Association facilitated the establishment of a new temple, even organizing the ritual transporting of a large bronze Buddha to the new site. About 100 brightly clad, chanting Cambodians marched in procession through Uptown playing gongs and drums. Street people and drifters looked on in disbelief. Despite these efforts, the temple schism hurt the Cambodian community. Feelings were so strong that some parents refused to let their children marry into a family that did not go to the same temple. When holidays occur, Cambodians in Chicago now choose between attending the "old temple" or the "new temple."

Institutions like the Buddhist temple are sources of stability for their community but also of conflict. Yet refugees establishing communities in urban areas must not only re-create and maintain community institutions but also negotiate relationships with other residents in their neighborhood.

Newcomers and Established Residents in New York City

In January 1983 a tenants' association in the Bronx started a rent strike in their building over lack of heat and general disrepair. A year later they succeeded in having the city appoint a manager to operate the building and collect rents—a major victory over the landlord. At one time the neighborhood was largely Italian, but blacks and Puerto Ricans replaced the whites who moved out during the 1970s. In the summer of 1981 an American voluntary agency (where I worked) began placing arriving Indochinese refugees in the building and, when the rent strike commenced, Cambodians and Vietnamese comprised about 40 percent of the tenants. The refugees' arrival required their black, white, and Puerto Rican neighbors to determine who these newcomers were in the context of local race relations. The advent of the rent strike required the refugees to decide if they would join blacks (the largest population in the building) in the collective action.

Many of the refugees were unprepared for life in a poor neighborhood in America's largest city. Five of the twelve households had farmed or fished in their homelands, and many of the younger adults had never held jobs because of the turmoil created by war and revolution. More significantly, some families had not arrived intact: three were collections of adult brothers and sisters, and two were single parents. The voluntary agency settled the refugees in the north Bronx because changing demographic conditions gave rise to apartment vacancies at reasonable rents. The director of the agency, the daughter of Russian-Jewish immigrants who arrived at the turn of the century, explained, "We try to put our clients in old, ethnic working-class neighborhoods. The young people there tend to leave if they can, but it's better than a fringe area which has a high crime rate." Once refugees begin living in a building more follow because Indochinese caseworkers encourage older arrivals to help newcomers, thus alleviating numerous phone calls and office visits. One Chinese-Cambodian caseworker stated, "I try to put all my clients together so that I can ask them to help each other out, even pick up new arrivals at the airport. It's easier for me that way."

But the racial dynamics of New York City neighborhoods also mean that the refugees are surrounded by tension. One day while returning from a park with a group of Cambodian mothers and children, I was hailed by a middle-aged Italian American as we entered the building. He was seated on a chair in front of an adjacent building and two young, well-dressed men were standing on either side of him. Describing himself as the "block leader," he asked me, "I've been seeing those people going in and out of this building. How many are in there anyway? I like to know who's living on my block, right? I've tried to talk to them but they're always afraid. You know, I can help if a Nigger or a [Puerto] Rican hits them up."

On another occasion I was stopped by a middle-aged white man who also inquired about the neighborhood's newest residents. After I explained that they came from Cambodia and Vietnam because of the war, he used American immigration history to place the refugees in a frame of reference: "Both my parents are from Ireland. My father came in 1921. My mother came later. I've always suffered because my father never told me about his life in Ireland. Well, I hope they tell their children about their past."

The Italian-American superintendent at the building adds another perspective of the refugees. He complained of the men wandering the hall in "skirts" (Cambodian men often wear sarongs at home) and children playing in the halls. He concluded, "I'm not blaming anybody but it makes my job harder. Their way of doing things may be different, but they live here now and have to learn what this society does. I know they've been through a lot but . . . I can't even talk to them!" Race, immigration, and culture were the idioms these whites used to understand who the refugees were and what they meant for the neighborhood.

Blacks and Puerto Ricans in the area were also trying to identify the refugees. A Puerto Rican boys' counselor at the local high school regularly visited the building. Drawing on his own immigration experience, he viewed the refugees as newcomers and emphasized the importance of language and residence: "I know what it's like being in a new country because I came here from Puerto Rico when I was 14. It's important to let Americans know that the refugees are here and they are going to stay here. I know some of the Vietnamese and Cambodians think they are going home, but hey, even my mother who has been here 35 years still talks about going home. At school I'm the Cambodian expert although I don't speak Cambodian. But I have them teach me some Cambodian and I teach them my language: Spanish."

Blacks I spoke to also used the idiom of "newcomers and established residents" to make sense of the refugees. But for them, newcomer was not associated with immigration. The one international perspective that some blacks had access to was the Vietnam War, and it was overwhelmingly negative. Southeast Asia had a personal meaning for one black man: "My brother went to Vietnam [as a soldier]. After he came back, he was never the same." Yet like whites, blacks emphasized cultural differences between themselves and the refugees. One black resident stated, "I know it takes time to get used to a new culture. Their culture is OK for them so long as it doesn't bother anyone else." Other blacks used the society's oppression of African Americans as a point of reference. Racial inequality weighed heavily on one middle-aged black woman in the building, erasing any positive disposition toward the refugees she might have felt because they, too, were nonwhite. And unlike the Puerto Rican boys' counselor, for whom language difference was positive, she was annoyed by the inability of most refugees to communicate with her, much like the Italian-American block leader and superintendent. This woman once commented, "Blacks in this country have their own private hell. I don't think because the refugees are new and have trouble that they shouldn't be polite, that's no excuse. Why did they all get dumped in this building anyway?"

Most important for the blacks I spoke to was the refugees' willingness to engage in collective action. A black man in his thirties led the tenants' association and took a special interest in the refugees during the strike. The association would have the greatest chance of success if the refugees could be convinced to withhold their rent. Native tenants feared that the white landlord might try to evict the activists and replace them with more refugees. Since a court date had been set and inspectors were likely to visit the building, the tenants' association also wanted the refugees to help keep the building clean as evidence that the landlord was at fault for its condition. The association leader stated, "You know how Americans are. If they see other people not caring about the building they'll follow and not give a damn. If they see the refugees working to make the building better, they'll do it too. I'd like to see the refugees show up to association meetings and pull together with the other tenants."

A black woman who worked at a city neighborhood stabilization program had already concluded that the refugees were hindering the rent strike. Her evaluation stemmed from the refugees' reticence to become politically involved. She cited cultural differences as a basic problem, yet she believed that newcomers demonstrated their membership in a neighborhood by a readiness to confront inequalities:

> The refugees in that building should get a representative who can speak English to work on their problems with us. If they don't get involved in the courts and with the tenants' association there's no way they're going to get services from the building. I understand that these people need time to learn the ways of a different culture and that cultural differences are responsible for the social problems that have arisen. But it's to the landlord's advantage to have refugees in that building because they don't openly complain.

The refugees did initially participate in the rent strike when it began in January. At least four of the twelve refugee households withheld their rent that month, and about one-half of the adult Vietnamese and Cambodian men showed up at one tenants' association meeting. Yet the refugees' participation lagged when the landlord made some repairs and winter turned to spring, temporarily resolving the problem of inadequate heat.

But factors other than the warm weather limited the refugees' activism. One Cambodian man who attended the tenants' association meetings was bothered by differences in political culture. He explained, "I don't like the meetings because they are disorganized. There is so much quarreling. The Americans all seem so angry and too many people speak at once." The native residents' tactic of using anger at the landlord to increase interest among other tenants failed to work with the refugees. According to the leader of the association, "The refugees are like the old type of tenants when the association was just getting started and nobody cared. We have to show the refugees that by helping the association they are helping themselves." Yet the refugees' prior experience with politics left disincentives to enter power struggles in the United States. In addition to experiencing a Communist revolution, about one-third of the adult males were former soldiers whose armies had been defeated in battle.

The recency of their arrival also meant that some refugees were still more attached to their homeland than to the United States. Minh, a Vietnamese man in his early twenties, had arrived with his sister and brother-in-law only two months earlier. He was four years old when his father was killed while serving in the South Vietnamese Army. In 1980 he and other relatives fled the country by boat, leaving many close relatives behind. Minh's migration was precipitated by imminent conscription into the army when he turned 18. He dwelled on his eventual return to Vietnam, a delusion that eliminated any chance of joining the rent strike: "I don't like the Communists, but I like Vietnam. I am a refugee, so I would like to go back when my country is free. I can't live here. I can't speak the language, and I don't know anyone in this building. I will live here a short time and then go back to my country to be with my family . . . my mother, my uncle." In fact, for many of the refugees the building was a way station rather than a permanent home, as it was for natives. Within a year of arrival two Cambodian families had joined friends in Virginia and another had gone to California to reunite with relatives; a Vietnamese family had moved out to be closer to their place of work.

Moreover, the newly arrived refugees were disoriented by the spatial dimensions of the building. None had lived in such a large structure in their homelands, and many had little awareness of what "their building" meant, since it took up half a city block and was separated by only a few feet from neighboring buildings. Some of the refugees were also perplexed by the building's internal layout. The long, dimly lit halls hardly encouraged contact between neighbors. During the day the building was eerily quiet, much at odds with the refugees' experience in their homeland, where neighbors worked and gossiped in a central location. The newest refugee household was an extended Vietnamese family, and soon after arrival a teenage grandson approached me with a question that revealed how alienating the building appeared to them: "Excuse me, but my grandmother would like to ask you something. Why do all the people in this building keep their doors shut?" The grandmother had apparently wanted to get to know her new neighbors, but interpreted their locked doors as a sign that they did not wish to be disturbed.

Nor would the sponsoring agency support the refugees' participation in the rent strike. The agency needed good relations with city landlords because it often asked for special favors, such as moving refugees in on short notice and filling rooms with more people than permitted by law to accommodate extended families in apartments designed for nuclear families. In addition, some landlords discriminated against minorities, as one Vietnamese caseworker's joke makes clear: "It will be easier to find housing for the refugees when the tan they got in the transit camps [in Southeast Asia] wears off and they turn more white."

But the agency also feared that if its clients became militant on the housing issue they might then organize around the issue of welfare. Whether newly arrived refugees should work or receive public assistance was the most contentious issue for the agency. The agency director described how the conflict over employment led many refugees to rebel against its resettlement plans: "In the summer of 1981 we were getting 150 refugees a month. Many were Cambodians, and they didn't come here with their families intact, they didn't have the support they needed, and they experienced more culture shock than previous groups. We now realize that the voluntary agencies treated them like the other waves, which had a welfare rate of only 20 percent. In the end the new arrivals united against us; they encouraged each other to go on welfare. Now over 75 percent are on welfare."

Past political experience, the migration process, and resettlement agency policy explains much of the refugees' reticence to join black tenants in the rent strike. But race relations also contributed because the Cambodians and Vietnamese had little understanding of African Americans and their history in the United States. One Cambodian teenager's misperception discloses how the refugees came to understand what black and white mean in American society. He had been in the United States for one year and attended a predominately black high school. We had just finished discussing the problem of gangs at the school when he asked, "What country do the black people come from? Do they speak English there?" He concluded that blacks were an immigrant group because they lived in a poor neighborhood like his own and did not speak English the way whites did.

Speaking English with an accent was among the primary criteria the refugees used to determine the identity of their neighbors. A conversation with a Cambodian man who lived near the building with the rent strike illustrates how the refugees use language to determine the group affiliation of other residents. For him, American meant English speaker, as the following dialogue reveals:

> Author: Do you know any of your American neighbors?
> Refugee: Yes, we are friends.
> Author: Are your friends black or white or Hispanic?
> Refugee: Spanish and American.

Race also shaped relations with neighbors, and the refugees were quick to stereotype all blacks because they became the crime victims of a few. Research has shown that whites in New York City responded to crime by abandoning liberalism—that is, by becoming less sympathetic to blacks' demands for affirmative action, school desegregation, and political participation (Reider 1985; Sleeper 1990). Refugees too experienced muggings and robberies by blacks, and some had responses similar to those of whites. In an unconscious reinvention of the cynical aphorism "A liberal is a conservative who hasn't been mugged yet," one Vietnamese woman simply stated, "I don't want to hate blacks, but I have to protect myself." Most refugees did not even attain this level of analysis. Instead, their concern was to quickly define friend and foe, and they often used the term "American" for the former. A conversation with a Vietnamese woman in the United States only a few months (but who had studied English in Vietnam) reveals how the refugees use both language differences and crime to determine relations with black neighbors:

> Author: Do you know any of your American neighbors?
> Refugee: No, I don't have any American neighbors. Only black people, Chinese, Vietnamese, Cambodian.
> Author: But the blacks are Americans.
> Refugee [Uncomfortable laughter]: I don't think they are American because. . . . Last month a black man broke into my apartment. My sister called the police and they caught him. Then my sister had to go to court.

In the end the tenants' association forced the landlord to improve the building. But the most important accomplishment of the rent strike was to introduce Vietnamese and Cambodian refugees to the diversity of urban America.

Conclusion

The American government had an interest in the location of Indochinese refugees during the war in Southeast Asia, and it continued to plan their geographic distribution once they arrived in the United States. This dispersal policy, which aimed at settling the refugees throughout the country, was motivated more by fiscal interests than the goal of assimilating the refugees. Public and private resettlement officials were concerned that large concentrations of refugees would adversely affect the social, health, and educational expenses of a few "impacted" counties. Dispersing the refugees was designed to disperse resettlement costs, not prevent the formation of ethnic communities. Despite this policy, Indochinese refugees largely have settled in locations of their choice. The strong kin ties between refugees overseas and their relatives in the United States forced resettlement agencies to locate new arrivals near their sponsors. Migration across the United States after arrival enables other refugees to settle where they perceive the greatest opportunities.

Indochinese refugees have overcome social policy and the unknowns of a new country in order to settle where they wished, but urban conditions determine in which neighborhoods they ultimately reside. In Chicago depressed property values and a reputation for poverty and deviance channeled the refugees into the Uptown area. The area had many apartment vacancies, good public transportation, and contained a community college that proceeded to offer classes in English as a second language. Several years after the first refugees' arrival a Southeast Asian shopping strip and the presence of many refugee families had transformed the area into a thriving community. Over time, however, many refugees have moved to better locations, while the number of businesses has continued to increase, particularly those owned by Chinese immigrants. The formation of ethnic communities is not only determined by the national response to the migrants, the migrants' class background, and labor market conditions, as suggested by the ethnic-resilience model, but by local urban conditions.

In Uptown, Cambodian refugees rebuilt a Buddhist temple that became the center of their community even though the temple and religious values never assumed the importance they had in their homeland. Contrary to the assimilation model, this temple was re-created in the United States rather than transplanted from the homeland. All the major participants in the temple assumed new, and more important, roles in the United States because so many knowledgeable laymen and monks were killed during the Khmer Rouge era. Yet rebuilding this communal institution inherently led to its change. American values of individualism and materialism eroded Buddhist values of communalism and simplicity among Cambodians. More important was the shift in the basis of religion from tradition to community support. Because the existence and continuation of the temple in Uptown now depended on the volition of community members, individuals and cliques were able to question religious doctrines and even establish a rival temple. By drawing an overly rigid distinction between homeland and host society, the assimilation model fails to capture the more complex process by which immigrants and refugees fabricate, rather than duplicate, communal institutions.

Because of their overwhelming urban residence, contemporary international migrants are as likely to interact with blacks and Hispanics as they are with whites of European ancestry. In a Bronx neighborhood, culture, race, and migration history shaped how whites, blacks, and Puerto Ricans identified Indochinese newcomers. The refugees used crime and speaking English with an accent to define the native groups they lived with. The advent of a rent strike in one building brought its African-American and Indochinese residents into much closer contact. The African Americans wanted the refugees to join the strike they had started, thus introducing the refugees to an American form of collective action against inequality—in this case a landlord neglecting the upkeep of a building.

The importance of African Americans and other ethnic minorities to the adaptation of immigrants and refugees at the neighborhood level reveals a new urban pluralism at odds with the assimilation model. In the context of non-European populations becoming the majority in many urban areas, the integration of immigrants and refugees can no longer be conceptualized with reference to a monolithic American culture and society.

five
___

Racism and Racial Conflict

A merican immigration history reveals that many newcomers have confronted hostility and even violence from natives. Indochinese refugees are
no exception to this pattern. Yet there is little evidence that anti-
Indochinese incidents result from the bitter legacy of the Vietnam War. Asian and
Hispanic immigrants have always experienced greater animosity than white
immigrants, and natives' negative reactions to Indochinese refugees stem from
prejudice in general. But the geographic distribution of anti-Indochinese incidents
is not closely related to the size of the Indochinese population in a given state. Nor
is the prevalence of hate-group activities, the most visible form of white racism,
linked with anti-Indochinese incidents. Instead, activities against the refugees are
closely tied to local conditions and take different forms among whites and blacks.

Conflicts with whites on the Texas Gulf Coast and with blacks in Philadelphia are revealing of these local conditions. In Texas the arrival of Vietnamese
seeking to reenter former occupations as shrimp fishers coincided with declining
shrimp catches. The Ku Klux Klan (KKK) used the resulting economic competition between Vietnamese and white shrimpers to foment racial hatred and
violence. In Philadelphia, Vietnamese, Hmong, and Cambodians arrived in the
context of declining entry-level industrial jobs and racial polarization of neighborhoods. In conjunction with the special services provided to the refugees by
public and private agencies, these conditions aroused hostilities among blacks.
The Texas case reveals how whites often resist the integration of newcomers,
contradicting the assimilation model that presumes that natives will allow
immigrants and refugees to participate in the society and culture. But the events
in Philadelphia evidence new forms of pluralism that are leading to equally profound conflict among ethnic minorities, in contrast to the image of dominant
versus subordinate groups portrayed by the ethnic-resilience model.

Patterns of Anti-Indochinese Incidents

Almost two-thirds of Vietnamese refugees expect to encounter discrimination
from whites, and 33 percent report experiencing racial discrimination (Roberts
1988). Among Indochinese refugees as a whole, slightly more than two-thirds
feel the Americans they know do not like them (Kim 1989). Because the
Vietnam War created such divisiveness in American society, it is commonly

believed that anti-Indochinese sentiments stem from events in the 1960s and early 1970s. Americans increasingly turned against the war in Southeast Asia after 1968. When the war ended in 1975, most felt it had been wrong for the United States to get involved. The Vietnam War powerfully influenced why refugees left Vietnam, Laos, and Cambodia and why the United States admitted so many.

But resentment over a lost war cannot explain the following incidents. In 1980 an anti-Asian rumor developed among whites in Stockton, California, that consistently contained these (false) elements: a woman "discovered that her expensive pet dog was missing; a boy in the neighborhood saw a Vietnamese family down the street eating the dog and reported the gruesome fact to the owner; the dog's head and fur were subsequently found by the garbage collector" (Baer 1982, 275). Nine years later a white man with an assault rifle killed five Cambodian and Vietnamese children in a Stockton school yard, wounded 30 others, and then took his own life (Reinhold 1989). A more familiar racial conflict occurred in Wausau, Wisconsin, in 1993, when five school board members who had advocated the bussing of white and Hmong children to promote integration lost their seats to challengers promising to reinstate neighborhood schooling (*St. Paul Pioneer Press* 1993a). Racial conflict, however, is not confined to whites. In 1979 Chicano youths in a Denver public housing project vandalized the cars and apartments of Vietnamese refugees, forcing 12 families to leave under police protection (Ivins 1979b). A similar episode involving black youths occurred in 1982 in San Francisco (Lang and Hsu 1982). Between 1989 and 1994 an Asian-Latino gang war in Long Beach, California, left 14 Vietnamese, Laotians, and Cambodians dead, although many of the victims on both sides were not gang members (D'Oro et al. 1994). As these incidents suggest, Americans' responses to Indochinese refugees are due to race and ethnic relations.

Americans with armed forces experience in Vietnam, elsewhere, or none at all differ only slightly in their "social distance" from the refugees—the degree to which they object to contact with Indochinese refugees at work, in public places, and as friends (Starr and Roberts 1981). When surveyed in 1980, self-labeled conservatives, moderates, and liberals had similar views on U.S. military involvement in Indochina: only between 17 percent and 22 percent agreed with the country's involvement. Twenty-five percent of conservatives, 33 percent of moderates, and 40 percent of liberals, however, agreed with the statement, "As a people, Americans should feel obligated to help refugees from Indochina." The study concluded that there is "no simple relationship between political viewpoint, pro- and anti-war sentiments and reactions to [Indochinese] refugees" (Starr and Roberts 1982, 176). Americans' attitudes toward the Vietnam War are too complex to be directly linked with attitudes toward the refugees produced by the war.

Instead, responses to the refugees are shaped by the degree to which Americans are prejudiced in general. A study sought to test this hypothesis in La Crosse, Wisconsin, where the Hmong constitute 5 percent of the city's population—a very high proportion in the context of a state with few minorities outside of its major cities. No minority populations resided in the city prior to the refugees' arrival. A racially motivated attack had occurred some years later, however: several white men beat two Japanese exchange students, believing them to be Hmong (*Leader–Telegram* 1990). The study found a strong relationship between negative attitudes toward Southeast Asians and general ethnocentrism (Ruefle et al. 1992). Ethnocentrism is an us-versus-them view of the world—that is, a personality that rigidly classifies people into in-groups and out-groups. The basis for distinguishing these groups may be race, ethnicity, or other social characteristics. In La Crosse ethnocentrism determined attitudes toward the refugees to a much greater degree than did age, income, level of education, or economic optimism.

Greater interaction and direct knowledge of a minority group can reduce prejudice and ethnocentrism among members of a majority group. This "contact hypothesis" is another explanation for antirefugee attitudes and was tested on a sample of Americans living on the Gulf Coast and in California (Roberts 1988). Of course, the willingness to contact a minority is itself related to sociological factors, and younger, more educated, and higher-income Americans had the greatest contact with Vietnamese refugees. Not all forms of personal contact lead to closer social distance between groups, however. Americans who had only general contact with Vietnamese (such as in public places) actually had slightly greater social distance than did Americans with no contact. But contact that occurred at home or in the workplace greatly reduced Americans' feelings of social distance from Vietnamese. Indeed, whether or not Americans had work contact with Vietnamese was more important in shaping their attitudes toward the refugees than their age, occupation, or income, and equal in importance to their level of education.

Unfortunately, Americans' treatment of Vietnamese, Laotians, and Cambodians goes beyond ethnocentrism and social distance. Vandalism, assaults, and even bombings have plagued the refugees from California to Iowa and Massachusetts. Nineteenth-century European immigrants encountered violence just as serious. Catholic churches and convents were burned in the 1840s; Jews were beaten on the streets of New York City early in the twentieth century; and Germans were lynched during World War I (Archdeacon 1983). Violence against nonwhites, however, has always been the most severe in any historical period. By the late twentieth century, ancestry rarely marked whites for discriminatory treatment, much less violence, but this was not true for Asians in general and the Indochinese in particular (U.S. Commission on Civil Rights 1987, 1990).

Although American hostility and violence against Vietnamese, Laotians, and Cambodians is part of American race and ethnic relations (not a legacy of the Vietnam War), this antagonism is highly localized. Activities by hate groups such as the KKK, Nazis, and Skinheads increased during the 1980s. The U.S. Department of Justice's Community Relations Service was alerted to 263 hate-group conflicts in 1985, and the number rose steadily each subsequent year, reaching 554 cases in 1990. But this rise in organized racism is largely unrelated to the Indochinese conflicts recorded by the Community Relations Service (see Table 5.1).

There are several federally designated regions where hate-group conflict is proportional to the Indochinese conflict, such as the Pacific Northwest (Region 10). But the regions where the refugees are most likely to experience conflict are not those where hate groups are excessively active. Region 9, which includes California, is similar to other regions in the level of hate-group conflict, yet it accounts for a large proportion of Indochinese conflicts. Similarly, New England produces a large proportion of conflicts involving the refugees, but hate groups are not particularly active there.

Table 5.1

Regional Distribution of Indochinese Conflicts, Indochinese Population, and Hate-Group Conflicts, 1985–1990 (in percent)

Federal Region	Indochinese conflicts	Indochinese population	Hate-group conflicts
1. New England (e.g., Massachusetts)	17	5	10
2. North-Central (e.g., New York)	2	5	9
3. Mid-Atlantic (e.g., Virginia)	8	8	11
4. South (e.g., Georgia)	9	6	11
5. Upper Midwest (e.g., Wisconsin)	9	11	11
6. Southwest (e.g., Texas)	12	11	6
7. Midwest (e.g., Kansas)	10	3	13
8. Plains (e.g., Wyoming)	5	3	3
9. California, Nevada, and Arizona	17	41	12
10. Washington, Oregon, and Idaho	13	7	15

N = 440 Indochinese conflicts and 2,280 hate-group conflicts
Source: U.S. Community Relations Service, 1985–90

The pattern of Indochinese conflicts is more closely related to the geographic distribution of the Indochinese population, but still does not perfectly overlap (see Table 5.1). New England has more conflicts than one would expect given the small proportion of refugees living there, as does the South and the Midwest. Conversely, the region containing California has comparatively little conflict although it contains slightly more than 40 percent of all Indochinese in the United States. The North-Central region also has a low proportion of conflicts given the size of its refugee population. Thus there are few national patterns to anti-Indochinese incidents. They are largely unrelated to negative feelings associated with the Vietnam War, have only a moderate correlation to the geographic settlement of the refugees, and have a weak correlation to the strongest manifestations of white racism.

Explaining conflict between the refugees and natives is best done at the local level, paying close attention to the timing of the refugees' arrival. The migration of Indochinese refugees to the United States occurred in three phases. First, the fall of pro-American governments in Vietnam, Laos, and Cambodia led to the arrival of 147,000 refugees between 1975 and 1978. Then political turmoil and persecution under the new Communist regimes produced 453,000 refugee arrivals between 1979 and 1982. Finally, migration primarily based on family reunification brought the arrival of 350,000 refugees between 1983 and 1990.

Using a variety of sources, I sought to quantify the actions during this period that aimed to harm or intimidate Indochinese refugees, whether conducted by

Table 5.2

Type of Anti-Indochinese *Refugee* Incidents *by* Year *(in percent)*

	1975–78	1979–82	1983–90
Protest arrival	67	15	2
Property destruction	0	11	22
Jobs and social services dispute	17	26	6
Harassment and altercation	17	11	22
Assault	0	22	45
Arson to home	0	15	4
Result in death*	0	40	60

* For either refugee or native; all categories are exclusive except for "result in death";
N = 6, 27, and 51 incidents in each period, respectively
Sources: Japanese American Citizens League 1985; *New York Times Index* 1975–90;
Newsbank Microform Index 1975–90; U.S. Commission on Civil Rights 1987

groups or individuals. The resulting list was derived from the *New York Times Index* and *Newsbank*, a microfiche collection of articles from more than 500 local newspapers. Reports on anti-Asian violence published by the Japanese American Citizens League (1985) and the U.S. Commission on Civil Rights (1987) added additional incidents. These anti-Indochinese incidents ranged from antiarrival petitions and arson to assaults and killings; there was a total of 84 incidents between 1975 and 1990.

Each wave is associated with a different pattern of aggression toward the refugees (see Table 5.2). The earliest period was marked by protest over the refugees' arrival. The next period produced conflict over jobs and social services—as large numbers of refugees arrived during a severe recession—and a rise in violence. The final period, when Vietnamese, Laotian, and Cambodian communities took root in the United States, is characterized by destruction of property, harassment, assaults, and murders. Rather than conflict peaking when natives first confronted the refugees and then subsiding, violence increased as Vietnamese, Laotian, and Cambodian settlement gained permanency.

Commentators on ethnic conflict in the United States have been quick to highlight the rise of hostilities among ethnic minorities, although instances of this tension—such as between native blacks and Caribbean immigrants—is hardly new. Yet Indochinese refugees did experience resentment from other minorities, not just whites. When asked if they would object to having Vietnamese neighbors, 17 percent of whites and 20 percent of blacks agreed, although levels of education and income revealed greater differences in opinion than did race (Gallup Poll 1990). When asked if the arrival of Vietnamese refugees had been a bad thing for the country, 38 percent of whites and 43 percent of blacks felt it had, but again education and income did more to shape

Table 5.3

Type of Anti-Indochinese Refugee Incidents by Race
of Native Group (in percent)

	White	Minority
Protest arrival	100	0
Property destruction	75	25
Jobs and social services disputes	40	60
Harassment and altercation	44	56
Assault	74	26
Arson to home	100	0
Result in death*	73	27

* For either refugee or native; all categories are exclusive except for "result in death";
N = 58 white and 26 minority incidents
Note: One-third of minorities are Hispanic; the remainder are black
Sources: Japanese American Citizens League 1985; *New York Times Index* 1975–90;
Newsbank Microform Index 1975–90; U.S. Commission on Civil Rights 1987

opinions than did race (*Roper Report* 1982). Yet what such surveys miss is differences in how whites and blacks acted out their resentment toward the refugees
(see Table 5.3).

Whites, rather than minorities, are responsible for destruction of property
and protesting the arrival of the refugees, in some cases in conjunction with
local government. Although many of the sources used to construct Table 5.3
report that minorities were dissatisfied with the refugees' presence in their communities, not one documented an organized effort to halt their settlement.
Whites also are disproportionately involved in the most serious conflicts, such as
assaults and arson (in a Chicago suburb three newly arrived Laotians died in a
fire). Conflicts resulting in death overwhelmingly involve whites rather than
minorities. It is conflict involving jobs and the supply of programs like housing
that tends to involve minorities, as does general harassment and altercations
like school fights.

The context of these conflicts also differs for whites and minorities (see Table
5.4). Incidents involving minorities overwhelmingly take place in large cities,
while more than one-half of those with whites occur in small cities. Schools also
are the setting for more than twice as many incidents attributable to minorities
rather than to whites. Significantly, youths are involved in almost two-thirds of
the conflicts involving minorities, compared with only 14 percent of conflicts
between whites and the refugees. Finally, whites reacted immediately to the
refugees arrival. But the first incident involving minorities was not reported
until 1979. The peak years for black and Hispanic conflict with the refugees
coincides with the peak period of the migration. Conversely, the peak year of

Table 5.4

Context of Anti-Indochinese Refugee Incidents by Race of Native Group

	White	Minority
Average city size (in 1,000s)	223	794
% Cities under 100,000	58	0
% In schools	5	12
% Youth in incident	14	62
First year	1975	1979
Peak year	1985	1981–82

N = 58 white and 26 minority incidents
Note: One-third of minorities are Hispanic; the remainder are black
Sources: Japanese American Citizens League 1985; *New York Times Index* 1975–90; *Newsbank* Microform Index 1975–90; U.S. Commission on Civil Rights 1987

conflict involving whites is five years after the great migration of 1980–81 (one-third of all Indochinese refugees arrived in these two years). White conflict with the refugees appears more deeply rooted in antagonism toward nonwhites in general. Conflict between the refugees and other minorities, however, is based on the perceived threat newcomers pose to institutions and resources, particularly among the most volatile age group. But all these conflicts are heavily determined by local race and ethnic relations and two cases deserve special attention: the Texas Gulf Coast and Philadelphia.

Conflict with Whites on the Texas Gulf Coast

The first Vietnamese refugees came to the Gulf Coast in 1975 to take jobs in seafood processing plants (Starr 1981). Their numbers were few, and most of the Vietnamese living on the Texas Gulf Coast by the early 1980s had migrated there after first settling in some other part of the country (Franken 1981). By 1985 there were approximately 2,000 Vietnamese living between Corpus Christi and Galveston Bay. This area became the scene for some of the most intense racial conflict between the refugees and natives. Before the conflict subsided in the mid-1980s, the KKK intervened, a white American died, and a dozen boats owned by refugees were burned.

Between 1978 and 1984 the number of shrimping vessels on the Gulf Coast increased by more than 1,000, and several hundred belonged to Vietnamese refugees (Van Praag 1985). The refugees usually arrived with some cash earned elsewhere and then bought small, used boats from white Americans for a few thousand dollars, often at inflated prices (Franken 1981). One white American in Kemah, a small town south of Houston that became the scene of conflict, describes how the Vietnamese purchased boats: "Americans were selling them boats that were worn out—nothing but plywood glued together—for $5,000 or

$6,000. I saw one piece of junk you couldn't give away. And the Vietnamese fisherman paid $7,500 for it. That boat was still fishing last year" (Sweeney 1982, 9). After a year or two the refugees tended to build bigger boats so they could sail farther from shore. The refugees also shrimped in groups of several boats, rather than alone like native-born Americans, and were thus able to use larger nets. Combined with long hours and unpaid work by family members, the Vietnamese proved stiff competition for native shrimpers. One refugee explained that his wife worked in a factory for the first time in order to raise money to repair a boat he owned with a partner. He, too, took a job in a factory for a time, but within two years the family had saved the $10,000 they needed for a boat of their own (Tenhula 1991).

The Vietnamese community in Palacios illustrates this process of economic adaptation (Van Praag 1985). The first six families to settle there in 1976 came from the same fishing village in the Mekong Delta of Vietnam. All were Catholics and had migrated from North Vietnam to the South in 1954 following the partition of the country when the French departed. The children continue to go to a Catholic school. For their first two years most of the men worked in a nuclear power plant and the women cleaned shrimp for native-born fishermen. But by their third year the families had saved enough money to purchase a used fishing boat.

Other Vietnamese families moved to Palacios, and by 1984 Vietnamese boats accounted for one-half of the town's fishing fleet. Some of the refugees migrated because they had relatives there, but others came because they placed a high value on self-employment. One refugee, originally settled in Seattle, left a job with Boeing despite having received training in electrical engineering. He arrived with $60,000 borrowed from friends and relatives. Six months later, he had built a shrimping boat with the help of experienced Vietnamese fishermen. By the end of his first fishing season he had earned enough money to pay back the loan. Shrimping has proved so profitable for the Vietnamese in the area that they have branched out into shrimp houses, restaurants, and food stores. Another Vietnamese refugee describes similar motives that led him to the coast after being sponsored by a church group in Dallas:

> The church gave me a job as janitor for the church, but I could not be a janitor. There was nothing for me to do in that job. All I knew was the sea and fishing. There, in Dallas, I was like a fish with no water. . . . I had a friend in Victoria, Texas, who moved to Port Luvaca. He was also a fisherman and he had a very large family—seven or eight children. All the time he talked about fishing along the Gulf Coast; there they have good shrimp fishing and this was the kind of fishing we did in Vietnam. The more he talked about returning to fishing, the less I could go on with my life in Dallas as it was. (Tenhula 1991, 99)

One of the earliest backlashes against the refugees occurred in Seadrift, a town of 1,200 inhabitants. The first Vietnamese came to Seadrift in 1976 after an American opened a crab plant, failed to find native workers, and then hired refugees just released from the mainland reception camps (Ivins 1979a). The manager of the plant stated, "Without the Vietnamese, this plant can't exist and my 60 other workers would lose their jobs" (Maxwell 1979, 12). But the Vietnamese men desperately wanted to work for themselves. Their wives started jobs in the plant, and the men pooled their money and bought some small boats. Within a few years, there were between 15 and 20 Vietnamese-owned boats in the town.

There had been some resentment toward the refugees in Seadrift and even occasional vandalism. In a town of 1,000 whites, the arrival of 100 Vietnamese was bound to cause some friction, especially when few of the newcomers spoke English. But in the summer of 1979 an incident began when a native fisherman "chased off" a Vietnamese boat that began lowering crab traps next to his (Milloy 1980). The Vietnamese boat returned with several others and rammed the American boat. When the white American later complained to the sheriff and Coast Guard, each claimed the other agency had jurisdiction. A month later the fisherman accosted two Vietnamese brothers who had been on the boats, stabbed one in the chest with a knife, and was then shot to death. A jury later found that the homicide was in self-defense.

The evening of the killing, several refugees were beaten, three Vietnamese boats and a trailer were burned, and an unexploded firebomb was found at the crab plant that employed the Vietnamese women. Two-thirds of the refugees in Seadrift left following the incident. Rather than being driven from the coast by the violence, the refugees moved 50 miles south to another fishing town and started over.

But conditions for a larger conflict existed all along the Texas coast. Native-born fishermen noticed a decline in the shrimp harvest both in 1979 and 1980, and they immediately accused the Vietnamese refugees for taking too many. In fact, bad weather and pollution from oil refineries and chemical plants were partly responsible (Franken 1981). But excessive fishing was also to blame. The Gulf of Mexico had experienced an increase in the number of fishing boats even before the Vietnamese arrived, from 5,000 licensed boats in 1966 to 6,500 in 1976 (Sweeny 1982). Over the next few years the number increased by more than 3,500. By the early 1980s about one-third of the 150 boats working the Galveston Bay were owned by Vietnamese. Even without the addition of the Vietnamese, more boats harvesting from a declining marine life population was bound to hurt local economies. The refugees were the most visible causes of the decline, and they became scapegoats for native fishermen.

Cultural conflicts added to the apparent economic conflict. Initially, the Vietnamese fished in areas that native fishermen had informally divided among themselves, and they also violated American sailing etiquette by bumping boats (Starr 1981). There were even legal infractions at first, since fishing was unregulated in Vietnam and the refugees had not yet learned of U.S. laws. According to a Vietnamese representative of the U.S. Office of Refugee Resettlement, however, "In the beginning, the refugees may have violated some of the coastal taboos through ignorance. Today, however, the Vietnamese can no longer be accused of technical cheating. It is ingenuity and family self-help that has enabled the Vietnamese to make it despite the depressed state of the shrimping industry" (Van Praag 1985, 14). Native-born Americans also resented the communal fishing practices employed by the Vietnamese (Mangan 1982, D4). Where natives would shrimp as individuals, the refugees cooperated. They tended to line up their boats and then sweep the waters with long nets. A white American shrimper complained, "These refugees are practicing communism. They all work together for the group. They are Communists in the purest way. I can't compete against that."

An eighteenth-century fishing law compounded the conflict (Starr 1981). In 1789 the new American government attempted to restrict foreigners' ability to communicate at sea with hostile nations. The law stipulated that noncitizens could not own boats more than five tons in weight or sail farther than three miles from the U.S. coast. The Coast Guard did not strenuously enforce the law in the Gulf, but off California they began fining Vietnamese boats $500 and eventually the case went to court (Bishop 1989a; *New York Times* 1989). The refugees contended that the law was being selectively enforced, and that only after they began to compete with native fishermen did the Coast Guard take action. The U.S. government argued that the law was still necessary: "In this modern age, rife with terrorism and threats to United States citizens from foreign extremist groups, the presence in United States coastal waters of foreign-owned and operated vessels has the potential to present a clear and present threat to the national security." To raise the question of the refugees' loyalty was a covert form of racism that evaluated Americans on their ancestry—the same sort of thinking that interned even second-generation Japanese Americans during World War II. But in 1989 a federal court upheld the law, and the fate of some 60 Vietnamese boats in California was put in jeopardy. The ban was finally lifted by the U.S. Congress in 1990.

The Texas government had always been reluctant to resolve the dispute by limiting the number of fishing boats (Van Praag 1985). Since hundreds of Vietnamese vessels were already registered, the policy would not have adversely affected the refugees. Rather, regulating the boats would have allowed all fishermen to obtain a profitable harvest. The government chose, however, neither to protect the marine ecology of the gulf nor to help diminish the economic conflict between white and Vietnamese shrimpers. Governor William Clements suggested that market competition would eventually force less productive shrimpers from the business and thus reduce the number of vessels. In the meantime, the conflict remained.

Following the acquittal of the two Vietnamese men in Seadrift, Vietnamese boats burned in the towns of Seabrook and Kemah in Galveston Bay, and a local fisherman asked the KKK to intervene (Southern Poverty Law Center 1981a, 1981b). The FBI had dealt some punishing blows to the KKK after 1964, applying the "disrupt and neutralize" tactics it had formerly used against Communists (Chalmers 1981). But the Klan had begun to reorganize during the late 1970s under the leadership of David Duke, who eventually became a state senator in Louisiana and won 60 percent of the white vote in 1990 when he ran for the U.S. Senate. Duke began appealing to the white middle-class and developing a political agenda to "protect the rights of white people." While moving into electoral politics, he trained other leaders who still sought to demonstrate Klan strength through violence and intimidation. One of these new leaders was Louis Beam, grand dragon of the Texas KKK. Vietnamese refugees competing with native shrimpers in a declining industry presented an ideal opportunity for Beam.

The Klan organized in Texas during the 1920s, rather than after the Civil War. But the Texas branch had the distinction in 1922 of having Earl B. Mayfield the first Klan member elected to the U.S. Senate. Although Klan presence in

Texas was small compared with that in Mississippi and Alabama, the cities of Houston and Beaumont were strongholds. Both were close to Galveston Bay. The KKK became active in the fishing conflict during February and March 1981, bringing in Klansmen from Galveston and Pasadena and recruiting local fishermen. A mock Vietnamese boat dubbed the *USS Vietcong* was burned at a rally that drew a crowd of 250. Robed Klansmen carrying rifles toured the Galveston Bay in a boat one day, coming close enough to Vietnamese boats and waterfront homes to shout racial epithets. Days later, burning crosses appeared near the homes of several Vietnamese shrimpers. Vietnamese-owned boats burned, and a white fisherman friendly with the refugees was threatened.

Even more troubling to those trying to defuse the conflict was the KKK paramilitary camp on the eastern side of the bay. One local fisherman reported that he and others had begun training there. Beam stated that unless the Vietnamese boats were gone from Galveston Bay by the start of the shrimping season, they would "enforce the law" to "protect" native fishermen. Such threats were taken seriously by local government agencies helping the refugees and the Vietnamese themselves. Beam had been forced to close one paramilitary camp after it was revealed that he had hired a convicted contract killer to instruct Boy Scouts in the use of firearms and hand-to-hand combat. More recently, a Dallas grand jury had indicted him for conducting paramilitary exercises in a federal park. The grand dragon told a crowd of native fishermen, "If you want [the country for whites] you're going to have to get it the way the founding fathers got it— blood, blood, blood" (Horton 1981, A14). Videotape recordings revealed that the Klan was indeed training two dozen men in guerrilla warfare (*New York Times* 1981).

Beam had fought in Vietnam and took a special interest in the conflict: "There are a number of Vietnam veterans like myself who might want to do some good old search and destroy right here in Texas. They don't have to ship me 12,000 miles to kill Communists. I can do it right here" (Milloy 1980, 57). Another figure in the controversy was Eugene Fisher of Kemah, a fisherman and former Marine. Fisher had been wounded in Vietnam and had many run-ins with the police and courts following his return to the United States. When the fishing controversy started he became an outspoken critic of the Vietnamese and eventually obtained a high position in the Texas KKK. Fisher's resentment of the refugees had more to do with the war than the economic plight of the Gulf fishing industry: "We didn't lose the war. The Vietnamese lost the war" (Sweeney 1982, 8).

Although the refugees had done no wrong, local and state government implicitly took the side of the disaffected native fishermen and, by extension, their Klan allies. Investigations began into allegations that the refugees were abusing the public-aid system in order to purchase boats; only one possible case was found. Large boats were checked for full registration, and some Vietnamese were found to have incorrect documentation. Still, an equal number of native fishermen also failed the inspection. These types of harassment were galling to the refugees, but a more serious threat came from Governor Clements. A special assistant to the governor toured the Texas coast and then left for Washington, D.C., to meet with representatives from the State Department, the Department of Health and Human Services, and several voluntary agencies. His plan was for the state to hire a broker to sell the boats for the refugees because "if there are not fewer boats in the water by May 15th [the start of the shrimping season], there will be violence" (Franken 1981, 2).

Many refugees did indeed express an interest in selling their vessels, but only because of Klan intimidation and the pressure from the government. The Southern Poverty Law Center, a longtime foe of the KKK, filed suit on behalf of the refugees to halt Klan activity in the bay. But a former ARVN colonel, who had become the leader of the refugee fishermen, stated, "The suit is just so we can get time to sell our boats and property. . . . [T]he violence I'm afraid won't go away" (Horton 1981, B1). About 50 refugees in Galveston Bay and other coastal areas offered to sell their boats but were unable to find buyers who would pay them a fair market rate (Lewis 1981).

A court injunction against the Klan and a state law limiting the number of fishing licenses for two years temporarily defused the conflict. But the next year during the first few weeks of the season, the Klan violated the court injunction by patrolling the bay from dusk to dawn, purportedly to prevent Vietnamese shrimpers from illegal night fishing (Hanners 1982). The Klan even offered a $500 reward to anyone aiding in the arrest and conviction of a refugee fishing illegally (Mangan 1982). A Vietnamese college student in computer science helping on his father's boat expressed fear of the Klan, but also took a long-run view of the conflict:

> We're scared. Even though I came from a country where they have a lot of violence, we don't like violence. I feel as though violence is chasing me from Vietnam to America. Shrimping is a hard job and it's not our first choice. It's just all that a lot of us know. I'm not an engineer, I'm not an auto mechanic, so I worked on a boat. My father is a shrimper all of his life. That's all my family has known, but you ask any of the Vietnamese if they want their children to be shrimpers, I'd guarantee you that they'd say no. (Hanners 1982, A4)

The KKK never succeeded in chasing the Vietnamese from the Gulf Coast. By the late 1980s there were more than 100 Vietnamese-owned boats in the lower bay area and 130 in Galveston Bay (Tenhula 1991).

Conflicts with Blacks in Philadelphia

Asian and Hispanic immigrants arriving in the United States during the 1970s and 1980s overwhelmingly settled in large cities. Beginning in the 1950s, whites began moving from central cities to the suburbs, and this migration increased during the 1960s and early 1970s. Blacks also undertook a historic migration during this period. Between 1945 and 1965 about five million blacks left the rural South for cities, primarily in the North. Although blacks represented only 12 percent of the nation's population, by 1980 they accounted for 22 percent of the population in cities with 200,000 or more inhabitants and 29 percent in the country's five largest cities. Unfortunately, the intersection of international migration from the Third World and the dynamics of white/black urban residence at times led to conflict between ethnic minorities. In Philadelphia (a city whose population was almost 40 percent black by 1980) a study of incidents of intergroup conflict found that whites were overrepresented as perpetrators and underrepresented as victims compared with the size of the white population (Goldstein and Yancey 1988). Conversely, blacks were disproportionately victims and less likely to be perpetrators. Action against Asians, however, was the one type of conflict where blacks were perpetrators in excess of their proportion of the city population.

The resettlement of 20,000 Indochinese refugees in Philadelphia between 1975 and 1985 was part of this conflict. Voluntary agencies aiding the refugees placed them in predominately black neighborhoods where inexpensive housing was available. In fact, the refugees faced many of the same problems as their poor black neighbors (Nordland 1983). For example, one Cambodian extended family of 12 in Philadelphia had only one wage earner, a son-in-law who worked at a minimum-wage job in a hotel. The father and mother subsisted on welfare because the former was 50 years old and had a back ailment that prevented strenuous activities. They paid $270 a month for a rowhouse with inadequate heat and in need of many repairs. But the son-in-law and his wife were planning to leave because their one income would affect the eligibility for the whole family after stricter public aid rules went into effect.

Sociologists studying the causes of poverty among urban blacks cite the changing mix of jobs in cities and suburbs as a leading cause (Wilson 1987). This "urban industrial transition" was especially severe in Philadelphia (Kasarda 1989). Between 1970 and 1980 the central city lost 75,200 blue-collar jobs, the type of work that both natives and immigrants with little education would have to take; the suburbs gained 29,500 blue-collar jobs during this period. More important, virtually all job growth in the city, and 62 percent of it in the suburbs, occurred in highly skilled work. Unemployment among black men without high school degrees reached 50 percent by 1980. Even if they had the skills, blacks remained in the city because commuting costs were too high, they could not afford to leave, or segregation prevented them from moving to the white suburbs.

The economic conditions of Philadelphia blacks set the stage for conflict with Indochinese refugees and other Asians. But of equal importance was the moral issue of newcomers receiving attention while established residents with equally pressing needs were neglected. One Cambodian stated, "Mostly we have trouble with blacks. We don't have problems with other Americans, because we always try to be nice, but black people, they feel we come here and some people go very fast from nothing to a better job. They feel the Cambodian people have a lot of help, and they say 'I'm here and nobody gives me anything'" (Nordland 1983, C2). The chairwoman of a neighborhood African-American mothers' organizations stated, "We have been here 400 years and what do we have? Nothing. They came yesterday and they will have all the rights and privileges today that we don't have in 400 years" (Nordland 1983, C2).

This accusation is not without foundation, since the federal government provides a grant of several hundred dollars to voluntary agencies for each refugee they sponsor. Even poor refugees have ties to social service agencies and sponsors who can provide resources or pressure governments to take action (Clancy 1979). For example, as the second wave of refugees began arriving in the fall of 1979, 40 families found themselves living in a run-down apartment building on the South Side. A sudden chill in the temperature led them to turn on the heat, and the furnace burst. Church groups and voluntary agencies that had sponsored the refugees immediately had city officials declare the building unfit for human habitation and began an investigation into housing conditions among refugees in general. At the same time, suburban clergymen began a clothing and furniture drive to help the refugees.

Similarly, when 78 Cambodian refugees from the same village were all settled in West Philadelphia, a social worker from a voluntary agency moved into the neighborhood, hired two translators, and helped the refugees settle in. The attention given the refugees must have reminded black residents of the War on Poverty. During the 1960s white liberals dedicated to ending poverty moved into ghettos, and community residents were hired by programs providing social services. Thus not only were the refugees competing with blacks for entry-level jobs, but they also competed for public assistance and social-service attention.

Aid from public and private agencies was not, however, the source of mobility among the refugees. Many refugees arrive with the ambition and skills to prosper in the long run. A former Vietnamese factory owner now living in the Logan area lost everything and was placed in prison when the Communists took over South Vietnam in 1975. To escape, he built his own boat and eventually sailed with his wife, two teenage sons, and many others. He now works at a minimum wage job in a Chinese egg-roll factory. Despite the problems in the neighborhood, he is determined that his children will succeed: "Some people are very worried about their children and what will happen to them; they worry about their kids being affected by American culture. But if they watch over them, it won't be too much of a problem. Make sure they study very hard and they can never get into trouble" (Nordland 1983, C3).

Refugees also worked in some of the lowest paid jobs. The Hmong in Philadelphia formed work groups, picked a foreman who spoke English, and left at 3 A.M. to pick blueberries in rural New Jersey (Kaufman 1984d). In fact, thousands of Indochinese from Philadelphia work in the blueberry fields for 25 cents a pint, replacing African-American and Puerto Rican workers as the industry's labor force (Pfeffer 1994). This transformation of low-wage agricultural employment resulted from the refugees' strong social networks, which enabled them to easily generate crew leaders and work groups from among friends and kin. At the same time, the decline in African-American migrants from the South, and Puerto Rican migrants from their island home, reduced the population of natives most likely to do farm work.

Korean immigrants, who have the advantages of bringing capital with them and planning their migration, created even more profound economic change. By the early 1980s Philadelphia had a Korean population of more than 40,000, and there were approximately 1,500 Korean-owned enterprises in the city. More than any recent Asian group, the Koreans have become self-employed, often buying failing businesses from Jews and Italians in black neighborhoods. Korean-owned small businesses became prevalent in New York City, Los Angeles, and Washington, D.C., by 1980 but did not become sources of contention for blacks until 1983–84 (U.S. Commission on Civil Rights 1987). Koreans accused black customers of shoplifting; black residents resented businesses that made money from the neighborhood but did not spend profits there or hire black workers. Sparked by alleged mistreatment of customers, the result was black boycotts of Korean stores, vandalism, and even firebombings. In a 19-month period beginning in January 1984, Philadelphia's Commission on Human Relations investigated 15 conflicts in which Korean merchants or their stores were subjected to arson, beatings, vandalism, and intimidation. At a meeting to discuss community relations one Korean stated, "Whenever the public speaks of Koreans in Philadelphia, the most frequent question centers on the Koreans doing business in the black neighborhoods: 'Why do so many Koreans come into black neighborhoods and establish businesses?' Many problems arise because of our excelling, we acknowledge that" (Philadelphia Commission on Human Relations n.d., 31).

The level of conflict peaked in 1984 when blacks assaulted several Southeast Asians. These attacks, however, followed the larger patterns found in Tables 5.3 and 5.4. First, they occurred well after the refugees' arrival. Philadelphia received 795 Vietnamese families when the refugees arrived in 1975 (Kelly 1977). About 2,000 refugees lived in the city by 1979, but the number jumped to 20,000 by the early 1980s. Many began leaving the city, however. For example, the Hmong population had dwindled to 300 by the fall of 1984 from a peak of more than 3,000 several years earlier (Kaufman 1984a). The second pattern is the predominance of black youths in the attacks and may be associated with gang activity that does not reflect the sentiment of the neighborhood.

Incidents began to multiply in the summer of 1984 (Kaufman 1984a, 1984b). In August a group of black youths cornered two Hmong men in West Philadelphia and told them, "We don't want people like you around here." When the Hmong ran to a relative's house the youths pursued them, attempted to break down the door, and threw rocks through the window. Several weeks later a Hmong man from Canada came to visit his brothers. After their car was vandalized and a call did not bring the police, the brothers started driving around the neighborhood looking for the vandals. A group of black men pulled them from the car and the visitor was beaten, resulting in two broken legs and brain injury. When one brother and a Catholic priest returned in a van the next day to look for clues, they were bombarded with rocks. The next week a black man threw a brick at an elderly Hmong man riding a bicycle.

The last week in August also saw assaults in the Logan community (Kaufman 1984c). A night of violence began when a group of black youths threw a bottle at a Vietnamese woman as she entered a relative's house. That evening the youths pulled a Vietnamese man from his car and beat him in front of the house. The youths then began throwing objects at the house for the next two hours. When a neighboring Korean merchant tried to pull a protective grate across his store the youths knocked him unconscious. By this time the Vietnamese in the house had called the police, but no assistance arrived; they called some Vietnamese friends to come to their aid. When the friends arrived in a van, the youths showered it with stones and bottles. The incident had begun at 6 P.M. and did not end until 1 A.M.

The official response to the assault on the refugees revealed the irony of American racial history (Kaufman 1984b). The FBI began an investigation into civil rights violations, and unlike similar investigation during the 1960s, this one pointed to blacks as the perpetrators. The Justice Department's Community Relations Service—a bureau established during the 1960s to resolve tensions between whites and blacks—also became involved. It proposed holding public forums for residents to discuss local issues.

Some blacks in the two neighborhoods were shocked by the violence. In West Philadelphia a woman who ran a block club quickly leafleted the neighborhood to prevent further conflict: "If the tables were turned we blacks would be yelling racism, racism, racism," she wrote (Kaufman 1984a, B10). She organized a meeting attended by several dozen blacks, but relations had so deteriorated that only two Hmong from a local mutual assistance association showed up. In the Logan neighborhood a black woman recalled similar problems when blacks first began to integrate Logan during the 1970s. She organized a petition in the neighborhood condemning the attacks, received 900 signatures, and read a statement to a crowd of 50 residents near the battered Vietnamese house (Sutton et al. 1984). Her analysis of the situation linked parents' stereotypes of Asians to youths' frustration over lack of jobs: "These youngsters who are doing things are learning at the dinner table—they're hearing adults say the Asians are taking jobs, they're all getting welfare, they're dirty" (Kaufman 1984c, B11). But she also urged Asians to become more politically active and help blacks solve the larger problems in the neighborhood: "We have to start getting people together to talk, and to see that the Asians aren't doing these things at all. And we have to convince the Asians that they have a stake here, they need to get involved too."

The Justice Department's forum was finally convened in late October, and more than 100 people turned out in a Logan church. A Cambodian resident explained his frustration with American prejudices against refugees: "When some of us receive public assistance, we are seen as a parasite on the community. When we secure employment, we are not praised but accused of taking jobs away from others" (Solovitch 1984, C6). A few black residents were unmoved by the refugees' plight. The leader of a local parents' group complained that attention had never been paid to problems among blacks but that federal, municipal, and voluntary agencies quickly came to the aid of Asians. She stated, "This hearing is a slap in the face to my community. Drugs, beer, rape and our old people being hit over the head—that's what we need the commission here for. We do not need you in Logan for this" (Solovitch 1984, C6). Other blacks were more conciliatory. Another woman at the hearing blamed the conflict on the tough conditions in the neighborhood that made life hard for all residents. But she, too, felt that the refugees should not place all the blame on blacks: "We need to interpret black feelings to our Asian neighbors, to explain to them that we're a hard-working people, that we built America into a country that they'd want to move to" (Solovitch 1984, C6).

Demographic dynamics underlie the conflicts in Philadelphia. The attack on the Vietnamese house and the Korean merchant occurred in the Logan neighborhood on 11th Street—an area that the U.S. Census calls tract 283. At the time the tract had almost 1,000 Asians, the largest concentration in Philadelphia: most were Vietnamese, Laotians, and Cambodians, but there were also Indians and Koreans. Asians, however, accounted for less than one in ten residents; blacks accounted for two-thirds of all residents. In the area to the north (tract 282) blacks and whites each comprised about 40 percent of the population, while Asians (largely Filipinos) comprised 10 percent. At one time the area had a Jewish community of Russian ancestry, and about 500 Ukrainian Americans still lived in tract 283.

The assaults in Logan occurred in the heart of the Asian community because neighborhood dynamics rather than economic competition were probably the root causes (see Table 5.5). The black populations of tracts 283 and 282 tended

Map 4

U.S. Census Tract Map of Philadelphia

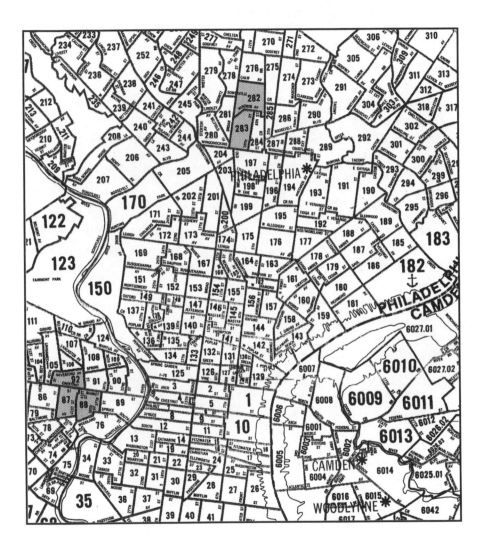

Table 5.5

Characteristics of Whites, Blacks, and Asians in Philadelphia and the Logan Community, 1980 (in percent unless otherwise noted)

| | Philadelphia | | Tract 283 | | Tract 282 | |
	Whites	Blacks	Blacks	Asians	Blacks	Asians
Managerial, professional	23	14	13	12	11	36
Technical, sales	36	30	29	23	28	25
Service	12	23	18	30	27	19
Production, repair	12	9	13	3	9	2
Operator, laborer	16	24	28	32	25	18
Unemployed	8	17	12	10	12	4
Weeks unemployed	18	23	22	12	24	8
Household income:						
< $7,500	25	39	28	44	26	15
≥ $35,000	10	5	2	3	4	22
Mean ($1,000s)	18.1	13.3	13.6	13.5	15.0	25.0
With public aid	8	31	28	21	19	9
Below poverty	8	29	26	37	20	6
Schooling:*						
≤ 8 years	21	22	13	19	10	12
12 years	35	34	45	47	48	14
≥ 16 years	14	6	3	12	6	46
Housing units:						
Built ≤ 1939	53	64	62	81	45	69
Median $ rent	207	128	172	164	178	206
Persons per						
room ≥ 1.01	2	6	8	39	6	33
Owner-occupied	66	54	58	16	71	49
Persons per family	3.16	3.59	3.91	4.13	3.81	4.09
Female-headed family	17	45	40	8	35	10
Males 15 to 24	9	9	10	8	8	4
Residence in 1975:						
Same	69	69	56	6	43	8
Abroad	**	**	**	87	**	77
Speak English						
not well/at all	**	**	**	42	**	15

* persons 25 years and older
** not applicable
Source: U.S. Department of Commerce 1980b

to work in less skilled occupations than blacks in the city as a whole, but they had lower unemployment, poverty, and public-aid rates. Although blacks in the city and the Logan area were far below the socioeconomic position of whites in Philadelphia, they were not disadvantaged compared with the 1,300 Asians in tract 283, where the violence occurred.

In comparison with their black neighbors, these Indochinese, Koreans, and Indians were able to work more frequently, and when unemployed they found new jobs in fewer weeks. The proportion with college degrees exceeded that of blacks as well. Yet these Asians hardly lived a life of which blacks could be envious. Over one-third were poor and they had a lower public assistance rate than blacks. Asian incomes were virtually identical to those of blacks, except that more earned under $7,500 a year. Their housing conditions were also below average: 81 percent of their apartments were in buildings more than 40 years old. And although Asian families were only slightly larger than those of blacks, almost 40 percent of their apartments were overcrowded. Finally, even in tract 283, almost 60 percent of blacks owned their place of residence, while only 16 percent of Asians had moved from renting to ownership.

The Filipinos and other Asians in the tract to the north (tract 282) had the economic prosperity that might have raised tempers in the black community. For example, almost 50 percent owned their own homes although less than one in ten had lived in the area more than five years. But they numbered only 600 and hardly posed a numerical threat. The area was also racially integrated, with about 80 percent of the population divided evenly between blacks and whites. Even these comparatively prosperous Asians lived in older buildings and in more crowded conditions than neighboring blacks. If the rapid mobility among Asian immigrants fueled black violence, it was more imagined than real.

What distinguished blacks in tract 283, where the violence occurred, was the social composition of the neighborhood. Male youths comprised a larger proportion of the black population; female-headed households were more prevalent. The blacks in tract 283 were also a more settled population than those in tract 282, and both paid considerably higher rents to live in Logan. Blacks in both areas were also newcomers, however. About one-half had moved from other parts of Philadelphia to their current homes in the last five years; about 20 percent had arrived between 1979 and 1980. By contrast, less than one-third of blacks in the city had changed residence between 1975 and 1980. Logan was a neighborhood in transition, and this caused the friction rather than the issue of economic mobility. In 1970 blacks accounted for only 7 percent of the population in both tracts 283 and 282, but by 1980 they represented 63 percent and 44 percent, respectively.

Asian immigrants and Indochinese refugees settled in Logan just as it was turning from white to black. Almost 90 percent of the Asians in tract 283 had arrived in the United States in the previous five years, and more than 40 percent spoke little or no English. These immigrants were probably not competing with blacks for housing, since they doubled up in old buildings. Nor is there much evidence of job competition, because almost one-third of Asians worked in services and only 3 percent in production and repairs. But they arrived quickly, in large numbers, and without the linguistic ability to explain who they were and why they came to the United States. Conflict between neighbors in Logan was caused by the family composition and settlement patterns of blacks, combined with direct migration from the Third World.

The assaults in West Philadelphia occurred on the outskirts of the Asian community, rather than in its heart, as in Logan. West Philadelphia represented the expansion of an Asian neighborhood into a long-settled black neighborhood. The attacks occurred in tract 92, which was 98 percent black in 1970 and 93 percent black in 1980. About 10 percent of the city's Asian population, however, lived in two census tracts just to the south (tracts 87 and 88). In 1970 these tracts had been predominately white, but as whites left the area over the next 10 years they were replaced by Asians, and the proportion of blacks remained virtually unchanged. Indochinese refugees entered tract 87 in large numbers, and Asians constituted 12 percent of the area by 1980. To the east, Chinese and Indians moved into tract 88 and with the refugees formed a ring around the whites living next to the University of Pennsylvania. The number of whites living around the school increased by 30 percent between 1970 and 1980. Just north of the campus whites had begun to settle an area that lost half of its black population in those 10 years. An adjacent census tract to the west had doubled its black population in the same period. Blacks in West Philadelphia as a whole were not among the poorest, but tract 92 was a pocket of poverty in a black neighborhood within blocks of the university. Asian immigrants had become the buffers for a white population increasingly concentrated around a major institution.

This ecological history of West Philadelphia gives new meaning to the fact that the attack on the Hmong occurred on Powelton Street, the border separating Asian and white neighborhoods from black neighborhoods. Blacks in tract 92 had less education, lower incomes, and higher rates of poverty and female-headed households than blacks in the city as a whole (see Table 5.6). They were also a much more settled population, since 75 percent had lived in their current dwelling for more than five years. And although black male youths were underrepresented in the tract, the large population of Asian male youths in adjacent tracts may have been a catalyst for conflict.

Conversely, the Asians were a very recent population. If the census data are to be believed, all of the Asians in tract 88 moved in during the preceding five years, more than one-half migrating directly from their homeland. The median rent paid by Asians in the two tracts was more than double that of blacks only a few blocks away—further evidence that tensions were caused by neighborhood dynamics rather than the economic leapfrogging of Asian immigrants over black natives. Indeed, these Asians afforded such rents not by having incomes higher than blacks but by crowding more people into apartments. Although over one-half of the Asians had at least a college education, none earned more than $35,000 from their jobs. The stability of black neighborhoods greatly determined the extent of conflict with newcomers.

The urban basis for the conflict between blacks and Asians in Philadelphia is further revealed by several incidents that preceded the August attacks (Nordland 1983). In South Philadelphia a neighbor objected to a Cambodian man parking a car in front of his house because the refugee was a tenant, not a homeowner. In West Philadelphia a Hmong man quit his job in a predominately black neighborhood after a black woman remarked, "See the Chinese taking our job"; the work in question was a newspaper route and symbolic of urban neighborhood identity. Changing the name of a local store from "Green's" to "Ho Hong's" also symbolized neighborhood transition for blacks in the area. Schools are even more central to the life of urban communities than parking spaces,

Table 5.6

Characteristics of Whites, Blacks, and Asians in Philadelphia and the West Philadelphia Community, 1980
(in percent unless otherwise noted)

| | Philadelphia | | Tract 92 | Tract 87 | Tract 88 |
	Whites	Blacks	Blacks	Asians	Asians
Managerial, professional	23	14	14	43	34
Technical, sales	36	30	43	35	27
Service	12	23	22	8	23
Production, repair	12	9	7	7	7
Operator, laborer	16	24	14	7	9
Unemployed	8	17	27	12	5
Weeks unemployed	18	23	24	23	7
Household income:					
< $7,500	25	39	60	48	42
≥ $35,000	10	5	3	0	0
Mean ($1,000s)	18.1	13.3	9.3	10.4	12.9
With public aid	8	31	48	10	9
Below poverty	8	29	46	33	35
Schooling:*					
≤ 8 years	21	22	28	23	10
12 years	35	34	26	3	5
≥ 16 years	14	6	4	62	54
Housing units:					
Built ≤ 1939	53	64	62	78	78
Median $ rent	207	128	96	196	195
Persons per room ≥ 1.01	2	6	10	33	31
Owner-occupied	66	54	34	4	0
Persons per family	3.16	3.59	3.31	3.87	3.20
Female-headed families	17	45	63	11	9
Males 15 to 24	9	9	7	13	26
Residence in 1975:					
Same	69	69	75	15	0
Abroad	**	**	**	43	53
Speak English not well/at all	**	**	**	38	16

* persons 25 years and older
**not applicable
Source: U.S. Department of Commerce 1980b

paper routes, and businesses. The principal of a West Philadelphia high school reported the reaction of black students to the arrival of the refugees: "The black [kids] were saying, 'They're coming into our community, they're taking over the businesses, and now they're taking over our school'" (Nordland 1983, C2). An explanation for the negative response of whites in Brooklyn to the arrival of blacks applies equally to blacks' reactions to the settlement of Indochinese refugees in Philadelphia: the newcomers became the symbols of and scapegoats for the larger political and economic changes that were adversely affecting the neighborhood (Reider 1985).

Conclusion

Vietnamese, Laotians, and Cambodians arrive in the United States as refugees, but they quickly become minorities whose lives are shaped by American race and ethnic relations. Although hostility and aggression against the refugees are commonly attributed to the divisiveness of the Vietnam War, they are in fact the result of racial prejudice—a major component of the ethnic-resilience model of immigrant and refugee adaptation. Common features of prejudice like social distance and ethnocentrism explain in part which Americans are likely to have hostile views of the refugees.

There are, however, few national patterns in anti-Indochinese incidents. The size of the Indochinese population in a given state is only a moderate predictor of these incidents, while the activities of hate groups are even less related. Anti-Indochinese incidents are closely tied to local conditions, suggesting that the ethnic-resilience model has exaggerated the extent to which the newcomer-versus-native conflict is a universal feature of migrant adaptation in the United States.

Moreover, this conflict takes different forms depending on whether the natives are white or black and Hispanic. Anti-Indochinese incidents involving whites are much more violent than those involving minorities. Whereas conflict between the refugees and other minorities tended to occur during the peak years of migration, those between the refugees and whites began early in the migration, continued through the peak, and became even more severe during the phase of refugee community formation. Most important, youths— the most volatile section of any population—are involved in the majority of anti-Indochinese incidents involving blacks and Hispanics but are infrequent participants in cases involving whites. Combined, these factors provide sharply contrasting portraits of native white and minority antagonisms with newcomers. The ethnic-resilience model presents as one-dimensional a conflict that in fact has at least two distinct facets, as exemplified by events in Texas and Philadelphia.

On the Texas Gulf Coast economic competition and the intervention of the Ku Klux Klan lead to animosity and violence when Vietnamese refugees became shrimp fishers. The incidents in Seadrift and Galveston are model cases of the ethnic conflict that forms the core of the ethnic-resilience model and reveals a major flaw in the assimilation model. The expectation of a gradual reduction of differences between the foreign-born and natives is to a large extent premised on the willingness of natives to treat newcomers as equals.

The ethnic-resilience model fails, however, to capture the contemporary diversity in American cities caused by continued segregation of blacks, the out-migration of whites, and the arrival of Asian, Hispanic, and Caribbean migrants. In Philadelphia black attacks on Vietnamese, Hmong, and Cambodian refugees occurred because of rising unemployment, perceptions that the refugees were receiving favoritism, and especially the changing racial and ethnic composition in particular neighborhoods. Although easily exaggerated, this racial conflict among ethnic minorities reveals a new form of urban pluralism that is absent from the ethnic-resilience model.

six
___

Leaders and Politics

Immigrants in the United States have historically taken active roles in shaping their adaptation. But the ability of Indochinese refugees to collectively manage their future is especially noteworthy because they had so little control over the events that brought them to the United States. Mutual assistance associations (MAAs) are the leading means of their participation in the adaptation process. Most MAAs provide social services or maintain cultural traditions, although some have social, political, and economic functions. Vietnamese, Laotian, Hmong, and Cambodian MAAs vary, however, in the functions they perform owing to the unique characteristics of each group's migration, homeland, and culture. Except for the role of culture in shaping self-help activities, this pattern is most consistent with the international perspective of immigrant and refugee adaptation offered by the ethnic-resilience model.

Yet, the activities of self-help organizations and ethnic leaders are often accompanied by intense conflict. As the relationship between a Cambodian MAA and a Cambodian temple in Chicago illustrates, refugee communities are divided between traditional and more Americanized leaders, one of the classic tensions depicted by the assimilation model. Such divisions are inevitable outcomes of the refugees increasing political activity in the United States. Despite experiences and norms in Southeast Asia that should hinder their political participation, the refugees have mobilized local protests, supported both political parties, run for office themselves, and shown a keen interest in shaping developments in their homelands. At least in the case of political interests and participation, the ethnic-resilience model is correct that culture does not provide an adequate explanation for immigrant and refugee adaptation. Nonetheless, the splits between leadership styles and political factions suggest that there is as much conflict within refugee communities as there is between the refugees and natives—a point overlooked by the ethnic-resilience model.

Indochinese refugees' involvement with the judicial system has been their greatest impact on American government institutions. They have been plaintiffs in important housing and job discrimination suits. But customs at odds with American law have forced courts to become arbiters of cultural conflict. Often the courts have taken homeland norms into consideration rather than adhere to a strict interpretation of the law. Where the need for judicial action against discrimination contradicts the integrationist assumptions of the assimilation

Table 6.1

Indochinese Leaders by Sector and Ethnicity (in percent)

	Vietnamese	Laotian	Cambodian	Hmong
Public	15	5	0	8
Private	18	15	23	8
MAA	56	75	77	77
Education	11	5	0	8

N = 82, 20, 22, and 12 leaders by their respective ethnicity
Source: IRAC 1986

model, the reshaping of American culture by the legal system contradicts the ethnic-resilience model's assumption that non-European newcomers are pressured to relinquish their ethnicity.

MAAs and Leadership

In 1986 a conference in Washington, D.C., on international and domestic issues facing Indochinese refugees drew more than 150 participants from 36 states. It was the largest leadership meeting since the refugee migration began in 1975. Conference participants represented a range of leadership sectors. Many came from MAAs—organizations operated by refugees using a mix of public and philanthropic funding. Other leaders worked in government offices, like the refugee resettlement coordinator in most states. Still others worked in the private sector, mostly for American voluntary agencies that have a long history of aiding refugees. Finally, some leaders came from the ranks of teachers and the coordinators of language and training programs.

The conference reveals that Indochinese refugees depend heavily on MAAs for their leadership base (see Table 6.1). Only the Vietnamese have significant proportions in all leadership sectors. Cambodian leaders are particularly confined to the MAAs, with none from educational institutions or the public sector. Laotian and Hmong leaders are more diverse, but still less so than the Vietnamese.

The diverse leadership base among the Vietnamese reflects a number of international influences, such as their arrival in large numbers before the other groups. Many Vietnamese also arrived with the job skills and educational requirements for administrative and social-service positions. Conversely, the Cambodians are more recent arrivals: their peak year of migration was 1981, compared with 1975 for the Vietnamese. Cambodians also are predominately from rural areas and most have only a limited education and few transferable job skills. Many of their traditional leaders were killed during the Khmer Rouge regime. Thus different migration histories and degrees of home country development (prior to

Table 6.2

Evolution of Indochinese Mutual Assistance Associations, 1980–1985 (in percent)

	1980*	1985
Ethnicity		
Vietnamese	68	53
Laotian	9	14
Cambodian	15	14
Hmong	6	15
Panethnic	2	4
Function		
Cultural	27	55
Social service	34	24
Special interest	23	11
Economic	0	4
Political	16	7

N = 70 in 1980 and 800 in 1985
* in Washington, D.C., only
Sources: Bui 1983; Khoa and Bui 1985

revolution) shape the formation of leaders among Indochinese refugees in the United States.

Despite this variation, MAAs are the central self-help organizations in Indochinese communities. Five years after the first Indochinese refugees arrived in the United States they had already created 500 MAAs. By 1985 there were 800, and by 1991 there were an estimated 1,200 (Abhay et al. 1991). The evolution of the MAAs reveals how Vietnamese, Laotian, and Cambodian refugees have organized to collectively shape the adaptation process rather than have decisions made by resettlement officials or individual refugees.

Yet the characteristics of the MAAs have changed over time. From 1980 to 1985 the ethnicity of these associations became more diverse, reflecting the arrival of groups from Laos and the formation of panethnic associations (see Table 6.2). Some ethnic groups, however, organize at a greater rate than others. In 1985 there was one Hmong association for every 478 Hmong, compared with a ratio of 1:832 for lowland Laotians, 1:1,024 for Cambodians, and 1:1,082 for Vietnamese. The greater mobilization among the Hmong reflects the transplanting of clan and political organizations from Laos to the United States, as well as special federal policies to promote self-sufficiency through refugee-operated social services (Hein 1992).

Table 6.3

Ethnicity of Indochinese MAAs by Function (in percent)

	Vietnamese	Laotian	Cambodian	Hmong	Panethnic
Cultural	60	63	53	39	29
Social service	13	31	32	43	41
Special interest	18	2	3	3	0
Economic	2	1	0	14	9
Political	7	3	12	1	21

N = 421, 108, 115, 122 and 34 MAAs by their respective ethnicity
Source: Khoa and Bui 1985

The function of refugee associations also evolved during the early 1980s. In 1980 (when more than 160,000 refugees arrived) the typical association provided a social service to resettle other refugees, such as employment counseling and translation. But by 1985 the majority had a cultural function, such as supporting religious activities or teaching children to read their native language. This evolution reflects the transition from meeting the needs of individuals and families to the larger goal of sustaining an ethnic community. Similarly, associations to support economic development did not exist in 1980 but became more common by 1984 because the refugees increasingly had the resources to open businesses. Special interest associations, such as a clubs for veterans, declined over time, reflecting increased interest in associations with the broader goal of cultural preservation rather than a status from the country of origin. Associations seeking to influence homeland politics also declined as conditions in the United States became more important for the refugees. Thus within five years of the peak of the Indochinese migration, about three-fifths of associations provided economic and cultural support for their communities. Previously, nearly three-fifths had provided services to solve social problems and meet the special interests of small groups of refugees.

Despite this trend in community-building, there are important organizational differences among the ethnic groups that comprise the Indochinese population (see Table 6.3). Hmong associations are unique in that close to one-half provide social services, and one in six have an economic function, far surpassing the proportions of any other group. Many of these economic associations manage collective enterprises like sewing cooperatives and gardens. This development reflects the extensive resettlement needs of a horticultural people from small villages now living in an urban, industrial society. The cultural uniqueness of the Hmong, however, also contributes to this pattern. Their clan kinship system creates bonds among all Hmong sharing the same last name, thus promoting collective solutions to many problems that other refugee populations solve as individuals or families. The comparative underrepresentation of Hmong cultural associations also reflects cultural influences. Hmong religious practices involve shamans—intermediaries who communicate with spirits—a much less

institutional approach to religion when compared with Buddhism among
Cambodians and Laotians and Catholicism among Vietnamese. The recency of
the Hmong written language, which was developed in the 1950s, and the consequent emphasis on oral forms of expression may further limit the need for for-
mally organized cultural activities.

There are strong parallels between Laotian and Cambodian MAAs, except for
the large proportion of political associations among the latter. The greater political activism among the Cambodians is due to the factionalism and instability
that characterized political conditions in Cambodia during the 1980s. The
importance of Buddhism for both populations explains why the majority of each
group's associations serve a cultural function. Economic associations are comparatively rare among Laotians and Cambodians. Social services account for
about one-third of their associations, reflecting the resettlement needs of these
predominately rural populations.

Vietnamese MAAs are distinguished by the large proportion of special interest associations. Clubs of former university professors, for example, are more
common among the Vietnamese because of their homeland's greater degree of
urbanization and modernity, which encourages the formation of associations on
the basis of achieved statuses. The small proportion of MAAs that provide services to refugees reflects the greater adaptability of many Vietnamese owing to
their urban backgrounds, prior knowledge of English, level of education, and
longer period of residence in the United States. Migration and homeland characteristics, as well as culture, shape the organization of self-help initiatives
among Indochinese refugees.

Despite the importance of MAAs for refugee communities, their very centrality often makes them the focus of community conflict (Abhay et al. 1991).
The first MAA established by a refugee community is typically an extension
of kin networks or a senior leader who established a reputation in the homeland. Such MAAs usually have a strong legitimacy in the community and a
large, representative board of directors. Yet they often lack the expertise to
provide social services. Other MAAs bear a greater resemblance to American
nonprofit organizations, which is one reason they are able to attract funds to
provide social services. This organizational strength, however, creates tensions between board members who are leaders by virtue of homeland characteristics and experiences and younger, professionally trained staff who obtain
funding and supply services.

Such conflicts are often resolved when the older leaders lose control and
the younger leaders transform the MAA into an American-style nonprofit
organization supplying social services through a combination of public and
philanthropic funding. In some cases the more traditional form of organization is retained. An MAA that is politically active on issues of importance to
the community will gain support even if it does not provide as much
resources as a more Americanized MAA. Greater selectivity in receipt of funding is a second route for an MAA to avoid Americanization. By working on
problems prioritized by the community, rather than providing any service a
funding agency will support, an MAA can balance the competing goals of tra-
ditionalism and modernism. A Cambodian leader in Chicago embodies many
of these communal conflicts.

Conflict between Traditional and Americanized Leaders

Sarun has dedicated his life to Cambodian politics and comes from a family that amply demonstrates leadership skills. His grandfather organized a farmers' group to protect their village against bandits. Sarun's father was a police officer who is proud of his ancestors' role in Cambodian political history. Sarun relates:

> My parents told me that my great-grandfather fought the French when they took over Cambodia. The French told the Cambodian people what to do and made them work. The people in my great-grandfather's village tried to fight them even though they only had axes and sharp sticks while the French had big guns. Maybe you won't believe this, but my parents told me my great-grandfather knew magic. When the French shot him he fell down, but the bullets only burnt his clothes instead of killing him.

Sarun graduated from Phnom Penh University in 1973 and was drafted into the army. After training he was given an officer's rank and put in command of 300 men who saw much bloody fighting before the war ended with the Khmer Rouge victory two years later. At one point he was even sent to Vietnam for special training by American officers. Sarun endeavored to defend the pro-American government of Lon Nol against the Communist guerrillas. But he remembered that the larger goal of the war was to save the Cambodian people. As Sarun explains:

> I always tried to do the best for my soldiers, not to cheat them like some Cambodian officers. Even after soldiers were killed officers kept their names on the books to collect their pay. Some even made their soldiers pay for boots and uniforms. The families of my soldiers also traveled behind us and I had to think about them. I remember helping one wife give birth to a baby in a house that was being shelled. I also had to decide what to do with Khmer Rouge prisoners. Sometimes soldiers would torture them and cut off their heads. I told them not to kill prisoners. Sometimes I would let them go back to their village if I thought they had been tricked into fighting for the Khmer Rouge. I thought that was the best way to make them accept our side. But I think it is also one reason that I was not killed, because I did not take their life [and obtained good karma from my good actions].

Sarun survived the Khmer Rouge regime although knowledge of his past would have meant instant death. After three years he escaped to Thailand, in the process again demonstrating his leadership skills. He and several other former soldiers had hidden weapons and were able to lead about 500 people into the mountains where they stayed for several months before crossing the border. Once in a refugee camp he quickly found a job with the American agency organizing the migration of refugees to the United States. He arrived in 1981 and was settled in Chicago. Within a year friends he had known at the university recruited him to the board of directors of the Cambodian MAA, the major provider of social services to Cambodian refugees in the city.

Although concerned about Cambodian Americans, one of Sarun's long-run goals is to help rebuild his country. Sarun has an international perspective of the adaptation process, however, that links homeland and host society. As he states it:

I want more Cambodians to come to the United States because it will be good for Cambodia. Here they learn English, that's the international language. They get an education and job skills. Right now there are Cambodians in France, Australia, Canada, and other countries. Each community will be able to contribute something to Cambodia in the future. I work as a supervisor for a Japanese company that makes televisions, VCRs, and cameras. I'm learning Japanese and I asked my boss if he would open a factory in Cambodia. You know, it's Japan, not the United States, which is the important country in Asia. That's how I'm trying to help my country.

Despite his wish to contribute to the rebuilding of Cambodia, Sarun is preoccupied with the the needs of the Cambodian community in Chicago. Since he works for an MAA, one of the greatest problems he faces as a leader is balancing competing resettlement goals. He describes the tension between meeting community needs, which supports the legitimacy of the MAA among Cambodians, while also providing services to individuals—an expectation of the public organizations that fund the MAA:

Right now we are having trouble with our funding: about 25 percent may be cut. Cambodians pay taxes so why shouldn't they get some back to fund the association? These [funding] organizations want us to provide job counseling and help with hospitals and public aid. But that's only some of what Cambodians need and really it's only for new arrivals. There are not many new refugees coming to Chicago anymore. We also need to provide services to help the community. Jobs only help individuals. Right now we provide bilingual education after school. On Saturdays we teach children to read and write Khmer. Citizenship is another way to help the community. We also work on the gang problem.

Gangs are a growing concern for Cambodian parents in Chicago, as they are for many Indochinese communities in the United States. Sarun carries a beeper 24 hours a day so that he can be contacted by the police when needed. He is especially alert during the spring, when many Cambodian wedding parties are held at local restaurants—events that often lead to gang confrontations. His description of handling gang members again reveals how refugees often view their actions in the United States from the perspective of events in their homeland: "I don't threaten them [gang members]. I just tell them that we know about them and that there are police at the party. If they make trouble and are caught it will be their own fault. I just warn them. I was in the army and know how to use a gun, but I don't carry one. I don't want any more killing on my conscience."

The political factions that plague many refugee communities are largely absent from the Cambodian community in Chicago. Some support Norodom

Sihanouk, the king of Cambodia until 1970 and then the head of the new government formed after the election in 1993. Others support Son Sann, a general under Prime Minister Lon Nol, who deposed Sihanouk in 1970. There are rumors that some Cambodians in Chicago are former Khmer Rouge cadre. Nonetheless, Sarun reports that factional fighting rarely disrupts his MAA: "I go to the meetings of both groups, those who support Sihanouk and those who support Son Sann. I don't think I'll ever go back to Cambodia to live, so it's more important to keep the community together in the United States. That's why I don't take sides. I even think the Khmer Rouge had some good ideas, like making sure that everyone had the same amount of money, making them equal. But I don't know why they killed so many people. That was terrible."

A greater problem for Sarun than political factions is the generational differences between Cambodian leaders. Younger leaders are more Americanized and base their authority on accomplishments in the United States. Conversely, older leaders are more traditional and attribute their positions to homeland achievements and age seniority. Sarun describes the conflict in leadership styles this way: "The old leaders have experience; they know more about Cambodia than I do. But I have more education and job skills. For example, I know how to use a computer and they don't. Even though I know what the community needs, I cannot make them accept my ideas."

The Cambodian MAA's greatest achievement for the community was sponsoring several Buddhist monks to the United States and purchasing a house to serve as a temple. The temple is now operated by the Cambodian Buddhist Association. Through donations, the MAA raised $60,000 to purchase a house near its office, the strip of Chinese, Vietnamese, and Cambodian stores on Argyle Street, and buildings that house many Cambodians. When the Illinois Department of Public Aid cut the MAA's funding, conflict erupted between the Cambodian Buddhist Association that operates the temple and the Cambodian MAA that founded the temple. Several leaders from the MAA (but not Sarun) met at the temple with a large group of temple devotees and the directors of the Cambodian Buddhist Association. Representatives from the MAA explained the funding cuts and proposed two solutions. The temple could use its plentiful savings to help fund the MAA. Or it could endorse an annual contribution of $20 from every Cambodian family, with the names of contributors recorded on a list. The temple representatives objected to using their institution's resources. An older director of the Buddhist Association proposed a solution in line with Cambodian traditions. He suggested that the MAA solicit funds the way Buddhist monks ask for alms: "You don't have to tell people how much to give. Ask for a donation and they will give some money." But a younger leader from the MAA, who had a more modern view of the problem, countered with a solution more like the "user's fee" in some American social-welfare programs. Stating that donations would never produce the needed sums, he concluded, "If people don't want to pay, then the next time they need someone to translate for them we will charge $50."

Some of the lay men and women who help with the temple upkeep supported the young leader's proposal to charge a fee for services. The MAA had helped many by providing translators for dealings with hospitals and the welfare department. But younger people recalled that when they needed employment the MAA put them in minimum-wage jobs with no health insurance.

Promises that work experience would lead to better jobs were never fulfilled. It became apparent that the temple was not going to relinquish any funds and that the MAA would have to ask for donations.

As several lay men and women finished recounting how the MAA had helped them, the young leader decided to seize the opportunity. He stood up and said, "Let's vote. Who wants to help the association? [Many hands rise.] Who will give money to the association? [Many hands rise again.] Then it's settled." Attempting to push through the decision caused some loss of support. One older woman objected that "it's not fair for us to vote for other people who aren't here. Anyway, people just raised their hands like the back wheels of a cart following the front wheels." The young leader retreated, conceding that the vote was only an endorsement to send letters out to the community. One older leader at the temple, in a final rejection of this impersonal approach derived from American social-welfare practices, pointed to the young leader and said, "Letters won't work. If you want people to give money you should go yourself." This conflict between the temple and the MAA illustrates how institutions in the refugee community provide both needed support and services but also collide because they differ in their degree of Americanization. Even greater conflict can occur when Indochinese refugees focus on politics rather than culture and social services.

Grassroots, Mainstream, and International Politics

A range of historical and cultural factors lead Indochinese refugees to be reluctant participants in American politics (Nguyen 1988; *Refugee Reports* 1986b). Cambodians recall indoctrination sessions and executions by the Khmer Rouge. During the 1960s many Vietnamese had to support both Vietcong guerrillas and the South Vietnamese government in order to avoid retribution from either side. The governments in Vietnam, Laos, and Cambodia before 1975 often were military dictatorships with little or no civilian control over the police and army. Southeast Asian values stress age seniority and respect for, not confrontation with, authority figures. Norms dictate that conflict should be muted rather than made public—the opposite of American democratic culture, which is based on contending interest groups. Factionalism within the refugee community also reduces interest in politics because involvement can have repercussions well beyond the immediate issue.

A study of political views among Laotian refugees found much evidence that their experiences in Laos have left them disinclined to participate in American politics (Harles 1993). In contrast to participatory democracy in the United States, political decision making in Laos was the province of elites rather than citizens. As a result, many Lao in the United States have a deferential view of authority figures: "The Lao respect those who are 'over them' more than do Americans. This has to do with good manners; children should have good manners toward older people, just as adults should have good manners to those who are over them" (164). This familial analogy appeared often in the interviews, indicating that the Lao view politics partly through the lens of kinship. Since the Lao have a hierarchical conception of the family, their views of citizens' relationship to government are similarly organized: "We must have a government that rules over the people. You can't just let the people rule over themselves; that would never work. It would be like a family. If you had children without parents to control them, it would not be good at all" (167).

Experiences under authoritarian and then Communist governments further contribute to the refugees' political timidity in the United States. Asked about his willingness to take even a minor political action, one Lao man responded, "I don't think I could ever present a petition to government officials [in the United States]. I don't think I would be brave enough. I was afraid to do something like that in Laos, and I guess I am still afraid" (179). Those Lao who have become politically active in the United States tend to be former elites. Their past activities in Laos create a disincentive for others in the community to become involved. As one refugee explained:

> The reason I don't go to these political meetings [by anti-Communist groups seeking political change in Laos] is that I know the people who are running the parties; I know their background. They were politicians in Laos, most of them, who made money from poor and uneducated people. They were people who used their power over people to control them. Here, in this country, they are doing the same thing. (174)

Finally, the very term *politics* has negative connotations for the Lao. Americans generally conceive of politics as a competition among groups formed of individuals with similar interests and aspirations combined with the guarantee of basic rights and protections. For the Lao, politics implies a dishonest and often threatening means for achieving one's goals at the expense of others. Political struggles in their homeland have left the Lao, like most Indochinese refugees, disillusioned with government institutions and politicians. The Lao interviewed for Harles's (1993) study stated, "When I think of politics I think of someone who is doing something underhanded" (171); "My parents taught me that I should never say anything wrong about politics because there was danger in that" (173); and, "There was a saying in Laos: If you play around with politics, pretty soon politics will play around with you" (172).

Yet some of the same factors that inhibit mobilization among Indochinese refugees are also the greatest catalysts for political involvement in the United States. For example, migrants from socialist countries become U.S. citizens at a much greater rate than others, and male (but not female) migrants who enter the country as refugees also have a very high naturalization rate (Jasso and Rosenzweig 1990). Indochinese refugees in particular naturalize much more frequently than immigrants from Mexico and Europe, although less often than other migrants from Asia.

Homeland politics provides Indochinese refugees with an even greater motivation for activism. In 1988 more than 2,000 Cambodians signed a letter to President Reagan—hardly evidence of political reticence. They voiced concern that the Khmer Rouge might use a proposed U.N. peace plan for Cambodia to regain territory and then seize power again (*Refugee Reports* 1988). In fact, the 1993 election in Cambodia proceeded with little violence, leading to the first democratically elected government in more than two decades. A Cambodian refugee living in Providence, Rhode Island, was even on the ballot (Ziner 1993).

Similarly, political, and even military, developments in Laos are of concern to Hmong refugees in the United States. A Hmong project in St. Paul, Minnesota, to provide health and educational materials to the Hmong still in Laos was opposed by other Hmong on the grounds that it would only stabilize and lend legitimacy to the Communist government. Opponents of the project gathered 1,200 signatures calling for its end (Lai 1992). General Vang Pao, the commander of the CIA-supported Hmong army during the 1960s, now lives in the United States but plans military operations for Hmong guerrillas in Southeast Asia. Reports suggest that he collects considerable sums of money from Hmong refugees to finance his military organization. There are allegations that the "contributions" are at times obtained through pressure and social sanction (Calkins and Rios 1989; Hammond 1989). But 5,000 Hmong protested in Milwaukee following attacks by the Laotian military against Hmong still in Laos, testifying to the refugees' sincere interest in their homeland (Klein 1990).

Political mobilization to influence events in the homeland is greatest among the Vietnamese. In 1981 there were at least six rallies throughout the United States by a Vietnamese organization supporting resistance fighters in the SRV, the Socialist Republic of Vietnam (King 1982). Two rallies in California drew crowds of about 3,000, including a former South Vietnamese prime minister and several hundred men in khaki uniforms. Since 1985 the National Congress of Vietnamese in America has organized against political repression in the SRV (AAP 1990). It also worked to end the recruitment of Vietnamese laborers (60,000 between 1987 and 1990) for low-paid factory work in the former Communist state of East Germany (Kinzer 1992). Following the collapse of communism in Eastern Europe and the former Soviet Union, Vietnamese in Western Europe and North America gathered in Washington, D.C., to promote concerted efforts among the "Vietnamese diaspora" to isolate the SRV (ABCN 1992a).

Vietnamese Americans' anti-Communist sentiments have at times led to conflict within the United States. For several consecutive weekends in the spring of 1985 (the tenth anniversary of the fall of South Vietnam), 200 Vietnamese protested outside the San Jose office of the Socialist Workers party, which was holding a workshop on Vietnamese history (Hill 1985). Two years later Vietnamese protested the commencement speech of California state assemblyman Tom Hayden, a prominent anti–Vietnam War activist during the 1960s. He was to address the graduating class at San Jose City College, which was 40 percent Vietnamese (Lane and Rockstroh 1987).

One of the most dramatic incidents stemming from Vietnamese political mobilization occurred in 1990. Nguyen Kim Bang, a Vietnamese journalist, committed suicide near the the the U.S. Capitol to protest political repression in the SRV (Kurtzman and McLaughlin 1990; McLaughlin and Kurtzman 1990). Bang had fought in the ARVN, and his grandfather, father, uncle, and younger brother had been killed in the war. Bang chose a method of suicide—self-immolation—used by Buddhist monks during the 1960s to protest against the authoritarian practices of the South Vietnamese government. A letter Bang wrote before his death read in part:

Our country is in shambles and our people in abject misery. . . . In many places around the world wherever we go we are mistreated, raped and persecuted on the seas around Vietnam, from Southeast Asian refugee camps to the workers' compounds in Eastern Europe. Acting on a small residue of moral conscience, I have therefore chosen to offer my little self . . . to my fatherland so that I may serve as a flickering candle shining into the darkest of tunnels in the hope that the civilized world may be awakened. (ABCN 1990, 26)

The depth of anti-Communist sentiments among Vietnamese refugees has even led to violence within Vietnamese communities, again dispelling the image of ethnic solidarity and political placidity. Since 1981 there have been more than a dozen politically motivated arsons, assaults, and murders, mostly in Orange County, California. The targets are Vietnamese who support the Communist government, advocate diplomatic contacts with the SRV, or simply visited their homeland to report on current social and political conditions (Wilkinson and Reyes 1989). In 1994 President Bill Clinton ended the American economic embargo against the SRV, thus undermining those in the Vietnamese community advocating an adversarial policy toward their homeland.

Vietnamese exhibit varying attitudes toward this violence within their community. Many of the refugees agree that advocating reconciliation with the SRV is like treason. A former officer in the South Vietnamese Air Force stated, "As long as the regime is suppressing people in reeducation camps with an iron will, people like me in the Vietnamese community will not give up the fight" (Wilkinson and Reyes 1989, C10). Others feel that events in their homeland should not remain of central importance for Vietnamese in the United States. Referring to the Vietnam War, a Vietnamese man who works for an American resettlement agency said, "It is an ugly scar we try to forget. If you keep touching a scar, you can't concentrate on the future. For the future generations, we have to divorce part of the past" (J. Steinberg 1989, E1).

There is some evidence that anti-Communist claims, while exaggerated, are not without foundation. A retired American CIA officer who worked in Vietnam believes that there are SRV agents in the United States: "I was in the business for more than twenty years, and the Central Bureau in Hanoi, which handles their foreign intelligence [does] just as any intelligence service does when they're running refugees out: they're running their own people in too. . . . That's a standard intelligence technique" (Fremstad 1981, A14). An FBI agent who heads foreign counterintelligence operations claims that the former Soviet Union used Vietnamese in the United States to collect information (Wines 1990).

But it is money, not politics, that is the best documented SRV activity in the United States (U.S. Senate 1984). A consultant for the U.S. Customs Service testified in Congress that the SRV, beginning in 1982, organized groups with relatives overseas to systematically write letters asking for money, relying on the strong obligations of Vietnamese family members to aid each other. At least 13 collection points in U.S. cities from Los Angeles to Arlington, Virginia, receive the funds and channel them to other centers in France, Canada, and some countries in Asia, which have monetary relations with Vietnam. The funds are then deposited in the SRV State Bank, and the government takes a large portion before passing the remaining sum to the relatives. At the time of the inquiry, it was believed that approximately $18 million left the United States each month in this manner.

Despite Indochinese refugees' strong interest in homeland politics, domestic issues are increasingly displacing their international concerns. In Denver 91 Vietnamese signed a petition criticizing the social-welfare services provided by the state of Colorado (Coakley 1982). They then translated the petition into English and published it in a local newspaper.

In San Jose, Vietnamese refugees occupied a Catholic Church to demand the creation of a separate Vietnamese parish within a diocese that contained about 7,000 Vietnamese Catholics (*New York Times* 1986; Rockstroh 1987b). Their actions came after the bishop suspended Vietnamese-language masses following disorderly protests at two churches. The dissidents then prevented a Vietnamese priest sent by the bishop from entering the church, prompting the bishop to order their eviction.

In Chicago more than 200 Cambodian and Laotian refugees protested when a landlord gave tenants 30-day eviction notices so that he could sell the building, which had greatly increased in value after recently being certified a historic structure (*Refugee Reports* 1986b). The refugees were eventually displaced by middle-class tenants who could afford the new rents, but the landlord was forced to extend the eviction deadline, return security deposits, and provide families with $200 to cover moving expenses.

In Lowell, Massachusetts, Cambodian and Laotian parents joined with Latino parents to force the local school committee to reform inadequate and seg-regated school facilities for their children (Kiang 1990). Antibussing candidates, however, swept to victory in the next school committee election. The top vote-getter had expressed the strongest anti-immigrant views. He won despite the fact that his son had racially insulted and then drowned a 13-year-old Cambodian boy a month before the election. As a result of this backlash, Cambodians in Lowell have begun mobilizing to influence the political process. These instances of grassroots activism, although far from pervasive, suggest that the inhibiting effects of homeland political cultures is not as great among Indochinese refugees as one would expect.

In fact, Indochinese refugees have entered the formal political process by forming Democratic and Republican support groups, with the latter gaining the most support. A survey in California found Republican affiliation at 47 percent among Asian Americans but only 42 percent among whites, 26 percent among Hispanics, and 5 percent among blacks (Cain and Kiewiet 1986). Former Vietnamese military officers, of which 11 past generals live in the San Francisco Bay Area, play a particularly important role as links to the Republican party (Rockstroh 1987a). A Vietnamese field representative for a Republican congressman explains the attraction of the GOP for the refugees: "The Republicans have a staunch anti-communist position. In essence, we are here because the communists drove us out. We know the Republicans will stand up to communists. The GOP's spirit of economic self-sufficiency truly coincides with the working ethic of small 'Mom and Pop' shops arising in the community" (*Refugee Reports* 1986b, 3). Sensing this attitude, Republicans have sought the Asian vote. At the start of the 1992 presidential campaign, Vice President Dan Quayle announced the formation of "Asian Americans for Bush-Quayle '92," proclaiming, "the Bush administration shares so many values with the Asian-American community, including an emphasis on entrepreneurship, close-knit families, crime prevention, hard work, and education" (quoted in O'Conner 1992, 17).

Increased political participation has led to the appointment of Indochinese refugees at the federal level. President George Bush picked Nguyen Ngoc Bich to be deputy director of the Office of Bilingual Education and Minority Language Affairs, a bureau in the Department of Education that develops policies to aid children with limited English proficiency. He also appointed Mary Chi Ray as deputy director of the Office of Refugee Resettlement, which sets national policy for the funding and provision of social services to refugees. Ray later resigned the post citing its limitations in really helping refugees.

Participation in local elections provides the final evidence of rising political interest among Indochinese refugees. In 1986 Nil Hul, the director of the Cambodian Association of Long Beach, California, ran for a position on the Long Beach City Council, the first electoral bid by a Cambodian in the United States. In 1990 Vu Duc Vuong sought election to the San Francisco Board of Supervisors, the first Vietnamese to run for political office in the United States. Although both lost, their initiatives marked the political maturation of Indochinese communities. In 1992, however, a Hmong woman named Choua Lee was elected to the St. Paul, Minnesota, School Board, marking the first electoral victory for an Indochinese refugee. Then Tony Lam won a seat on the Westminster, California, City Council, becoming the country's first Vietnamese elected official. But it has been the legal system, not conventional politics, where the refugees have had the greatest struggles and some of the greatest gains.

Inequality, Culture, and the Courts

Although Vietnamese, Laotians, and Cambodians are among the most recent ethnic minorities in the United States (few lived in the country before 1975), they have already used the courts to challenge racial discrimination. In 1986 a manufacturing company in St. Paul fired more than one-half of its 130 Vietnamese, Cambodian, and Hmong workers after they attended a union information meeting (ABCN 1992b). It then began hiring native workers to replace them. The National Labor Relations Board brought charges against the company, which settled the case by reinstating some workers and placing the rest on a preferential hiring list. But company records also revealed racial discrimination in pay and promotion, leading the Equal Employment Opportunity Commission to file suit on behalf of the refugees.

The first decision regarding housing discrimination against Southeast Asians occurred in Appleton, Wisconsin (*St. Paul Pioneer Press* 1993b). A Hmong man sought to rent a house in a predominately white neighborhood. While he was scouting the neighborhood, a white woman approached him and stated that "his people were not allowed to live on that block." The man felt especially insulted because his father had worked for the CIA during the Vietnam War. A judge fined the woman $12,000 in damages and penalties.

A more significant legal precedent was set by a Cambodian refugee, a former naval officer who was in the United States for training in 1975 when the Khmer Rouge took over Cambodia, killing his family in the process. He sued his employer, a bank, charging that he had been denied promotions because he spoke English with an accent. A lower court agreed that an employer who used a worker's foreign accent to make workplace decisions was guilty of discrimination based on national origin, which is prohibited by the Civil Rights Act of 1964. The bank was fined $390,000, and the Washington State Appeals Court upheld the decision (AAP 1992). That same year three Vietnamese won a suit charging that the Defense Department discriminated on the basis of national origin (Hoang 1992). The case concerned a Defense Department regulation that banned security clearance for high-level jobs for migrants from Communist countries, with Vietnam, Laos, and Cambodia specifically cited. The U.S. District Court in Washington, D.C., ruled the that policy was discriminatory.

American courts have been important allies of Indochinese refugees in combating housing and workplace discrimination based on race and national origin. But migration to the United States from Asia has raised new and complex cultural issues for the courts as well. Intent is an essential point in American law, and planning to commit a murder is much more serious than killing someone by accident or during a period of mental illness. But should courts consider a person's cultural background when determining their innocence, guilt, and punishment? Many lawyers believe they should and have increasingly relied on a "cultural defense" to win cases for Asian clients (*Judicature* 1988; Sheybani 1987).

One of the most famous cases that centered on cultural differences occurred in Los Angeles. When a woman from Japan learned that her husband was having an affair, she purposefully drowned her two children and tried to drown herself (Oliver 1988). A petition defending the woman circulated in the Japanese-American community and received 4,000 signatures. The petition explained that in Japan parent-child suicide was a historical custom permitted a wife whose husband committed adultery. According to custom, a mother who committed suicide and left her children alive was considered disgraceful. In the end, an American court found the woman guilty of manslaughter, not murder, which follows Japanese law. She was sentenced to one year in jail and five years of probation with psychiatric treatment.

A similar case occurred in Connecticut after Binh Gia Pham, a Vietnamese refugee who had lived in the United States for 11 years, immolated himself (Sege 1993). Pham, a devout Buddhist, chose this method of suicide to call attention to religious oppression in the Socialist Republic of Vietnam. Six men, four of whom belonged to a Buddhist youth association founded by Pham, assisted in the suicide. They allegedly drove him to an isolated location, poured some of the gasoline on him, and videotaped his death. A district attorney charged the men with second-degree manslaughter. Vietnamese Buddhist monks appealed for clemency, however. They argued that Western views of suicide were inconsistent with those of Buddhism, which under unusual circumstances views it as sign of selflessness and willingness to sacrifice on behalf of others. Thousands of Vietnamese across the United States signed petitions urging Connecticut authorities to cancel the prosecution of Pham's companions.

More than any other new immigrants, the Hmong have confronted cultural conflicts with the judicial system. In some cases the courts have not taken culture into consideration, instead adopting an assimilationist approach to the adaptation process. For example, a Hmong father and son in Chicago were accused of aggravated battery against a white motorist following an argument over who had the right of way. At the trial the Hmong men requested that the judge allow them to enact a ritual used to resolve disputes among the Hmong in Laos. A rooster should be slaughtered, they explained, and some of its blood put in glasses of water for both parties to drink. For the Hmong, the rooster is a mystical animal that can communicate with spirits. A person who lies after drinking rooster blood will be put to death by spirits. The defense presented an anthropologist who testified to the authenticity of the ritual and also discussed how the Hmong had been American allies during the Vietnam War. Both the Hmong men on trial had rescued American pilots as part of their military activities. The judge barred the ritual, however, and later found the two Hmong men guilty. His sentence—probation with the understanding that they would study the English language and American culture—revealed how American courts have become sites for resolving cultural issues raised by immigration from the Third World. The judge explained his sentence: "I recognize that they come from a different society and a different culture, and one that unfortunately experienced violence on a daily basis. . . . But the two defendants should be assimilating our culture, and they should realize we live in a society of law and order" (Wilson 1988, 1).

In many more cases, however, the American judicial system has interpreted the law in ways giving priority to Hmong culture, such as possession of opium. In Laos the Hmong grew opium for medicinal purposes (they had no other pain-killers), but also for profit since it can be chemically converted into heroin (Westermeyer 1982). Before Laos gained independence from France in 1953, the French secret service encouraged the opium and heroin trade to make hidden profits, as did the American CIA during the 1960s and early 1970s (McCoy 1972). Some Hmong have continued to grow opium in the United States, while others have received opium from relatives in Thailand (Schmickle 1983). After discovering several opium packages in the homes of Hmong in Minneapolis, a U.S. attorney declined to prosecute since he believed the Hmong did not realize opium was illegal. Asked how he would have defended the Hmong in a court, a public defense lawyer stated: "These people come from a culture where opium is regularly used as a medicine, a laxative, to sleep and to make old age better. At least until they become acculturated it's a reasonable exercise of prosecutorial discretion not to prosecute them" (Anderson 1984, D3).

Courts have also restricted Western medical practices to accommodate Hmong culture (Ziner 1990). In Providence, Rhode Island, a Hmong family requested that a hospital not perform an autopsy on a recently deceased son. When the son's body was on view at the funeral, however, the family discovered the stitched wounds indicating an internal medical examination. The doctor who performed the autopsy stated that he was medically obligated to determine the cause of death, especially since the son had died in his sleep without any previous sign of illness. Over 100 Indochinese refugees, mostly Hmong, have died from what the U.S. Centers for Disease Control terms Sudden Unexpected Nocturnal Death Syndrome (Munger, 1986; Lemoine and Mougne 1983). The Hmong attribute these deaths to evil spirits. Social workers (Tobin and Friedman 1983) and anthropologists (Adler 1991) have linked this folk belief with traumatic flight and culture shock to explain how mental states can cause physiological disorders.

The Hmong object to autopsies because they violate their religious beliefs (Bliatout 1993), one of many conflicts between Hmong and Western medical practices (Deinard and Dunnigan 1986). A mutilated body prevents the spirit from moving to the next world. A spirit that cannot make this transformation will stay to haunt the family. In the Providence case, this was the fourth member of the family's clan (households sharing the same last name) to die, and autopsies had been performed on the first three. The clan concluded that an angry spirit was responsible for the fourth death. The American Civil Liberties Union argued the case on behalf of the Hmong family and asked for $2 million in damages. A federal judge agreed that the hospital had violated the Hmong family's First Amendment rights to freedom of religion when it performed the autopsy.

A similar case occurred in Fresno, California, and again illustrates how contemporary cross-cultural conflicts in the United States are often brought to the courts. American social workers discovered a Hmong boy with two clubfeet and obtained a court order for an operation over the protest of the parents and the Hmong community (Kurtzman 1990). The boy's parents believed that the deformity actually represented good luck rather than an abnormality. According to Hmong religious beliefs, clubfeet are a sign that an ancestor's feet wounded in battle have been healed. As a result, the son is considered a blessing rather than a deviant. While living in a Thai refugee camp the family had allowed doctors to partially correct the son's handicap. Then two other sons were born with cleft palates because, the parents explained, they had displeased their ancestor. The Hmong family appealed the court-ordered operation all the way to the Supreme Court, which refused to hear the case. Despite a court ruling in their favor, social workers had been unable to find a doctor willing to perform the operation against the family's wishes. When the case returned to the lower court, the social workers abandoned their plans for the operation. In this case, courts did not use the First Amendment to shield Hmong culture.

Yet it is courtship practices, not religion, which have been the basis for the most publicized cases of conflict between Hmong culture and the American legal system. On several occasions, single Hmong men have been accused of kidnaping and even raping single Hmong women. In defense of their actions some of the men explain that in Hmong culture there is a ritualized elopement or abduction of a bride termed bride theft. In Laos, an unmarried Hmong woman was expected to resist the attention of male suitors lest she give the impression of sexual interest. In this context, Hmong youths might have several motives to enact the ritual. A woman might encourage abduction by a man she wishes to marry but who is disapproved of by her parents. A man may want time alone with the woman to convince her of his good attentions. A ritualized theft of the bride allows the woman to maintain a display of chastity and high moral standing. It also would place the young man in a better position to bargain for a lower bride price, the precious metals and animals given the bride's parents to compensate them for the economic loss of their daughter's labor. Although uncommon even when the Hmong lived in Laos, in "a culture where marriage was the main avenue to socially recognized adulthood . . . bride theft could thus be viewed as a viable alternative in the face of parental or bridal opposition, or limited bride price resources" (Scott 1988, 144).

Detailed accounts of Hmong bride theft in the United States reveal how the Americanization of gender roles creates a cultural conflict requiring the intervention of the criminal justice system (Goldstein 1986; Oliver 1988; Scott 1988;

Sherman 1986; Sheybani 1987). Many Hmong women embrace the greater equality accorded women in the United States and view bride theft as abduction without any justification based on cultural misunderstandings. Hmong males, however, show a greater reluctance to adopt new gender roles, and some resort to bride theft. In Laos marriage by capture was tolerated when a woman's parents asked an exorbitant bride price or if the couple wanted to marry without parental permission. In the United States males appear to resort to bride theft because they cannot accept the new independence of Hmong women.

Although bride theft clearly contradicts American law, courts have shown surprising tolerance for the practice, consistent with their neglect of violence against women in general. In one bride-theft case in Fresno, California, a Hmong man was convicted of kidnaping and rape, but the judge sentenced him to only 120 days in jail with a $1,000 fine. The judge acknowledged that this was a light sentence but claimed that it gave him "leeway to get into all these cultural issues and to try to tailor a sentence that would fulfill both [American] needs and the Hmong needs" (Sheybani 1987, 775). Another case in Minnesota involved a female minor and was resolved with a fine of $1,000 and no jail term. In these and other cases involving the Hmong, courts have become not only the arbiters of justice but key sites for regulating cultural conflict between new immigrants and American society.

Despite the leniency of the courts in bride-theft cases, Hmong clan leaders seek to resolve these and other crimes within the community. Male elders have a special leadership role in the Hmong clan system. A clan has particular customs and oral histories and is expected to practice exogamy (marriage outside of the group). A Hmong proverb signifies the importance of clan membership for individuals: "One person can't be a household. One household can't be a village. One village can't be a city" (Lyman 1990, 342). Elders avoid the intervention of American organizations to preserve their traditional dominance over disputes. The village mediator who presides over conflicts ranging from theft and adultery to murder is an honored status in Hmong society—one that is eroded when American judges, police officers, and social workers decide right and wrong.

But the parties in the dispute may also want an internal resolution. In Laos disputes were settled through formal apologies and banquets for minor offenses, payment of money or material goods in more serious cases, and communal beatings and even death as the most extreme punishment (Silvers 1992). American courts use jail terms and fines that may not directly benefit the abducted woman or her relatives. Hmong clans continue to mete out justice to members in the United States. Clan leaders settled a case of adultery in Sheboygan, Wisconsin, by requiring the accused man to pay $1,000 to the family of the man whose wife he had slept with. Unfortunately, this punishment did not end the affair. The two men eventually agreed to fight a knife duel for the woman. After the husband stabbed his rival to death, police arrested him on charges of first-degree intentional homicide.

In some instances, however, the Hmong may have used the American judicial system to reinforce their sexual codes in cases of rape that do not involve bride theft (Hammond 1993). In two rape cases in St. Paul, the accused Hmong men claimed that their acts with married Hmong women were consenual and thus constituted adultery and not sexual assault. Because Hmong custom severely punishes adultery while American law does not, they argued that these women were pressured by husbands and family to make the charge of rape. Only a conviction on rape charges would bring about a punishment consistent with Hmong sanctions as practiced in Laos. Both cases did in fact end in convictions despite a great number of discrepancies between the Hmong interpreters' translations of prosecutors' questions and plaintiffs' answers.

A final illustration of the new role of courts in determining the legitimacy of U.S. and Southeast Asian norms involves a case against two Cambodians in Long Beach, California, accused of slaughtering a dog for food (Bishop 1989b; *Chicago Tribune* 1989; Haldane 1989). Neighbors of the two men called the police after hearing squeals coming from their apartment. The police found a dead and partially skinned German shepherd and arrested the two refugees. Food preferences vary all over the world (horse meat is commonly eaten in France), and dog meat is eaten in parts of Asia, although rarely in Cambodia. The defense lawyer argued that since dogs were a culturally sanctioned food in their homeland, the two refugees were being tried for their ethnic cuisine. He stated, "When you bring someone into this country you take the whole person. . . . You don't just extract them from their culture, you bring the culture with them" (Haldane 1989, A6). But animal-rights groups following the case disagreed. The prosecuting attorney argued that killing the dog constituted cruelty to animals, although agreeing that the dog had been killed in a manner no worse than for livestock in American slaughterhouses.

Once again demonstrating how courts are evaluating American values and norms in response to cases involving Third World migrants, a Long Beach judge ruled that California had no law against eating dogs and that the animal had been killed in a humane way. An assemblyman in the California Legislature immediately sponsored a bill to prevent future acquittals in such cases. In 1981 the California Assembly had examined (and defeated) a similar bill in response to rumors that refugees were killing and consuming animals in San Francisco's Golden Gate Park. Indochinese MAAs lobbied against the 1989 bill, arguing that associating Asians with bizarre food preferences is an anti-Asian prejudice that can be traced to white resentment of Chinese immigrants in the nineteenth century. They failed to sway the assembly. In California it is now "a misdemeanor to possess, sell or give away for the sole purpose of killing for food any animal 'commonly kept as a pet or companion'" (Bishop 1989b, 22).

Despite victories in discrimination suits, judicial leniency in cases of cultural conflict, and increasing political activism, Indochinese refugees in California could not prevent codification of one of the oldest and most virulent anti-Asian prejudices (Baer 1982; Mitchell 1987). In an indirect attack on Hmong religious practices, the Fresno City Council proposed in 1992 to make illegal the killing of an animal without a permit from the Health Department (Pulaski and Dudley 1992). The legislation came in response to constituent concerns about the health hazards posed by slaughtered animals. For the 30,000 Hmong in the city, however, it threatened the practice of animal sacrifice by shamans at healing rituals. A 1993 Supreme Court decision unanimously ruled that a city could not ban sacrificial killing of animals for religious purposes. The case involved Miami and a Caribbean cult known as the Santeria, indicating how Third World migrants in general, not just the Hmong, are using American courts to settle cultural conflicts.

Conclusion

The hardships of migration coupled with an official resettlement program could have left Indochinese refugees with little collective control over their adaptation in the United States. Instead they have formed numerous self-help organizations and sought to influence the political system. Ethnic associations and leaders enable the refugees to play an active role in the adaptation process.

Yet Indochinese refugees' self-help and political activities in the United States are shaped by conditions in their homelands. These international influences are unexpected from the viewpoint of the assimilation model, which examines the adaptation process from a domestic perspective. But homeland political conflict, economic development, and level of modernization are included within the ethnic-resilience model's more global view of migrant adaptation. Similarly, the very rapid shift in refugee associations' goals from social service provision to cultural preservation confirms the ethnic-resilience model's prediction that migrants' interest in their ethnicity increases over time. Vietnamese, Laotian, Hmong, and Cambodian associations differ, however, in the degree to which they pursue cultural preservation, in part because of the groups' different cultures, a factor neglected by the ethnic-resilience model.

The ethnic-resilience model also says little about conflict within refugee communities. A case study of two Cambodian MAAs in Chicago—one that provides social services, the other operating a Buddhist temple—reveals that self-help initiatives can be sites of intense conflict among refugees. Conflict also arises among refugee leaders because some have positions of authority owing to accomplishments in their homeland, while others have skills derived from experiences in the United States. This tension between traditional and modern leaders exemplifies the collision of homeland and host society that is at the core of the assimilation model.

The domestic and international political concerns of Indochinese refugees further reveal divisiveness within their communities. Support for policies of rapprochement with the Socialist Republic of Vietnam causes intense disagreement among Vietnamese Americans, at times even leading to murder. Political diversity and discord within refugee communities suggest that the ethnic-resilience model has overemphasized the salience of conflict between natives and newcomers as the defining feature of immigrant and refugee adaptation. Indeed, the strength of Republican support among the Indochinese and Asian Americans in general, in sharp contrast to the Democratic leanings of African Americans, is not what one would expect if the ethnic-resilience model is correct in portraying Asian immigrants and refugees as new minorities.

The assimilation model presumes that natives allow newcomers to enter American society as equals. Indochinese refugees' interactions with the courts, a nascent form of politicalization, suggest the contrary. The refugees have used the courts to win important, even precedent-setting, legal victories against job and housing discrimination. At the same time, the refugees' interaction with the legal system also belies the ethnic-resilience model's characterization of non-Europeans as holding an inferior status in the American ethnic hierarchy. Particularly for Hmong refugees, courts have assumed the role of cultural arbiters, such as deciding whether defendants should be given a lenient sentence because their behavior was acceptable in their homeland. In a number of cases, judges have been persuaded by this cultural defense, thus using the legal system to redefine American norms.

seven
___

Family and Kinship

N o aspect of the refugee experience better illustrates the importance of
groups in the adaptation process than the family and kinship. Perhaps
the greatest advance of the ethnic-resilience model over the assimilation
model is this recognition that migrants adapt as members of groups with collective strategies and goals rather than as isolated individuals facing the host society alone. An important coping mechanism that works through families is kin
and fictive kin relationships, exemplified by an ethnography of how a fragment
of a larger Cambodian family regrouped its members in a city near Boston and
then forged links with more isolated Cambodians.

Yet paradoxically, research using the ethnic-resilience perspective has given
little attention to immigrant and refugee families and kin relations. This omission is linked to the model's conceptualization of ethnicity without culture.
Culture is a necessary concept in the study of the adaptation process because
values (ideals of good and bad) and norms (rules concerning appropriate and
inappropriate behavior) explain in part why relations between husbands and
wives, children and parents, youths and seniors, differ in the United States
and Southeast Asia. As a result of viewing ethnicity as nationality rather than
culture, the ethnic-resilience model exaggerates migrant's resistance to adopting elements of American culture.

The attractiveness of some elements of American culture for Indochinese
refugees is most evident in changing gender roles. Women in the United States
have more egalitarian roles within families and greater freedom to define their
roles without reference to the family than has traditionally been true for women
in Vietnam, Laos, and Cambodia. Equally profound changes occur in family life for
children and parents, since Southeast Asian cultures use age to establish seniority
and thus the right to make decisions for others. Changing gender and age roles is
accompanied by intense conflict, as revealed by an account of the intergenerational tension between a Cambodian widow and a prospective Cambodian son-in-
law over courtship and marriage customs. But the maintenance of age seniority in
the United States can have negative outcomes, such as parental pressure on
teenage girls to marry before they are "too old," which if successful often pre-
cludes the girls from completing high school or entering college. Immigrant and
refugee adaptation is not fundamentally a conflict between newcomers and
natives, as depicted by the ethnic-resilience model, because American culture contains values and norms that many migrants find worthy of adoption.

Kin and Fictive Kin, Family, and Community

Yay and her husband are the core of an extensive Cambodian network in a city near Boston that has attracted immigrants since the industrial revolution (Yay is a respectful term in Khmer for "old woman"). Yay and her relatives illustrate how Cambodian refugees build households into extended families, and in turn how these networks of kin become the foundations of the community. Isolated individuals and fragmented families attach themselves to a family, either by close friendship, marriage, or fictive kinship—the practice of using kin names for people not related by blood or marriage to signify a close, protective relationship. When asked how many Cambodians live in a city Cambodians usually respond with the number of families rather than the number of people, indicating that the basic unit of the community is a kin group rather than the individual.

At first it is difficult to understand why other refugees would create bonds to Yay and her family. In Cambodia they were poor peasants who survived only by the generosity of a wealthy landowner. He took pity on the family, giving them land in return for a share of their harvest. Yay's response to a question about her memories of Cambodia emphasized the family's prior status as poor farmers:

> First there were the French. They made the high taxes. Taxes were so high it took three or four years to pay for one year. Some people were put in jail or lost their land. In the year of the goat the Thai came [in 1940 Japan took Indochina from France and ceded part of Cambodia to Thailand]. When the Thai came they freed the slaves and the servants. The Thai stayed in the market, they didn't go into the country like the French. One time there was a big bomb in the market. Then the French came back but there was also the Issarak [a Cambodian independence movement during the early 1940s]. They fought with the French and killed their spies. It was just like the Khmer Rouge: Cambodians killed Cambodians. Sihanouk came and life was easier, but then he lost to the Khmer Rouge. After that there were the Vietnamese and another war. I have lived through four wars.

The experience of Yay's oldest daughter, Bopha, is revealing of the family's socioeconomic position in Cambodia. She worked in the home of the landowner's cousin and reports being treated badly. On one occasion the wife in the family threatened that her husband (the mayor of the town) would have Bopha jailed if she disobeyed a command. Bopha secretly prayed that disaster would befall the family. When the Khmer Rouge conquered Cambodia in 1975, they immediately executed the husband, and the wife lived in poverty until committing suicide in the late 1980s when relatives discovered she had been stealing their rice. Bopha says she is "happy things turned out the way they did," referring to the revolution that destroyed Cambodia's elite. But she also takes pride in how her family achieved a higher social status in the United States than they had in Cambodia.

Yay's family did not achieve this status through education, occupations, or wealth—the typical routes to a higher social class for Americans. A son and two sons-in-law work at jobs that are unlikely to provide an opportunity for mobility: work at a yogurt factory and stripping asbestos in building renovation. Yay and her husband receive social security, while the two daughters get public assistance because the welfare department believes their children were fathered by boyfriends who have since disappeared. Only the children speak English well. Housing is perhaps the worst part of the family's life. The apartment has three bedrooms, a large living room, and a spacious dining room. But Yay and her husband live there with their son, two daughters, two sons-in-law, six grandchildren, and a female boarder. There is one bathroom for these 14 people. Paint peels from the walls, there are several species of roaches, and the unlighted staircase is hazardous at night.

Refugees attempting to live in extended families face many difficulties in the housing market: declining apartment construction; new buildings containing units with one rather than several bedrooms; the conversion of large apartments into condominiums; and landlords who insist on one bedroom for each person (Haines 1980; Ragas 1980). In rural Southeast Asia houses often consist of two large rooms—one for cooking and eating, and the other where the whole family sleeps, perhaps in separate corners. The American conception of housing with distinct areas for activities and individual sleeping quarters does not mesh well with traditional Cambodian household life. Cambodians emphasize communality, rather than privacy, and regard as akin to solitary confinement the American custom of having young children sleep in their own rooms.

It is not material conditions that make Yay a leading figure in the Cambodian community but the social relations she weaves between family and friends. One of her favorite pastimes is hosting card games. Cambodians drive for miles to play, and hundreds of dollars can change hands in a night. Yay also is among the oldest members of the Cambodian community and thus respected for her opinions, wisdom, and especially sense of humor. She almost always will be asked to attend a wedding, since her presence will bring other guests, while a refusal could doom the whole event.

Seniority and recreational activities contribute to Yay's prominence in the Cambodian community. Of more importance is her ability to reproduce the close bonds—the blurring of friendship and kinship—that were so much a part of community life in Cambodia. But before Yay could help rebuild the community, she had to piece together her own family, which had been dismantled during migration to the United States. When Yay arrived in 1982 she was accompanied only by her husband, a daughter, and a son. Although Bopha, Bopha's husband, and their four children stayed with Yay in a Thai refugee camp, American immigration officials split them into a separate family. Bopha and her family arrived the same year as Yay did, but were sent to a southern state while Yay was sent to Massachusetts.

Within a year of arrival, Bopha's family had moved into Yay's apartment. Yay was especially eager to live with them because one granddaughter had been born during the Khmer Rouge period and survived against all odds. Bopha reports that the forced agricultural labor she endured was so severe that she was unable to produce milk to breast-feed the baby. Instead, she fed it small shrimp gathered from a swamp and mashed into a paste. Not long after Bopha arrived, Yay's younger daughter married, and her husband moved in as well. Each household occupied one room in the flat, and although massively overcrowded by American standards, this arrangement fit Cambodian custom. Yay had rebuilt her family, transforming an isolated household constructed by American immigration officials into an extended family containing not only grandparents and grandchildren but married siblings as well.

The next additions to Yay's network were a distant female relative of her husband, and this woman's recently divorced daughter named Chhonn. Chhonn survived the Khmer Rouge period with her husband, even experiencing the death of a child born in 1975. But she divorced him shortly after arriving in the United States and moved with the two remaining children and her aged mother from her initial settlement site to the city where Yay lives. Chhonn hoped to make a new start with the help of her relatives.

Chhonn's mother introduces Yay's husband as her "brother." The Khmer language has two words for "relative." One contains the words for body and blood, while the other means the seniority relationship between older and younger siblings, husband and wife. Cambodians add a prefix to the latter term for relative to create a new word meaning "friendship like that of close relatives," or fictive kinship. Thus Chhonn's mother places herself in a subordinate position in Yay's kin network in order to attain a degree of status (so lacking in her own family) by association with Yay's family. The irony of this new relationship is not lost on Yay and Bopha. In Cambodia, Chhonn's mother had a very high social status because her husband was a local government official. In the United States she needs the close bonds offered by a family of former peasants to which she is only distantly related.

Some time later Chhonn allowed a Cambodian boyfriend named Dara to live with her. Bopha and others tried to convince Chhonn that Dara was probably a scoundrel looking for a woman to live off. He was accompanied by a young boy he claimed was his son (the story was that his wife died in Cambodia), but he sent the boy to a relative when he moved in with Chhonn. Other relatives felt he probably adopted the boy while in a Thai refugee camp in order to increase his chances for admission to the United States, since single men have a lower immigration priority than do families. Chhonn's relatives also are suspicious of Dara's fluency in English, although he claims to have just arrived to the United States (some suspect he left a wife in California). As if to symbolically offer greater support as Chhonn entered what her relatives believed was a doomed relationship, Bopha left Yay's home and with her family moved into the apartment above Chhonn.

A final addition to Yay's network is a female boarder who moved into Yay's apartment with her eight-year old granddaughter following a tragic series of events. This woman's daughter learned that her husband was having an affair and unsuccessfully attempted to kill herself with an overdose of pills. She was pregnant at the time. Eventually she gave birth to a daughter who was disabled. Problems in the family continued, and the Massachusetts Child Welfare Department considered placing the child in a foster home. Before they could make a decision, the grandmother took the disabled child to live in Yay's apartment.

Yay's acceptance of the two might seem charitable, but the border is a fortune-teller and thus adds greatly to the prestige of Yay's network. Cambodians come to consult her about the fate of relatives missing since the Pol Pot years, money problems, prospective spouses, or simply when they are bored and want to hear a good story. According to Cambodians, many of her predictions come true, and Yay consulted her when selecting a wife for her son.

Yay calls the boarder her "cousin," using fictive kinship to incorporate an iso-lated individual into her social network. For Cambodians "individual" connotes vulnerability, not independence, as it does for Americans. This value extends into naming practices. Rather than using personal names, which are highly individualistic, Cambodians tend to use kin and age names that have meaning only in relation to someone else. Thus Cambodians use fictive kinship less for sentimental reasons than to expand their social network (the kin-name giver) and to gain an identity and access to other people through the host family (the kin-name receiver).

A man who drove from an adjacent city to play cards at Yay's apartment illustrates how Yay's family is an entry point into the Cambodian community for those with weak kin ties. His response to a question concerning his relationship to Yay's family at first seems to indicate an inability to express himself in English. In fact, he is trying to describe fictive kinship to an American he pre-sumes is ignorant of this type of relationship: "They are my grandparents. . . . I'm their nephew. . . . My wife is their niece. . . . I don't have any family here and they are very nice to me." Communality rather than privacy, extended rather than nuclear residence, and the conversion of friendship into kinship enables refugee families to mitigate the hardships in the United States by adapting as groups rather than as individuals.

Changing Gender Roles for Husbands and Wives

Fictive kinship minimizes the shock of migration and resettlement for Indo-chinese families, but conflicts over the liberalization of gender roles are not so easily resolved. Women in Vietnam, Laos, and Cambodia experience more subor-dination to men than do women in the United States. When Vietnamese refugees in a Malaysian camp were asked to anticipate changes in their lives after their arrival in the United States, the subordinate status of women registered the sec-ond greatest change out of 10 areas of social and cultural life (Henkin and Singleton 1992). More than 97 percent of the refugees agreed that women had a subordinate status in their homeland, but only 58 percent expected it to continue in the United States—a decline of 39 percentage points compared with the aver-age decline of 16 percentage points for all areas. Only the dominance of family interests over individualism registered a greater decline (54 percentage points).

Just how different the role of women in Southeast Asia is compared with that in the United States is illustrated by a single Vietnamese man in his twen-ties. Asked by social workers what things he misses about Vietnam, he begins with food. But his response quickly turns to gender roles, implying that the con-tinuation of Vietnamese traditions in the United States requires Vietnamese women to be submissive: "I miss a variety of salted fish. I miss Saigon with the traditional [women's] robes fluttering in the wind. In this country, the American girls are difficult to deal with. They don't have the shyness of Asian girls. All these differences cause me to feel that I lose and miss a lot of things" (Matsuoka and Ryujin 1989–90, 36).

A more direct statement on the subordinate status of women in Southeast Asia comes from a Laotian man describing life in Laos to an anthropologist. He begins with the community but ends discussing the family and finally the posi-tion of women, as if gender relations were the root of Laotian culture:

Even though we did not have a lot of material things, we were happy and we had good neighbors. People who lived close by always helped each other when they were in need. When the parents were old and incapable of working, they depended on their children for physical and financial support. Usually the oldest in the family became the head of the household to make the decisions for the rest of the family. In my country, divorce was very rare and women did not have the freedom to do anything they chose. In Laos, a woman had to be submissive to her husband. (Rutledge 1990, 365)

Although changing gender roles and marital conflict are important for Indo-chinese refugees, they are only two of many traumas these people face (see Table 7.1). Clearly, Cambodian women in the United States experience a great amount of stress. More than one-third of them have lost a family member or close friend, and others have witnessed atrocities. But trauma continues for many of the refugee women after their arrival (see Table 7.2). Refugees are highly mobile, and setting up a household again in a new city is likely to be especially stressful to women, since they have responsibility for domestic chores. Although domestic violence, divorce, and separation are fairly prevalent, the family is not reported as a major resettlement problem. Cambodian women are probably underreporting domestic violence because they do not yet identify the family as a public problem, as they do with language and feeling homesick.

Table 7.1

Traumatic Experiences among Cambodian Women in the Boston Area (percent agreeing, multiple responses accepted)

Moved to new U.S. city more than twice	35
Death of family member or close friend	34
Widowed	25
Major illness	24
Hospitalization	20
Domestic violence by spouse	13
Domestic violence by other	13
Divorce or separation	13
Assault, robbery, car accident in United States	12
Witnessed torture or killing in homeland	11
Rape or torture of self or family member	9

N = 92
Source: Waldron 1987

Table 7.2

Resettlement Problems among Cambodian Women in the Boston Area
(percent agreeing, multiple responses accepted)

Language	85
Homesickness	48
Housing	43
Health	25
Money and jobs	24
Child care	16
Transportation	13
Loneliness	12
Violence	10
Family	7

N = 92
Source: Waldron 1987

Marital conflict is a resettlement problem that is frequently obscured by the well-known difficulties of jobs, housing, and language (Lovell et al. 1987; Luu 1989; Walter 1981). Some conflicts develop over ideal family size, with refugee women wanting fewer children than expected in their homeland and husbands wanting the same number or only slightly fewer. Another source of tension is the expectation that women will perpetuate cultural traditions in dress, food, and child care, while men have the freedom to Americanize. The sharply higher rate of English-as-a-second-language class attendance among refugee men compared with refugee women may indicate a combination of family obligations and reliance on husbands for linguistic expertise (Tran 1988). Women also find that they cannot call upon mothers, sisters, and sisters-in-law for help, since in many cases their extended family did not migrate with them. Some younger women even become responsible for siblings in the absence of their mother. Refugee women living in extended families work less during their first three years in the United States than those without these kin, perhaps because additional household responsibilities prevent entry into the labor force (Bach and Carroll-Seguin 1986).

Through work or eligibility for public aid, refugee women gain a degree of economic freedom in the United States that was often denied them in Southeast Asia. One Cambodian woman describes how poverty necessitated her economic independence but also caused marital problems: "We needed two incomes and I went to work. I know my husband did not like it, but it could not be helped. The journey here created problems for us and this work situation was one of them. I could work easier than he could and I began to do well and I supported the family. I became the breadwinner. He had bad feelings about this, I understood this, but the feelings got worse. . . . I understood his pain but there was nothing I could do about it to help him. Eventually, we were divorced" (Tenhula 1991, 180).

Many marital conflicts lead to domestic violence rather than divorce. Some husbands abuse their wives because they cannot accept new roles for women and feel threatened by the woman's power to get a divorce, which rarely occurred in their homeland. One Cambodian woman, a caseworker for refugee families, reports, "Traditionally, Cambodian women stay at home with the children. In the United States, we go to work and everything changes. We become independent, self-sufficient, and equal to men. This is the source of a lot of fights in our households" (Dunwoody 1982, 1). Other men are abusive because they are frustrated with their failure to achieve resettlement goals, such as entering a former occupation and learning English. Another Cambodian woman who directs a women's self-help project describes how uprooting leads to family conflict:

> The most obvious problem I see is violence—I mean family violence, wife and child abuse. Yes, the woman has not been liberated and she is a second-class person, but the physical harm done to her here in the United States is unlike that in Cambodia. I have seen women with terrible wounds on their faces and arms, teeth missing, and much more. For me, it's even harder to understand when the children, I mean small children, are harmed. All of this is a combination of grief and guilt and somehow there is depression that makes these people violent. (Tenhula 1991, 156)

Although Cambodian women help each other resolve problems in the settlement process, the development of informal self-help groups is best documented for Vietnamese (Kibria 1990, 1993) and Laotian (Muir 1988) women in the United States. Many Vietnamese women belong to social groups of six to ten members, and overlapping group membership links women throughout the Vietnamese community. Groups meet in apartments but also in restaurants, ethnic stores, and hair salons. Through these groups Vietnamese women exchange food, material goods, and information on jobs, public assistance, and schools. They also support women who want to work over the objections of a husband, and they share advice on how to cope with domestic violence. Occasionally, these social groups will even confront men. Friends or kin of a woman with a family problem may speak directly to her husband or use gossip to hurt his status in the community.

Laotian women have developed a similar network of support. At mixed-gender gatherings the women tend to segregate from men and behave aloofly and with great deference. But when in all-female company their interaction turns more boisterous, and heated conversations develop about men and family life. Physical interaction is minimal in the presence of men, but amongst themselves the women will greet each other with a hug and style each other's hair. Such personal interaction among Laotian women takes on a communal significance because their bonds are among the most stable in a community where men divide into factions in pursuit of personal gain. Relationships among Laotian men tend be competitive. But Laotian women use their networks to facilitate child care, mate selection, shopping, and other communal activities. Unlike those of the Vietnamese, the social groups among Laotian women are more defined by kin, proximity, and age.

Interviews I conducted with twelve male and six female Indochinese case-workers on husband and wife conflict among refugees reveals much about the causes of the problem but also some differences between male and female per-ceptions of the problem. The caseworkers were employed among seven resettle-ment agencies in San Francisco to help other refugees with problems ranging from sponsoring relatives to the United States to finding jobs and resolving family conflicts. During interviews I described a hypothetical case involving moderate domestic violence and gender-role change that I had constructed after reading hundreds of case files at one resettlement agency. I asked the case-workers: "How would you handle a case where a wife comes to you saying she wants a divorce from her husband because he sometimes hits her? He's jealous because she sometimes goes out without him, and has a man as a friend at school. She says that in the United States she can do what she wants. The fami-ly is on welfare and the husband doesn't always give the wife enough of the money to feed the children." Many of the caseworkers immediately responded that they had cases like this one. Their proposed solutions raised three issues regarding marital conflict: whether the cause was economic or cultural, the legitimacy of changing gender roles for women, and the viability of divorce.

About one-half of the male caseworkers attributed the conflict to the fami-ly's being on welfare and the husband not working. One Chinese-Vietnamese man felt economic and intergenerational problems caused husbands to become abusive: "The man is the king in our country. He supports the wife. Here the wife has to work and loses respect for him. If the family is not working children feel ashamed of their parents. Parents even have to ask children to help trans-late when they go shopping. Children are now first to give their opinion." Conversely, the female caseworkers overwhelmingly pointed out that this was a case of cultural change in gender roles. A Laotian woman stated, "I would help them get back together, but they are in a new culture now. The husband will have to accept that, the new and old culture are 50-50. It's nothing for his wife to sit next to a man in an English class."

With a few exceptions, both male and female caseworkers supported the lib-eralization of women's roles for Indochinese in the United States. But many of the men were quick to point out that the woman in my case was becoming too Americanized. A male Vietnamese caseworker gave this analysis: "I would explain the laws and roles in America to the husband. If he beats his wife it's a crime. But the wife has to moderate her freedom. She is not an American right away, she has to maintain cultural traditions, she has to adjust gradually." Another man responded, "It's a cultural crisis. I would tell the husband to change his attitude. He cannot maintain the old ways. But I would also tell the wife to be careful. She can go too far with freedom. Freedom has limits."

While male caseworkers were more likely than female caseworkers to feel Indochinese women were gaining too much equality in the United States, there was no pattern in the caseworkers' views of divorce: equal proportions of men and women supported and disapproved of it. A Chinese-Vietnamese man simply stated, "My principle is to keep the family together. The second generation can live like Americans. We have our own traditions and customs for the first gener-ation so the American ones don't apply." A Chinese-Laotian man who thought gender roles should change for refugee women nonetheless felt divorce was wrong. He explained, "I had a case like that. In Laos, the husband gets the money and spends it for the family. Here it's the wife who gets money from welfare for the children. In my case, the wife said the husband spent all the welfare money, only gave her $20 for a month's food. I told them they have to try and respect each other, to stay together, and remember that Lao culture doesn't want families to break up."

A Chinese-Cambodian woman was also against divorce for the hypothetical couple, but for a different reason: "Their life is hard now, but they should take care of the children, they should teach them. The children are growing up in a new country and there will be no future for them if the parents divorce." Even the female caseworkers who approved of divorce felt both husband and wife should agree to it. A Laotian woman who supported divorce gave this insightful explanation of how marital conflicts were handled in Laos, suggesting that divorce was only appropriate when the decision was made collectively, rather than by an individual: "In Laos, the couple would come from the same village, and going to court for a divorce would give them a bad reputation. If she wants a divorce she will have to talk with her relatives first, she cannot just divorce right away. If it's more serious her parents and his parents will talk. The parents have to talk since it was an arranged marriage. If the parents don't like the son or daughter-in-law they may support the divorce. Finally, they can go to the village chief. If they both want a divorce they can get one."

The views of these caseworkers indicate that changing gender roles causes marital conflict among Indochinese refugees. The male caseworkers tend to stress the greater economic power of women, whether as workers or welfare recipients, as the source of this change. Female caseworkers emphasize the egalitarian gender roles in American culture, at least by Southeast Asian standards. But both male and female caseworkers are reticent to resolve family conflicts through divorce. They view divorce as an American practice empowering individuals and thus ill-suited for Asian families, which prioritize the group. Like relations between husbands and wives, relations between generations are also changing and often become a source of conflict.

Changing Relationships between Parents and Children

During an interview a historian asked a Vietnamese woman, "What was your first great cultural shock [in the United States]?" Her response did not cite political freedom, racism, or even gender roles, but relations between generations: "It was with my sponsor, with whom I stayed for six months when I first arrived. It was the first time when I heard the young daughter of the sponsor shout back at her. When I heard this, I was in total disbelief. You see, obedience is taught to be a virtue in our culture. Well I thought this was a terrible, horrible thing. But believe it or not, a few years later my oldest daughter shouted at me in the same way" (Tenhula 1991, 26).

Most of what is known about the adjustment of Indochinese refugee youths comes from three studies commissioned by the U.S. Office of Refugee Resettlement. Although conducted in Philadelphia (Peters 1988), San Diego (Rumbaut and Ima 1988), and Minneapolis–St. Paul (Baizerman and Hendricks 1988), the studies reached many similar findings concerning the family life, educational

Table 7.3

Family, School, and Career among Indochinese Refugee Youths

	Laotian	Cambodian	Hmong	Vietnamese	Chinese
Parental authority	Weak	Weak	Moderate	Strong	Strong
Family form	Nuclear	Nuclear	Clan	Extended	Extended
Peer group	Strong	Strong	Weak	Weak	Weak
Interest in homeland	Strong	Strong	Strong	Weak	Weak
Career goal	Clerical, health	Clerical, teaching	Science, police	Science	Science
Major problem	Counter-culture	Single parents	Early marriage	Parental hopes	Parental hopes

Sources: Baizerman and Hendricks 1988; Peters 1988; Rumbaut and Ima 1988

progress, and career aspirations of teenagers from Vietnam, Laos, and Cambodia (see Table 7.3).

Vietnamese parents place an especially high importance on the educational attainment of their children. They realize that allowing them to study now and work later will pay off in the long run. Vietnamese youths generally expect to attain levels of education and jobs above those of their parents. Many parents have been unable to reenter prestigious occupations held in their homeland, and their children feel a special obligation to succeed. Although parents also have high hopes for their children, many are unable to help them negotiate the American educational system and job market. Instead, older siblings, peer groups, and native school advisers replace parents as guides. Indeed, the San Diego study found that Vietnamese youths often reported that their best friends and role models were siblings. Nonetheless, Vietnamese youths still maintain strong bonds with their parents and feel little pressure to leave home. One study found that 70 percent of Vietnamese parents believed that their children would live with them until they got married, as opposed to the American ideal of children forming their own households soon after becoming adults (Simon 1983).

The tenacity of the Vietnamese family does have drawbacks. The Philadelphia study found that parents expect children to support them even after establishing their own households, which may not be consistent with the expectations of Americanized youths. The Twin Cities study discovered that the strong entrepreneurial pursuits among Vietnamese and Chinese Vietnamese could restrict the occupational and educational choice of youths. Parents who own a small business may expect children to study business, accounting, and other skills likely to help the family enterprise. Parental authority can be both supportive and confining for Vietnamese youths.

A comparative study of mother-daughter relations among Americans and Vietnamese refugees provides greater insight into the question of parental control and expectations (Simon 1986). In contrast to Americans, Vietnamese mothers and daughters have very different expectations about future jobs, education, spouses, and ideal number of children. The daughters tend to be more optimistic than their mothers about completing college and attaining professional employment. Nearly 60 percent of Vietnamese mothers want a Vietnamese son-in-law. Only 40 percent of daughters prefer a husband of the same ethnicity, and 30 percent feel ethnicity and religion are unimportant (none of the mothers agreed). Where American mothers and daughters were in almost complete agreement about the number of children, 45 percent of Vietnamese daughters wanted no more than two children, while 50 percent of their mothers wanted four or more grandchildren. Although Vietnamese children may remain with their parents until married, this living arrangement can cause conflict as youths Americanize more rapidly than their mothers and fathers.

The age at which refugee youths arrive in the United States greatly affects their relationship with parents. Those who arrived as teenagers tend to have lower career expectations and show greater independence from parents. Vietnamese youths in this age group often seem trapped between two cultures, unable to fit into either. They observe, "It's better to be younger when you come here" and "The older you are, the harder it is to change" (Baizerman and Hendricks 1988, 27). This feeling of being caught between two cultures, rather than blending elements of both, led the San Diego study to call this age group the "1.5 generation." Like the first generation born in Southeast Asia, refugee teenagers experienced adolescent socialization prior to migration. Yet like the second generation born in the United States, these teenagers must cope with major life-course changes in American society, like working for the first time and starting a family.

The refugee youths who arrive in the United States with few or no relatives find this break in the life course the most difficult. This population, which is primarily Vietnamese, includes orphans but also youths sent by parents as "anchor children" in the hopes that American immigration officials will eventually allow relatives to join them in the United States. Many of these children did not know of their departure until it was happening and consequently resent their parents in Vietnam. Others feel an intense responsibility to do well in the United States so they can send money to their family and eventually sponsor them. Even when accompanied by their families, youths can lose respect for fathers who must take jobs much beneath their skill level and mothers who depend on their children for English translation. Both the Philadelphia and San Diego studies reported that gang and crime problems were most serious among the Vietnamese (and to some degree the Lao), but it was youths from broken families who tended to have the greatest problems with the educational and criminal justice system, regardless of ethnicity.

Amerasian youths (the offspring of Vietnamese women and American soldiers) experience particular adaptation difficulties. These youths, who usually range in age from 15 to 25, experienced much discrimination in Vietnam due to their mixed racial background and because they symbolized the American presence in the country. Living without a father is particularly difficult in Vietnam because Vietnamese culture determines descent through males. Although many arrive in the United States with brothers or sisters, most have only a mother. Few are reunited with their American father, although the mother usually knows his name. Amerasian youths often report that their primary reason for migrating to the United States was the hope of finding their fathers. A survey of Amerasians prior to arrival in the United States found that 63 percent had positive feelings toward their fathers and 54 percent wanted to be reunited with them (Felsman et al. 1989). Yet when asked what they knew about them, 56 percent responded "nothing." A survey of Amerasians in the United States found that 15 percent thought of themselves as Americans, 25 percent as Vietnamese, 40 percent considered themselves to have a mixed identity, and 20 percent were unsure (U.S. Catholic Conference 1985). Amerasians whose fathers are black are much more likely to identify themselves as "American" than are those with white fathers. Amerasians in general, however, tend to adopt American culture more readily than do Vietnamese youths (Tien and Hunthausen 1990).

Many Cambodian youths share one characteristic with Amerasians: an absent father as a result of killings during the Khmer Rouge regime. So many live with widowed mothers that the Twin Cities study termed these youth a "transitional generation," since only with their children will Cambodians fully reform the two-parent family. The San Diego study found that only 49 percent of Cambodian youths lived in families where both father and mother were present; 40 percent lived with widowed mothers.

Unlike the Vietnamese, many Cambodian youths have low career expectations and cannot draw upon family members for support. Girls are especially likely to have diminished confidence levels. Many Cambodian parents had little or no education in their homeland and consequently have low expectations for their children in the United States. For example, parents' only experience with American schools may be English-as-a-second-language classes, and they often do not understand the importance of college. Instead, they prefer youths to contribute to the family income as soon as possible. Many Cambodian parents still arrange marriages, especially for daughters, and this practice further disrupts the transition from high school to college or full-time work.

Both Cambodian boys and girls, however, show a stronger attachment than do Hmong, Laotian, or Vietnamese youths to their culture. They also exhibit a greater interest in their country's recent political history. In 1993 more than 150 Cambodian youths responded when the Cambodian-American National Development Organization called for 25 volunteers to work with social-service and human-rights groups in Cambodia (*Refugee Reports* 1994). Many of these youths had completed college in the United States and thus were willing to forgo employment in order to assist with the rebuilding of their homeland. As a result of these interests, many Cambodian youths seek human-services jobs. The San Diego study found that Cambodians often described the value of jobs with reference to social interaction—an indication of how their refugee experience shapes choice of occupation in the United States.

The aspirations and achievement of Hmong youths was the one area of disagreement among the studies. The San Diego and Philadelphia studies found much evidence of success, although significant out-migration of Hmong from these cities may have biased the sample in favor of the well adapted (who would be less likely to move). Both noted that a strong clan organization helps parents deal with problem children. As a result, Hmong students have few academic or disciplinary problems in schools, and even less trouble with the police.

The Twin Cities study reached much more pessimistic conclusions, perhaps because many Hmong have migrated there after being resettled in other regions. In Minneapolis and St. Paul, Hmong youths experience the most difficult transition to adulthood, and high school dropout rates are quite high. Some males even dress as "punks." Hmong welfare rates are nearly 80 percent. Although many parents and community leaders emphasize that youths should complete high school and aspire to stable employment, there are few role models for youths. In fact, many do not feel stigmatized by public assistance, believing that it is a type of compensation from the American government for the loss of their homeland. Many Hmong parents have unrealistically high expectations of their children's careers, putting pressure on the youths to attain something beyond their means. Like the Cambodians, many of the Hmong boys felt a strong attachment to their homeland and respected the military achievements of their male elders. Indeed, the San Diego study found that 22 percent of Hmong youths aspired to jobs in law enforcement or the military, compared to 11 percent of the Lao, 6 percent of the Vietnamese, and 0 percent of the Cambodians.

All three studies agreed that early marriage and childbearing is detrimental to Hmong women, an example of cultural values and norms from Southeast Asia hampering the adaptation process. In California, where 52 percent of the Hmong population in the United States lives, clan leaders estimate that between 30 and 50 percent of Hmong girls marry before the age of 17, although other estimates are higher (Arax 1993). While not common, some Hmong men marry girls as young as 12 or 13. One indicator of the frequency of teenage marriage is the high proportion of births to Hmong mothers 18 years old and under. In California the rate is 15 percent for the Hmong, compared with 12 percent for blacks, 11 percent for Latinos, 5 percent for Anglos, and 3 percent for all other Asians.

Culture is the primary reason that Hmong girls tend to marry by age 16 and boys several years later (about eight years earlier than the U.S. average). The Hmong culture has little or no period between adolescence and adulthood. Single Vietnamese children over the age of 18 can live at home while attending college or working, but Hmong children, especially daughters, are rushed into marriage. Reflecting on the pressure to marry young, a 21-year-old mother of two says, "Hmong females have no rights. We're just supposed to have babies, be housewives, do what the husband says to do. It's a very sad life" (Arax 1993, B2). Another woman, a 17-year-old high school student with plans to attend college, puts the problem in a cultural context but reaches a similar conclusion: "There is a lot of good in our culture. You know there's no such thing as a Hmong convalescent home. Or a Hmong homeless person. So I want to keep my language. I want to keep my customs and music. But this early marriage stuff has got to change" (Arax 1993, B3).

Just how difficult it is to change these cultural norms is made evident by the results of counseling sessions to encourage delayed marriage in St. Paul, Minnesota (Rolnick 1990). After completing the counseling, 60 percent of parents, 39 percent of junior high school students, and 27 percent of high school students still reported that marriage should take place before the age of 21. Significantly, the study also found that 70 percent of parents felt they could communicate well with children about dating. Only 25 percent of their children agreed. A study in which Hmong high school students in Boulder, Colorado, rated their own and their parents' views of 18 forms of acculturation found that decisions about the timing of marriage was the area of greatest disagreement (Rick and Forward 1992).

Tradition, however, is not the only reason for the early marriage of Hmong girls and women. In some cases early marriage results when parents push sons and daughters into matrimony at the slightest hint of "unconsulted dating." Some girls feel that parents pressure them to marry to gain the $3,000 to $4,000 bride price given by the groom to the bride's parents. But marriage also allows girls to escape parental authority and live more independent lives, which they observe among American women. Combined, these factors make high school a very stressful period for Hmong girls (Goldstein 1989).

A study of educational aspirations among Hmong girls in Wisconsin directly addressed the consequences of early marriage for educational achievement (Yang 1990). When asked what prevented Hmong women from obtaining education beyond high school, about one-half agreed that they were afraid of being considered "old maids" if they were not married by the age of 18. One-half, however, agreed that many girls did not know about opportunities for work and education (multiple responses were accepted). About one-third also indicated two other barriers to attending college or vocational school: financial problems and traditional gender roles.

Early marriage is clearly a leading cause of preempted educational attainment among Hmong women, and the study sought the girls' explanations for why so many married by age 18. The leading cause was pregnancy before marriage (46 percent), followed by peer pressure (38 percent), and parentally arranged or forced marriage (37 percent). Many also made remarks that support the studies in Philadelphia, San Diego, and the Twin Cities, which found that family problems led to early marriage. Some of the girls explained, "They get married to escape problems at home," "When things are rough they need someone there," and "Their parents get divorced, and they don't have places to go." Nonetheless, 60 percent of the girls reported that parents encouraged them to continue their education, while 36 percent reported support from teachers, and 22 percent from peers (multiple answers were accepted).

Laotian youths are the least studied population, with only the Twin Cities study giving them full attention. They generally expected to get relatively unskilled jobs that did not require education beyond high school. Some even seemed to resist the higher expectations of their parents, who hoped their children would get professional jobs. All three studies noted that some Laotian boys adopted counterculture dress and demeanor, such as ripped clothes and spiked or dyed hair, which alienated their parents and others in the Laotian community. In fact, conflict between Laotian parents and their children was more pronounced than among any other ethnic group.

The San Diego study went the furthest in suggesting how similarities and differences among these Indochinese populations affect parent-child relationships. The Hmong, Vietnamese, and Chinese Vietnamese have extended families that place great emphasis on filial piety and ancestor worship. Youths from these ethnic groups are subject to much greater group conformity, and thus children experience greater discipline and parental expectations. Conversely, Cambodians and Laotians have nuclear families that are more female centered and place little emphasis on common ancestry. Laotian and Cambodian youths are allowed more individuality and are given greater freedom from parental authority. For example, the use of fictive kinship is more common among Cambodians than Vietnamese. While it gives Cambodians a greater sense of community, it also limits the authority of kin, since individuals can re-create kinlike relationships with others.

The consequences of these family forms for scholastic achievement is that peer groups compete with parents for the allegiance of Laotian and Cambodian youths, while Chinese, Vietnamese, and especially Hmong parents face little challenge. Homeland experiences also shape parent-child interactions in the United States, such as the added stresses in the case of Cambodians who survived genocide under Pol Pot. Class factors are important as well, and the Westernized elites of all ethnic groups exhibit many similarities. Yet the San Diego study found that among all Indochinese ethnic groups, mothers had a greater impact than fathers on children's achievement in schools. Mothers' level of education, work experience, and English proficiency heavily determined the performance of their children.

Despite the comparatively greater family organization among the Vietnamese, intergenerational conflict is still a problem. Traditional family values are a particular source of conflict (Nguyen and Williams 1989). For example, Vietnamese parents are much more likely than their children to agree with statements like, "Family members should prefer to be with each other rather than with outsiders" and "Grandparents should have more influence than parents in family matters." Over time, Vietnamese girls' belief in such values declines much more rapidly than that of Vietnamese boys. Vietnamese fathers and sons, however, are two to three times more likely to report disagreements than are Vietnamese mothers and daughters (Simon 1983). But the leading cause of intergenerational conflict for both sexes is parents' complaint that children did not listen to their advice.

One Vietnamese man in his seventies explained that Vietnamese parents are always praising their children in public. He felt that only his children had changed until he talked more informally with other elders:

> When they discussed their sons, daughters, and daughters-in-law, it was very different: bad behavior, how wives cheated on their husbands, how children disobeyed and showed no respect, how they told their parents not to interfere in their lives because it's none of their business, how they said that they had a higher regard for their spouse than their parents. When I heard all that, I did not feel so bad. In America there is nothing to hold our family together. In this city alone, my family numbers some sixteen people spanning three generations: we live in different locations in the city. We also have others of our family living elsewhere in America. Even so, we have nothing to look forward to. If I returned to Vietnam, the Communists would put me in a reeducation camp, which would kill me. But here in America, my wife and I will die a lonely death, abandoned by our children. (Freeman 1989, 367–68)

This passage indicates how the liberalization of age roles for youths and children has negative consequences for senior citizens and parents. Indochinese refugees are a young population. Surveys indicate that their median age is about 20, and only approximately 3 percent are over 60 years old (Gozdziak 1988; *Refugee Reports* 1987). But homesickness, isolation, and acculturation problems are quite common among the elderly, compounding physical health problems they are likely to experience. A common fear is dying in a hospital rather than at home with relatives present. Vietnamese highly value burial next to ancestors, while Cambodians prefer specialized cremation rituals that are not part of American funeral home practices. In comparison to black, white, Hispanic, and Native American seniors, Indochinese seniors report more health problems, greater isolation from friends, lower incomes, and the most difficulty with daily activities like shopping (Chase 1990). They are the least likely of all groups, however, to live alone and the most likely to live with their adult children, once again indicating the strength of family and kin ties among Indochinese refugees.

Food is a common problem for Indochinese seniors. One study of food habits among Cambodian and Hmong refugees found that 32 percent of parents felt it was very important for their children to continue eating native food, and another 42 percent felt it was somewhat important (Story and Harris 1989). Yet three-quarters of Cambodian and Hmong teenagers prefer to eat both native and American food, although only 9 percent exclusively prefer American food (Story and Harris 1988). This dietary conflict is exacerbated among the elderly, who have the most traditional food preferences. A Vietnamese social worker reported that one elderly Laotian man developed psychological problems in part because he wanted "his food cooked as it was in Laos—outside, over an open wood fire—but laws prohibit the practice. Consequently, he eats very little" (Kane 1987, D7). A Vietnamese woman, who lives in a rural area, reports that her mother also complains about the poor quality of food in American supermarkets: "She wanted to buy live chickens. Would you believe we now have twenty-one . . . in our back yard? She wanted to raise a pig, but I just couldn't have that" (Wilstach 1976, E11).

A more serious problem for refugee seniors is a much more limited ability to speak English than other age groups (Tran 1992). Language barriers mean greater dependence on other family members for even simple activities like shopping, as well as more complicated activities like interactions with the health and social-welfare system (Tran 1990). Unlike other refugees, whose lives generally improve the longer they reside in the United States, for the elderly time only exacerbates their difficulties. One Chinese-American consultant for the National Institutes of Health succinctly summarized this dilemma: "In the old country, it is to your advantage to be old. Here, it is to your advantage to be young" (*Refugee Reports* 1987, 2). One of the greatest conflicts between young and old is the Americanization of courtship and marriage practices.

Generational Conflict over Courtship and Marriage

The funeral for Um was marred by a serious family squabble (Um means aunt in Khmer, and is used for middle-aged women instead of their personal name). Um was one of the most active women in the Cambodian community in Chicago's Uptown. She sent her children to learn the Khmer language on Saturday mornings and attended meetings of the Cambodian MAA to raise money for refugees and prevent gang activities. She also was very religious, regularly attending services at the Buddhist temple. Um had a unique reaction to a schism that occurred at the temple in the early 1980s. Unlike most Cambodians, Um took neither side in the dispute and participated in services at both the old and new temples. When she died of a stroke in 1989, both temples held funeral ceremonies, a rare honor. Older women remarked that Um's death had been swift and painless because she had so little sin to account for.

Unfortunately, the service was disturbed by a quarrel between Um's oldest son and her son-in-law. It revealed the conflicts that had troubled Um's family ever since her oldest daughter had married several years after they arrived in the United States. Um's husband died suddenly in a Thai refugee camp, leaving her with six children, two of whom had been born during the Khmer Rouge period. Just after the father died, however, the family "got their name to come to America," refugees' expression for finding their name on a list of families accepted by American officials for resettlement in the United States. Um's husband had always wanted to resettle in the United States, while Um argued that the family should return to Cambodia. The family initially migrated to Thailand to find food when Cambodia was experiencing famine in 1979. To fulfill her husband's wish Um decided to leave. Without a husband it had been difficult for Um to negotiate a marriage for her oldest daughter. In fact, she always felt that she had been tricked by her son-in-law, Sok, into accepting the marriage. This conflict over the marriage explains the scene at the funeral and illustrates how the liberalization of age and parental roles is accompanied by much tension between Indochinese youths and seniors.

After the traditional money donations for the family were accepted (several of the poorer Cambodians gave their food stamps) Sok stood up and stated that the funds should be kept by the Cambodian Buddhist Association. But Um's oldest son immediately exclaimed that he and the remaining four children desperately needed the money as they were penniless. Um had been hard pressed economically ever since she arrived in the United States. She found an apartment for herself and the six children, and the oldest daughter began working at the minimum wage in a jewelry warehouse sorting earrings. Um also received $290 a month in food stamps and $380 a month from public assistance. But she paid $320 a month in rent, leaving her only $60 to cover other expenses. When she died, her remaining children were left with nothing more than a few pieces of gold jewelry. What little savings she had were loaned to Sok to pay for a wedding, which should have been his responsibility. Sok never repaid the money.

As the son and son-in-law argued, people at the service whispered, "Sok just wants the association to have the money so he can try to get it later." Other people yelled, "Let the children keep the money," although a few felt the teenage son was too young to be given several hundred dollars in cash. In the end, some of the money was given to the children and the rest deposited with the association for future use. To the Cambodians present, the conflict at the funeral exemplified one of the worst things than can happen to Cambodian families in the United States: a widow cannot control the marriage process and her daughter marries a bad man.

Um had been tricked by Sok into accepting the marriage. Worse, she learned after the marriage that he already had a wife and children in Cambodia. It is not uncommon for married Cambodian men to remarry in the United States. Some find new wives because they were separated from their first wives during the

Khmer Rouge period and, having had no contact with them for years, believe they are dead, missing, or remarried. Then one day a letter arrives from Cambodia from the old wife, or a newly arrived refugee knows of her whereabouts. Others, like Sok, left their wives in Cambodia to find food in Thailand during the famine and never went back. Instead, they became caught up in the migration process and the dream of coming to the United States.

It was not polygamy that bothered Um, since many Cambodian men in this situation still become good fathers and sons-in-law. It was the fact that Sok had outwitted her during the courtship and marriage process. For Cambodians, marriage is not only an important ritual event but also the end of a negotiation between two kin groups that will now have a common bond. In addition to kin ties, marriage also is a financial deal to be struck. Even in the United States, the groom will usually pay a bride price of several thousand dollars to the bride's parents, in addition to jewelry and fine clothes for the bride. Not only must all parties involved feel that the price and kin bonds are to their liking, but an intricate body of lore prescribes how prospective brides, grooms, and parents-in-law should arrange a marriage. Those who enact this drama well are praised in the community for their skill. Those who fail will be long remembered and used as an example of all that can go wrong.

Um began the marriage process at a disadvantage because she had no husband, the principal negotiator on the bride's side. Nor did she have any relatives in Chicago, such as a brother or uncle, who could use their network of friends and relatives to learn the moral quality of the prospective groom and his family. Finally, as a pious widow, Um had very high standards to live up to as far as the Cambodian community was concerned. Sok managed to marry Um's oldest daughter, Maly, without any bride price. Moreover, he tricked Um into paying for a traditional Cambodian wedding when this is the groom's responsibility, and he soon left the city with his wife, thus depriving Um of a much needed source of income. Only an outright elopement could have been worse from the standpoint of Cambodian marriage etiquette.

This tragedy began with a rumor in the Cambodian community that Maly had slept with Sok when they first met. Although unfounded, it was especially hurtful to Um, who was a regular at the temple, the moral center of the Cambodian community. Maly had been taking driving lessons from Sok. For Sok, like many Cambodian males, teaching women to drive is an ingenious strategy to have an unchaperoned "date," when traditionally courtship is closely regulated. In fact, it was Um who suggested that Maly learn to drive so that the large family could avoid public transportation expenses. Although it is changing in the United States, Cambodian custom dictates that unmarried men and women should not fraternize unattended. Even in the United States it is not uncommon for a bride and groom to meet for the first time at the ritual where the groom's parents bring gifts asking permission for marriage. Unfortunately, Sok later boasted of his fictitious sexual conquest to friends, thus starting the rumor. Um was beside herself. Believing that Maly was no longer a virgin, and thus an unlikely marriage partner already at the "advanced" age of 20, she put pressure on Maly to marry Sok, explaining that she had forfeited her chance for a respectable marriage. Sok, promising a formal marriage ceremony when he saved up enough money, moved into Um's already overcrowded apartment. Um resigned herself to Sok as a son-in-law but hoped that a splendid Cambodian wedding would salvage her status in the community.

But after several months Sok showed no signs of planning the ceremony. Worse, he started talking about taking Maly to an adjacent state with better job opportunities. This move would have constituted elopement, the greatest fear of Cambodian parents. It would not only reflect badly on them but also end contact with grandchildren and destroy the family lineage. Worse still, the daughter might return home alone and pregnant, forever dependent on the parents. Um begged Sok to hold the wedding as he had promised, insisting that Maly could not go with him unless they were married.

To keep Maly with him and comply with Um's demand, Sok resorted to a deviously clever trick that took advantage of Cambodians' bicultural position in American society. Cambodians in the United States often get married in two stages. The first is the traditional marriage ceremony officiated by monks from the temple, and the second is a marriage at city hall to obtain a certificate. Many Cambodians never proceed to the second stage since within the Cambodian community the religious ceremony is considered more significant. Sok learned from a friend that a church group in an adjacent state was helping refugees get factory jobs with starting pay at $6 an hour and good benefits. But according to this friend, the church group would only help married couples, not men and women living together (as he was with Maly). The friend gave the church group Sok's phone number, but when a pastor called and learned that Sok was living with Maly he told Sok that the church would not help. Sok solved this dilemma by getting married at city hall and then presenting the marriage license to Um. She protested that it was not a Cambodian wedding, but Sok replied that this was not Cambodia and the license proved he was the husband. He had obtained a wife for about $35, instead of several thousand, with the added benefit of now being eligible for a much higher-paying job through the aid of the church group.

Before Sok and Maly left, Um extracted a promise that once he saved up some money the couple would return for a traditional ceremony. Um still desperately wanted Sok and Maly to have the formal wedding that would legitimize their "American" marriage. For older-generation Cambodians, a marriage license from city hall is no substitute for the four- or five-hour ritual supervised by monks, followed by a lavish party at a Cambodian restaurant. Again several months passed with no progress toward the wedding. Only when Um agreed to loan Sok half the cost did he allow her to begin preparations. At the last minute, however—literally as the guests and monks were arriving—Sok said he would not go through with the wedding unless Um paid for it all. The only way to avoid an even greater scandal was to agree. Um did not even have enough money to pay the restaurant and Cambodian band in advance, and was humiliated when Sok opened the envelopes containing gift money at a table in the corner before the guests had even left.

The conflict between Um and Sok illustrates the problems facing Cambodians who expect marriages in the United States to proceed as they did in Cambodia. Young men and women can defy the older generation because of the decline in seniority by age. Where the local temple was once the only institution that could confer marriage there is now an alternative: the American justice of the peace. Finally, the custom of a bride price is difficult to transplant to the United States because the Americanization of courtship prioritizes the prospective bride and groom as individuals over their parents and the kin groups they represent.

Conclusion

Like immigrants and other refugees, Indochinese refugees adapt as groups rather than as individuals. Membership in a family and kin group leads the refugees to develop collective approaches to solving problems raised by migration and resettlement. Indeed, one of their primary problems is the family. As illustrated by the extended Cambodian family in Massachusetts, refugees will move across the United States to reconstitute families that have been split by migration or the decisions of American immigration officials. The resulting households may contain three generations, married siblings, and even friends who are unrelated by marriage or kinship but are nonetheless treated as part of the family. This practice of fictive kinship is more common among Cambodians and Laotians than among the Vietnamese, ethnic Chinese from Vietnam, and the Hmong. Nonetheless, using kin terms to designate the closeness of unrelated individuals is widespread among Indochinese refugees. Among Cambodians, it enables isolated individuals or members of fragmented families to gain protection and social prestige by association with a strong family. In turn, these networks of real and fictive kin become the basis of the ethnic community. One of the primary failures of the assimilation model is its focus on the individual characteristics of migrants when in fact migrants are enmeshed in social networks.

The insight that migrants adapt as members of groups may be the greatest contribution of the ethnic-resilience model. While research using this model has given considerable attention to ethnic communities and businesses, it has largely neglected the family and kin relations. This omission is due to the absence of culture from the model's conception of ethnicity, which deprives it of such crucial concepts as values and norms. Cultural ideals and conceptions of appropriate behavior are essential for understanding the collective adaptation of immigrants and refugees precisely because groups like the family are changing. The most pronounced changes concern gender and age roles.

The greater equality of men and women in the United States, in contrast to Southeast Asia, liberalizes gender roles within Indochinese refugee families. Wives assume a greater economic importance when they work or receive public assistance. Husbands no longer have the same degree of decision-making power on family issues, such as the wife's education and number of children. Like women, youths are accorded greater autonomy in the United States, which can lead to conflict with parents. In some cases parents seek to control children as they did in their homeland, such as arranging marriages. In other cases family bonds are disrupted by the inability of parents to advise their more Americanized children about life in the United States. Changing familial roles create the most problems for seniors. Unlike women and youths, older refugees experience a loss of social importance in the United States. Their problems include greater difficulty learning English and stronger attachment to the homeland than among the younger generation, although Indochinese seniors have more familial support than the seniors of other ethnic groups in the United States.

These problems resulting from changing gender and age roles indicate that conflict between newcomers and natives—the focus of the ethnic-resilience model—is not the primary concern of Indochinese refugee families. In fact, the greater freedom of Indochinese women and youths in the United States indicates that the refugees seek to blend elements of American culture with their own, rather than reject assimilation outright.

eight

Work and Social Class

Employment, wages, poverty, and public-assistance use are among the most important areas in which Indochinese refugees differ from other Americans. Some of the refugees, particularly members of the Vietnamese middle and upper class who arrived in 1975, have made substantial economic progress. But most Vietnamese, Laotians, Hmong, and Cambodians work in jobs that earn less than those of whites, and they are more likely than whites to be poor and thus require public assistance. To the extent that pluralism is based on differences in socioeconomic status, the ethnic-resilience model is correct in portraying the immigrant and refugee experience as one of conflict and inequality.

Still, work is more than a means of material survival for refugees and immigrants. Migrants are re-creating their lives in a new country, and employment or public assistance, blue- or white-collar work, determines not just economic achievement but many aspects of cultural integration. Indochinese refugees who farmed or fished in their homelands have difficulty adjusting to the work routines of factories and low-skill service jobs in the United States, as well as the importance of money in American life. Job selection among Vietnamese wives and mothers is based not only on economic considerations but on cultural values governing gender and familial roles. A comparison of two Cambodian women illustrates how refugees can arrive in the United States very much alike, subsequently find blue- and white-collar jobs, and end up with very different ways of understanding their place in American society, such as the meaning of being an ethnic minority. A case study of a Cambodian man who works at a lathe in a factory reveals the workplace to be a site for learning about American culture, such as the value placed on competition, but also a place for blending American with Cambodian culture. Work cannot be separated from culture, as it is in the ethnic-resilience model.

Employment, Poverty, and Public Assistance

Adult Indochinese refugees arrive in the United States with various levels of human capital: skills and knowledge derived from schooling and work experience. The first refugees to arrive in 1975 had a great deal of human capital because they were from their homeland's middle or upper class. Among the 125,000 Vietnamese who arrived after the fall of Saigon, the proportion with professional and managerial skills was about three times greater than among

Americans (Kelly 1977). Many also spoke English, and about 40 percent were Catholic rather than Buddhist—four times the proportion of Catholics in the Vietnamese population as a whole. The higher class status of the first Vietnamese resulted from the evacuation of army officers, government officials, and others with ties to the South Vietnamese and American governments. In contrast to this "first wave," Vietnamese refugees arriving in the late 1970s and early 1980s (the second wave) had fewer years of education, lower occupational skills, and less ability to speak English (Nguyen and Henkin 1982).

Despite the higher class status of the first wave, these refugees had great difficulty finding employment. An American caseworker vividly described this problem one year after the arrival of the first Vietnamese refugees: "I have top people. Top generals, judges, factory owners, bank owners, people trained and employed by the American government, a chief of the taxation service and a man who has translated many of the major American classics into Vietnamese. I have Ph.D.s, professors, and administrators . . . you name it. But they can't get jobs" (Salisbury 1976, D6).

The employment problems of the first-wave refugees were partly the result of the severe recession in the U.S. economy during the mid-1970s. Eventually, most of these refugees did find work, but they rarely entered occupations commensurate with their level of education and prior work experience (Stein 1979). About 30 percent of the first wave were professionals in Vietnam; only about 14 percent were blue-collar workers. After more than two years in the United States only 7 percent found professional jobs, while 24 percent worked in blue-collar jobs. This process of downward mobility is common among middle-class refugees. A reporter investigating the resettlement of the first wave made this discovery in a town near Los Angeles: "Behind the counter of a small liquor store in Norwalk the former Premier and Vice-President of South Vietnam, Nguyen Cao Ky, and his elegant wife, Mai Ky, tend local customers with beer and cigarettes, gum and magazines. 'Sorry, we're out of beef jerky,' said the soft-spoken lady who used to entertain diplomats and heads of state" (Bernier 1977, A12).

Despite their initial hardships, by 1984 the first-wave Vietnamese had the same median income as the U.S. population (U.S. Office of Refugee Resettlement 1987). On the tenth anniversary of the fall of Saigon, the American press seized upon the accomplishments of the first wave as another instance of immigrant success in America (Doerner 1985; Greenberg 1985). A headline in the *Wall Street Journal* extolled that Vietnamese "early arrivals make it in entrepreneurial jobs; values that spell success: work, school, thrift, family" (Hume 1985). The refugees deserved to be praised because they were rapidly gaining economic equality with natives. But attributing their success to values added the Vietnamese to the myth that Asians are a "model minority," an ethnic group whose economic achievements are the result of culture rather than the human capital they arrived with and, in the case of the Indochinese, assistance provided by public and private social-welfare agencies. In fact, most Indochinese refugees have yet to experience the economic stability of the first-wave Vietnamese.

A study of economic achievement among Laotian and Vietnamese refugees found that 80 percent of their households were below the poverty level during the first year in the United States (Caplan et al. 1989). Only 30 percent, however, were still poor after three and one-half years. Although a dramatic reduction,

Table 8.1

Characteristics of Indochinese Refugee Households by Source of Income

	Only cash assistance	Cash assistance and earnings	Only earnings
Average number of persons	5.7	6.1	4.4
% Household members:			
Under the age of 6	20	8	6
Under the age of 16	46	25	18
% Households with at least one fluent English speaker	8	22	29

Note: national sample in 1991 of 608 Indochinese refugees who arrived in the United States from 1986 to 1991
Source: U.S. Office of Refugee Resettlement 1992

the poverty rate (at the time of the survey) was 12 percent among whites, 31 percent among Hispanics, and 36 percent among blacks. It thus took Indochinese refugees several years merely to reach the economic status of America's poorest ethnic minorities. For this reason, some researchers are pessimistic about the economic future of the refugees, fearing that in the years to come their socioeconomic status is more likely to resemble that of blacks than whites (Gold and Kibria 1993).

One result of the refugees' high poverty rate is that Indochinese refugees have rates of public assistance significantly higher than natives and other immigrants (Jensen 1988). The refugees' use of welfare is a particular concern to state and federal officials. According to the U.S. Office of Refugee Resettlement (1988, 157): "Welfare dependency is probably the most commonly used measurement to assess the status of the domestic refugee resettlement program and the progress that refugees are making in becoming self-sufficient." The emphasis given to welfare rates by resettlement policy reflects the fiscal costs to the resettlement program, but also the stigma attached to public assistance in the American social-welfare system (Hein 1992). Refugees' use of income-support programs is not a public policy issue in France. Unlike its American counterpart, the French social-welfare system does not presume that people receiving aid lack a work ethic.

The study of Vietnamese and Laotian refugees found that over 90 percent of their households received cash assistance their first year in the United States (Caplan et al. 1989). After three and one-half years only 45 percent of households continued to receive public aid. Despite this decline, the refugees remain heavily dependent on the social-welfare system (U.S. Office of Refugee Resettlement 1989). During their first five years in the United States, about one-third of Indochinese refugee households depend exclusively on cash assistance for support. Approximately 22 percent of households have some members

Table 8.2.

Patterns in the Adjustment of Indochinese Refugees
by Months of Residence

	7–12	19–24	31–60
Unemployment rate (%)	29	13	18
Weekly wages	$179	$206	$249
Speak English well or fluently (%)	29	33	41
In English training (%)	37	30	21
Other training or schooling (%)	29	24	21

Note: national sample in 1991 of 608 Indochinese refugees who arrived in the United States from 1986 to 1991
Source: U.S. Office of Refugee Resettlement 1992

receiving a form of cash assistance and other members working. About 45 percent of households receive all of their income from employment. Thus during the early stage of their adaptation, slightly more than one-half of Indochinese households receive all or a portion of their income from the social-welfare system. Only about 7 percent of white households and 27 percent of black households receive cash assistance.

These three types of Indochinese households are considerably different (see Table 8.1). Households receiving cash assistance are larger than those whose income is derived only from earnings. The greatest difference, however, is the ages of household members and if the household has a member fluent in English. Households receiving income only from cash assistance are almost totally deprived of a member fluent in English. Children, particularly those under the age of six, account for a large portion of members in these households. Conversely, there are comparatively few children in households whose income is derived only from earnings. After length of time in the United States, the number of young children in a family is the best predictor of public-assistance use among Indochinese refugees (Rumbaut 1989).

Indeed, many indicators of economic status improve the longer the refugees reside in the United States (see Table 8.2). The unemployment rate among refugees declines dramatically with the passage of time. But the high rate among those in the United States 31 to 60 months indicates that refugees' employment is often unstable. Nonetheless, there is a uniform rise in refugees' wages and English proficiency during their first five years of resettlement. Despite these gains, refugees continue to enroll in English-language and job-training courses and other forms of education. Although these social services are most often used during the early phase of resettlement, about one in five refugees takes courses even after residing in the United States more than two and a half years. Other studies have suggested an even higher rate of use of programs specifically for job training (Strand 1984).

English proficiency is an important but complex factor in refugees' economic progress. When asked why they are not seeking employment, younger refugees cite education, those between the ages of 25 and 44 cite education and family needs, and those over 44 cite health problems (U.S. Office of Refugee Resettlement 1991). Inability to speak English has never been a major reason given by refugees for not seeking employment. Indeed, English proficiency is unrelated to employment among refugees arriving in the United States between 1980 and 1983, although it was for refugees arriving between 1975 and 1979 (Bach and Carroll-Seguin 1986). The fact that refugees with varying levels of English found jobs at about the same rate during the early 1980s, but not during the 1970s, has been attributed to the development of ethnic communities and social services in the latter period. The earlier wave of refugees could not draw upon these resources to find jobs. But the advent of social networks and job-placement programs enabled refugees to locate work even when they spoke little English. The primary effect of English proficiency is on refugees' earnings (Rumbaut 1989). Compared with refugees with no English proficiency, those who speak a little English earn about $2,000 a year more in wages, while those who speak English well earn more than $3,700 a year in additional wages (U.S. Office of Refugee Resettlement 1992).

The major determinant of earnings, of course, is not English proficiency but type of job. Indochinese refugees residing in the United States less than five years are overwhelmingly concentrated in jobs that pay low wages (see Table 8.3). Fewer than one in five of the refugees have white-collar jobs. Almost 40 percent work in unskilled and semi-skilled blue-collar jobs, compared with only 14 percent of all Americans. Not only are the refugees overwhelmingly employed in blue-collar jobs, but this industrial work is initially unfamiliar to them. The data in Table 8.3 do not indicate which occupations these new blue-collar workers had in their country of origin. But almost 40 percent of all the refugees were farmers or fishers before arrival in the United States. Thus many refugees are moving from work in agriculture to work in factories—an experience similar to that among European immigrants and rural Americans during the nineteenth century.

Nationality is an important factor in evaluating the degree to which blue-collar work represents a dramatic break with past work experience. The different levels of urbanization and economic modernization in Vietnam, Laos, and Cambodia constitute important differences in the backgrounds of refugees from each country (Haines 1989). Similarly, the degree of military mobilization in each country leads to variation in the proportion of Vietnamese, Laotian, and Cambodian men whose prior employment was as a soldier (Strand and Jones 1985).

Refugees from Vietnam tended to live in urban areas and be literate in their native language. Sales and clerical work accounts for the largest occupational background for both men and women. About 18 percent of heads of households were in the military—a low proportion in comparison to other refugees. These characteristics suggest that Vietnamese refugees experience little social dislocation when entering the American workplace. As noted earlier, however, middle-class refugees usually confront a difficult downward mobility. One study suggests

Table 8.3

Previous and Current Occupational Status of Indochinese Refugees
(in percent)

	Homeland	United States
White collar		
Total	35	17
Professional and managerial	9	1
Sales and clerical	26	16
Service workers	8	18
Blue collar		
Total	18	63
Skilled	14	24
Semi-skilled	4	35
Laborers	0	4
Farmers and fishers	39	1

Note: national sample in 1991 of 608 Indochinese refugees who arrived in the United States from 1986 to 1991
Source: U.S. Office of Refugee Resettlement 1992

that dissatisfaction with less-skilled jobs leads middle-class refugees initially to have a higher job turnover rate than refugees with less prestigious occupational backgrounds, who do not consider blue-collar jobs demeaning (Tang and O'Brien 1990).

Lowland Laotians and especially Cambodians are more likely to have lived in small cities, towns, and rural areas. About one-quarter to one-third of heads of households were in the military, and a similar proportion of all Laotians and Cambodians now in the United States are illiterate in their native language. Many Laotian and Cambodian women were farmers, while Laotian and Cambodian men tended to be farmers or were sales and clerical workers. In contrast to the Vietnamese, entering the American workplace is likely to be more traumatic for lowland Laotians and Cambodians. One Cambodian woman in the United States described the hardship of making the transition from farming to wage work in a low-skill service job:

> When we lived on a farm, before the war, it was easier to feed the family than it is here now. But the war and killing changed all that, and our past is gone. Now I work many hours in a hotel laundry to buy food and pay the rent. My husband works until late at night. It's hard when school starts because my oldest son won't be able to take care of

my little one. I can't afford to quit my job and I can't leave my five-year-old alone after school. I don't know what I'll do. Every night I wake up in bed and worry. (Kalergis 1989, n.p.)

Locating and maintaining employment in the American economy is the most traumatic for the Hmong. Because they lived in the highlands of Laos, Hmong refugees' origins are overwhelmingly rural. They did not have a written language until the 1950s, and as a result most are illiterate in their native language. Almost all Hmong women and most Hmong men farmed for a living, but about two-thirds of the men also were in the military. A Hmong man expresses what it feels like to move from an autonomous, rural existence to an economy where survival depends on employment by other people:

Over there [in Laos] you had to go into the jungle, cut a tree and work very hard in raising chickens and all that just to eat. And you don't have a car and so many mosquitoes come into your house. But even though it is a poor country I could take care of myself there. Here you work day-to-day and year-to-year and you worry too much about your job and you hurt and you're scared. . . . Everything is money here. Over there even if you don't have a job there is still a lot of land and you can grow potatoes and corn and rice and raise chickens and you are free yourself. (*Denver Post* 1985, G9)

Thus the transition from public assistance to employment that occurs for most refugees within the first few years after arrival is the beginning of a profound change in the meaning of work. Americans, particularly those in the resettlement program, equate "self-sufficiency" with employment. But refugees whose prior work experience was in agriculture find that employment in blue-collar or low-skill service jobs makes them feel less independent. Gender roles within Indochinese families is another area in which employment has cultural, not merely monetary, significance.

Work and Family Roles among Vietnamese Women

Vietnamese women have long had important economic roles in their homeland. In both urban and rural areas, it was not uncommon for women to own property and run businesses. During wars the women assumed even greater responsibility for the household economy when husbands departed for the army or were killed (Hickey 1964). This tradition of independence has been transferred to the United States (Haines 1986). The employment rate of Vietnamese women is closer to that of American women than is the rate of Vietnamese men to that of American men. In contrast to men and women from other Indochinese groups, Vietnamese men and women have the lowest disparity in levels of education and types of occupations in their homeland. In the United States they also are closer in labor force participation rates when compared with Cambodians, Laotians, and the Hmong.

Although distinguished by their entry into the work world, Vietnamese women often have low-paying jobs. Many work in the informal economy (jobs that do not meet government standards, such as sewing clothes at home) or have low-paying service jobs, such as hotel maids (Kibria 1989, 1993). In Philadelphia 30 percent of employed Vietnamese women work in such jobs, compared with only 13 percent of Vietnamese men. Little education and few job skills limit the women's opportunities for employment. But the structure of the Vietnamese family also leads the women into this line of work.

Vietnamese women explain that such jobs, while low-paid, allow them to keep receiving public assistance and the medical benefits that go with it. Since they are generally unqualified for jobs that provide health insurance, and in many cases their husbands do not get insurance at their jobs, it is the women who provide medical benefits for the whole family through their eligibility for public aid. Working at home sewing clothes for the garment industry also allows the women to take care of young children. Finally, work as waitresses in ethnic restaurants or as domestics allows quick entry and exit from the labor force. This flexibility is consistent with the experience working women had in Vietnam, where a cycle of family needs determined the timing of wage work.

The relationship between Vietnamese women's employment and family roles varies with labor market conditions. When refugees enter highly competitive labor markets, as in San Francisco, Vietnamese women often find employment before their husbands (Gold 1989). Jobs as house cleaners and hotel maids are readily available, leading many Vietnamese women to initially take on the breadwinner role. In addition, wives may support the family while their husbands study for professional employment. Vietnamese women had considerable discretion over the family budget in their homeland, and they now operate many groceries and restaurants in "little Saigons." The business is viewed as a ticket to complete self-employment for the family, if it is successful, or as a safety net should the husband lose his job.

The familial role of working Vietnamese women changes when there are many opportunities for husbands to work (Benson 1990). Under these conditions a Vietnamese family will use the husband's income for living expenses. The wife's income may be saved for a future investment, such as a business, college tuition, or purchasing a home. In many cases, however, the wife's income is what keeps the family from becoming part of the working poor. Dual wage-earning families are able to cover unexpected expenses like car accidents and health problems without going into debt. Some families may take in boarders or have another family share a residence with them in order to gain additional income. Since the wife is responsible for household chores, in effect it is she who earns the money the family receives from sharing its residence. Women are thus essential components of the Vietnamese household economy. As workers, they seek to balance cultural values from their homeland with economic conditions in the United States. For refugees working in the formal economy with white American workers, the blending of cultures is even more pronounced.

Cambodian Working-Class Culture

When Sombat arrived in the United States his prospects seemed very bleak. He was only 14 when the Khmer Rouge came to power in Cambodia. As a result, his education stopped at the ninth grade. Moreover, many of his close relatives died between 1975 and 1979, when he escaped to Thailand. His wife gave birth to their first daughter in a Philippine camp where refugees stay for six months for language and cultural orientation prior to entering the United States. Neither he nor his wife had any relatives in the country, and his sister-in-law was part of their household.

To make matters worse, Sombat's family was sponsored by a voluntary agency in Chicago. Lacking relatives to provide support, refugees like Sombat hope they will be sponsored by an American family or church group. Refugees prefer private sponsors because they provide more resources and individual attention to refugees than do voluntary agencies, which receive a federal grant for each refugee sponsored. These agencies do employ caseworkers from all the major ethnic groups arriving from Vietnam, Laos, and Cambodia. But refugees want private sponsors because they can form a relationship with them that resembles those with kin or traditional authorities in their homeland (Ledgerwood 1990; Mortland and Ledgerwood 1987). Sombat described the differences between agencies and private sponsors this way: "A private sponsor is better than an agency. They help more because they care more about the refugees and know more people. If you have relatives here it's easy to get started, to share money. But without them it's very difficult. A friend of mine now owns a doughnut shop. He started working at the same factory that I do, but he has relatives in California who run a doughnut shop. He saved up money, went to visit them, learned how to run the business, and then started one of his own."

Economic conditions in the United States posed an additional hardship for Sombat. The country was experiencing the worst recession since the 1930s. Yet between 1980 and 1981 more than 300,000 Indochinese refugees like Sombat arrived in the United States. The refugees' lack of English and job skills, combined with the country's high unemployment rate, meant that many of the refugees had to receive cash assistance. The voluntary agency arranged for Sombat's family to receive public aid, but Sombat intensely disliked having to get money from the government when he knew he could work: "Cambodians had to work very hard under Pol Pot for no money and almost no food. We know how to work, and if there are jobs we can do them."

Hardship in Southeast Asia is only one reason refugees are motivated to work in the United States. In Sombat's case, his family background raised his aspirations. His mother came from a wealthy family and was so educated that she spoke French and Thai. His father, however, had been born into a poor peasant family, but through hard work he eventually owned a small construction company. Sombat's father, a brother, and a brother-in-law starved to death during the Khmer Rouge revolution, leaving his mother, a sister, and a sister-in law with little means of support when the Vietnamese forced the Khmer Rouge from power in 1979. This need to aid relatives still in Cambodia, the example of his deceased father, and the knowledge that he could work hard drove Sombat to seek better opportunities than were present in the Indochinese neighborhood of Uptown where the agency initially settled him.

When Sombat learned that a friend of his had found a factory job paying more than $6 an hour in a suburb of Chicago, he moved out of Uptown and stayed for one month in the friend's apartment before a woman from a church group that had sponsored other refugees helped him get a job in the factory. His wife and sister-in-law also found jobs in the factory. Sombat now runs a lathe and says of his calloused and red hands: "I have a harder job than any Cambodian I know. My hands look as bad now as they did during the Khmer Rouge."

With three steady jobs the family took out a bank loan to purchase a house for $60,000 on a typical suburban street. Only one other Cambodian family lives near them. A van sits in Sombat's driveway and, except for several pictures of kin in Cambodia, the house is decorated in the style of a midwestern suburb. Conspicuously absent are the ornaments that adorn the apartments of Cambodians in Uptown: posters of Vietnam War movies, Thai food, the Buddha at various stages of his career, and the famed Cambodian temple of Angkor Wat. Instead, an idealized portrait of Jesus greets those entering the house. The family occasionally goes to church, but Sombat confided, "I go to pay respect to the woman who found me this job, not really because I'm Christian." During the Persian Gulf War he flew an American flag and attached a yellow ribbon to a tree in front of his house.

Sombat's status at the factory adds to this picture of rapid integration into the American working class. Although there are about 20 Cambodian workers at the factory, Sombat is the only one who joined the bowling league, a fixture of blue-collar culture in the Midwest. He regularly goes fishing with some of the older American men, saying he prefers their fishing trips to those of the younger men who drink a lot of beer. Sombat also is the unofficial foreman for the other Cambodian workers, and he is always invited to attend meetings with managers to discuss job and production issues. Recently, although he has yet to learn the game, factory management gave him a set of golf clubs for consistently high productivity.

Sombat's home life appears equally Americanized. His two daughters speak unaccented English and wear the latest T-shirts and sweaters bearing cartoon characters. The older of the two speaks some Khmer, but the children speak English to each other. Sombat and his wife speak Khmer to each other and use both languages for the children, although Khmer is used for disciplinary purposes. Americanization extends to the couple's gender roles. Sombat explains, "I don't like the Cambodian custom of the man being the boss. I try to share with my wife, and we talk things over when there is a problem. Men aren't the same as women. Women seem to think more short-term, and they get jealous easily. But the man cannot say do this or do that like in Cambodia. We have to respect our wife and give an example to our children." Sombat is studying to become an American citizen, but is waiting until his wife can pass the test with him.

Entry into the American working class has not been without difficulty for Sombat. He is aware that although he may try to act American, some native workers resent his presence at the factory. On the racism of some white co-workers, Sombat has this response:

When I do something wrong it's because I'm Cambodian. When an American does something wrong it's only because they're Mike or John. That's prejudice, isn't it? I tell new Cambodian workers that Americans are watching them and that they will judge all Cambodians by what they do. They may get mad at the Americans, but I tell them that if they care about the name of the Cambodian people they will have to work harder. That's how to handle it. If some American says something bad about me, I'm still polite to him. But I will try to work harder than him. Each time we get paid there's a list posted telling us who is producing more than 100 percent. I'm always over.

Being an ethnic minority is only one factor that prevents Sombat from feeling that he is fully part of the American working class. Despite considerable integration into American society via his suburban factory job, much of Sombat's life remains centered around Cambodia and Cambodian culture. His understanding of work and wages is shaped by experiences in Cambodia, while the greatest comparison for his American neighbors might be other jobs in the United States. Sombat comments on the meaning of income and possessions in his homeland and adopted country: "In Cambodia, you could have money, but there was nothing to buy. In the United States, there are many things to buy but we don't have the money." Like other refugees, Sombat has difficulty adjusting to the importance of money in the United States. The absence of a consumer culture in Vietnam, Laos, and Cambodia means that many refugees do not fully accept the value placed on materialism and acquisitiveness by American culture.

Further distancing Sombat from American working-class culture is his strong interest in Cambodian politics. He hoped (until his wife dissented) to become a U.N. observer during the 1993 elections in Cambodia. Many Cambodians are reluctant to become politically involved in the United States because they are embarrassed by mistakes in speaking English and do not come from a political culture where citizens confront leaders. Yet Sombat called an Illinois senator to ask about U.S. policy toward Cambodia and eventually telephoned the State Department. He spends much time reflecting on the fate of his country, and it makes him bitter:

> Cambodian leaders have never cared about the country, they have always looked out for themselves. Even Sihanouk who tried to keep Cambodia neutral eventually made a deal with North Vietnam. Some Cambodians say it's because one of his wives is Vietnamese, but I think it was because he wanted to get land in South Vietnam that used to belong to Cambodia a long time ago. I feel so bad for my country because it used to have enough food for everyone. It's not like the United States, where you cannot eat most of the plants. In Cambodia, almost all the plants grow a fruit or vegetable to eat, and many of the flowers and leaves can be used for medicine.

Sombat's ties to Cambodia are more than romanticized reminiscences: he sends over $1,000 a year to his relatives even though the courier takes 20 percent. One Cambodian leader in Chicago criticized Sombat for sending money to his relatives, saying that it only supported the Vietnamese-backed government (which ruled Cambodia from 1979 to 1993). Sombat said he came "this close" to telling him off: "He was one of the intellectuals who left with all his relatives in 1975 so he doesn't have to worry like I do. The intellectuals in Cambodia should have done more for the country. It was people like him who didn't take responsibility and they should have because they had more education."

Sombat's strong kin ties also reflect his attachment to Cambodian culture and only partial integration in American working-class culture. His sister-in-law has lived with his family since they arrived in the United States, and he helped arrange her marriage. As he explained, "It was an arranged marriage, not a marriage for love, although they do love each other now. The groom sent some friends to see me to see if my sister-in-law wanted to get married. In Cambodia marriages are arranged by the parents and other relatives, but I told them it was up to her, that I couldn't decide for her. But she wanted my opinion since I knew this man. I said that I had never heard anything bad about him, and then the parents and the son came over with gifts."

Sombat then contacted an *ajcha*—a layman who acts as a go-between for the relatives of the bride and groom, knows the Buddhist chants for engagement and wedding ceremonies, and will organize the monks at the local temple to come to the bride or groom's house to perform the wedding. He even bought the *ajcha* a cooked pig's head, a very traditional gift. Sombat gave his sister-in-law the bride price of several thousand dollars given him by the groom's parents. The young woman and her husband, in turn, continued to live in a basement room in Sombat's house. They remained there even after the birth of a daughter, and paid Sombat $300 for rent and food.

Sombat also plays in a Cambodian band once or twice a month. Several times a year, the band performs at Cambodian wedding parties or concerts, earning several hundred dollars at each event. They play mostly American music, but they know traditional Cambodian dance tunes and tend to blend the styles together. Sombat's band even advertised in a national Cambodian newspaper and were invited to perform a concert in Montreal attended by more than 400 Cambodians.

Sombat's life as a semi-skilled blue-collar worker in a Chicago suburb blends together American working-class culture with Cambodian tradition and the refugee experience. He consciously selects the best elements from both cultures and uses them to reinforce each other. From Cambodian culture he takes the value of "respect," while from American culture he takes the value of "competition." Sombat described this mixing of cultures and experiences in this way: "Cambodian people are too passive, not aggressive enough. That's what I've learned from Americans. You get to be your best by competing with other people. Cambodians just accept things the way they are, and maybe that's why our country has had so much trouble. But Cambodians also know how to respect. We teach our children to care for their parents even when they are old. They have to respect their teachers too. Without respect you start feeling too important."

As Sombat's experience demonstrates, workplaces are important sites for blending cultures. Yet cultural integration through the workplace, particularly the formation of an ethnic identity, varies with the type of work and the degree of ethnic diversity among co-workers.

Blue-Collar and White-Collar Lives

Phea and Chanta were childhood friends in Cambodia but were separated following the revolution in 1975. Both had no prior work experience and little schooling when they arrived in the United States, since they were children when the Khmer Rouge transformed Cambodians into slave laborers. But their work careers in the United States took very different paths. Phea works in a Chicago warehouse bagging candy for the minimum wage. Chanta is a nurse's aid, works in a Minneapolis senior citizens' home, and earns more than twice the minimum wage. Their distinct positions in the American labor market is primarily the result of the timing of their migration to the United States. The resulting differences between the two workplaces profoundly affected their integration into American society and culture.

Phea arrived in the United States above the legal age at which she could enter high school. Instead, she attended English-as-a-second-language classes at a local community college. At the time, federal resettlement policy provided one and a half years of public aid to refugees so they could improve their linguistic skills and receive needed social services. When this period ended, federal policy dictated that Phea go to work. With no job skills and only basic English, Phea was only qualified to work in the secondary sector of the labor market: minimally skilled blue-collar jobs that pay about minimum wage with slow or no pay increases, few or no benefits (such as health care), and little chance for moving up to a better job.

Only one year younger than Phea, Chanta arrived in the United States young enough to start junior high school, greatly improving her chances of entering the primary sector of the labor market: skilled white-collar jobs that pay high wages, have benefits, and are part of a career track that enables workers to improve their skills and earnings over time. But entering an American school was not easy. Chanta was placed in the seventh grade even though she was 17. When her family moved from Washington, D.C., to Minnesota one year after arrival, the new high school moved her into the tenth grade because of her advanced age. Although now among her peers, Chanta had to complete school work beyond her abilities. She could not repeat any grade because 21 was the maximum age for a high school student under Minnesota law. Through hard work Chanta graduated the month she turned 21.

Phea's and Chanta's different educational backgrounds not only affected their entry into the labor market but also shaped their attitudes toward work. Phea had an instrumental approach: work was a monotonous necessity and not central to one's life. Chanta, however, selected work that fit her personal interests and had an important social function. One of Chanta's first neighbors in the United States was an African-American woman who encouraged her to become a nurse. They frequently discussed health, doctors, and hospitals because of the neighbor's illness. Although this experience led Chanta to aspire to become a nurse even before she had finished high school, without a diploma she would have been unable to fulfill this aspiration. Following graduation, she obtained additional training and then worked in several hospitals and old-age homes—jobs she found through want ads in newspapers. After three attempts at the nurse's aid test, she finally passed. This new qualification raised her hourly wage from $8.50 to $10.25, and her present employer provides a generous benefits package.

Phea's selection of a job occurred in a very different way. After finishing English classes, her caseworker at a Cambodian MAA sent her to a warehouse that sorted inexpensive jewelry for customer orders. This job lasted only a few months, and the association then found Phea a job packaging cheap candy and children's toys (the type one sees at the exit of supermarkets) at a warehouse where all the workers were women. The job paid the minimum wage ($3.25 an hour in 1985), with a 25¢ raise every two years up to a maximum of $5 an hour. There were no health benefits and only a few paid vacations. The warehouse was cold in winter and hot in summer, and the only water available came from a rusty sink in the bathroom; workers had to bring their own cups. But the greatest hardship was working "the line"—an assembly belt that passed candy in front of workers at a rapid pace. Workers had to quickly pack the candy or else disrupt the work of others farther down the line.

Being a nurse or warehouse worker has led Chanta and Phea to have distinct forms of class consciousness: recognition, particularly among wage workers, of their collective economic function and frequent exploitation by employers. Chanta has the more politicized awareness of her class, in part because of a difficult period early in her marriage. Her husband had to hide her income in order to qualify for a tuition reduction at a local college. Chanta resented the system that forced this deceit. Her husband worked eight hours a day (at a job that did not provide health insurance), took engineering classes at night, and still had time to work in his parents' store. Reflecting on their situation, Chanta commented, "It seems like the middle class has to pay for everything. All the benefits and programs are to help the really poor, but there's nothing to help people like us. My sister lives in France, and taxes are higher there. But at least you get something for them. In France, the health care covers everyone and all workers get one month vacation in the summer."

Unlike Chanta, who expressed dissatisfaction with her class status in a very political way, Phea simply treated work in the candy warehouse as a routine. But both did bring an international awareness to their work. For Chanta, it was the contrast with conditions in France, where she had visited a sister resettled there. For Phea, it was the experience of working under the Khmer Rouge. Although Americans might consider invalid the comparison of slave labor in Cambodia with work in the American secondary sector, it was a meaningful contrast for Phea. She comments, "This is an easy job. In Cambodia I had to work outside in the rain or hot sun with no food."

Although Phea was less politicized in her views, her workplace could be the scene of brief but intense conflict between workers and supervisors, which was absent from Chanta's nursing home. In the context of the warehouse, Phea earned a reputation for being one of the few militant workers. During Phea's first months on the job, an older American woman worker was often temporarily in charge. She would yell, "OK Cambodians, get over here" as an instruction where teams of workers should move. Incensed at being herded by ethnicity, Phea finally responded, "Don't call us like that. Our parents gave us names and you should use them." There was a stunned silence, and Phea saw several American workers beaming at her and silently clapping their hands to show approval. The older woman never spoke like that again, and in fact became quite friendly toward Phea, often teasing her about the day she "stood up to the boss." On another occasion Phea rebelled against a male manager who came down once a month from the main office. On one of these visits he harangued the female workers about being slow, and Phea replied, "You don't pay us enough to work that fast. I worked as a slave for the Communists for four years. I don't have to work like that here."

Phea came to realize that other workers had a special regard for her because she would confront supervisors. Once when returning from a vacation, she was immediately told by a co-worker: "There was another one like you." A male supervisor had grabbed the hands of a woman and said: "Faster! Just throw the candy in like this. Don't arrange it." The woman, a Native American, had been complaining about the job since her arrival. She responded, "OK, I'll throw it" and then threw the box of candy at the supervisor, punched her time card, and was never seen again. In contrast to Chanta's more policy-oriented class consciousness, Phea's experiences in a secondary-sector job led to a more militant, yet highly localized, conception of class inequality.

Although Chanta clearly has the better job with respect to pay, benefits, prestige, and working conditions, she has become increasingly disillusioned with her work, even doubting her choice of nursing as a career. Some problems concern the service she provides. The doctors she works with often resent her calling them late at night when a patient is ill. Chanta dislikes how they only stay a few minutes with each patient. When she learned that Medicare pays them per visit to a patient, regardless of how long they stay, she became angry with the health-care system. Other problems arose from the workplace itself. She normally works from six o'clock in the evening to two o'clock at night—hours that leave little time to spend with her husband and son. The nursing home often expects her to fill in for an absent worker and work additional hours as needed.

Chanta also discovered an unexpected drawback to the nursing profession. Moving from job to job in search of better pay and benefits results in few close ties to the people she works with. Even at the nursing home where she has stayed the longest, frequent changing of shifts and staff turnover has left her without social ties to co-workers. The fact that almost all of her co-workers are white Americans sometimes makes her "feel like an outsider."

Chanta's experience as an Asian in a predominately white workplace magnifies her awareness of being an ethnic minority. She has vivid memories of past experiences with prejudice, reporting that when she first arrived in Minnesota whites "yelled at me when I drove a car, saying the government gave refugees money. But I worked during the summers for that car. The first one I bought was in such bad shape that it could only drive in reverse." Returning from a trip to Canada, Chanta and her husband were detained by U.S. border police when they could not produce U.S. passports. Since this document is not required for trips within North America, she concluded that they were stopped because they are Asian. The couple watched while white Americans entered without interruption. Finally, the police located their names in a computer file: "They said we were lucky the computer wasn't busy that day, otherwise we might have waited the whole day." She recounted this story while holding her two-month-old son and concluded, "He won't have it easy even though he was born in this country. People will look at his black hair and know that he is Cambodian." Although Chanta has not experienced prejudice at her various workplaces, the scarcity of other Asian workers and the weak ties to white American workers reinforce her feelings of being an outsider in the United States.

While Chanta became disillusioned with her work, Phea discovered some positive aspects of employment at the warehouse. Phea learned about American holidays and customs at the warehouse that were not observed in the predominately Indochinese neighborhood where she lived. On Halloween black and Hispanic children in the area came by the warehouse to ask for candy. On April Fool's Day co-workers played a trick on her. Phea knew she could leave the warehouse whenever she wanted, while Chanta was expected to have a commitment to her work. Workers could also take home small amounts of candy for their children or friends. But Phea found that the greatest advantage to work in the secondary sector was the ethnic diversity among co-workers.

Where the ethnic homogeneity of Chanta's workplace reinforced her alien-
ation from American society, the Assyrians, Mexicans, and other immigrants in
Phea's workplace led her to understand being Cambodian in the United States
primarily by comparison with non-Europeans. Assyrians from the Middle East
were the largest ethnic group employed at the warehouse. Phea learned that
unlike the Cambodians, who were placed there by an MAA that received public
funding to employ refugees, the Assyrians found work there through relatives.
Many were related by marriage. During the summer high school students joined
their mothers and grandmothers. Most of the Assyrians lived near the warehouse, which was one reason they valued the job. Even those living farther
away would walk in large groups to save money on public transportation.

The Mexicans at the warehouse found their jobs through friends. Like the
Cambodians, the Mexicans had the least proficiency in English and changed
jobs frequently. An older Chicana woman born in Texas became one of Phea's
best friends. From her Phea learned that some people in the United States also
had lives as difficult as those of Cambodian refugees. The Chicana woman
recounted picking cotton and vegetables as a child and described how planes
sprayed pesticide even when there were workers below. The work precluded
attending school, and this woman was barely able to read. Phea had great
respect for her: "She had to work like a slave when she was young. But she's so
kind. She's friendly to everyone and never gets angry."

Phea was surprised that some white Americans also did what she called
"refugee work." The white Americans worked at the warehouse for a mix of reasons. Some only wanted to work part-time, and the warehouse provided flexible
hours, albeit at low pay. Others were in between more permanent jobs. One
American became Phea's best friend and taught her English in spare moments.

Finally, there were other Cambodians who found jobs there through the
MAA or occasionally through friends. When a friend needed a job, Phea was
able to get work for her at the warehouse. The informality of the secondary sector, while negative in some respects, also leads many employers to hire workers
when they are vouched for by a current employee, which reinforces ethnic networks. For example, an older Cambodian woman befriended Phea, who, lacking relatives in the United States, was only too happy to have this relationship.
When the woman had a hospital appointment, Phea took the day off to trans-
late for her, refusing when the woman offered to pay her the missed wages.

The ethnic diversity of warehouse workers created a valuable social dimension to an otherwise dull job. The fact that all of the workers were women added
to the solidarity of workplace culture. From their frequent weddings and ethnic
celebrations the Assyrians brought food for other workers to try and provided
recipes when asked. Phea learned how to make grape leaves and peppers stuffed
with rice and meat, a typical Middle Eastern dish. The Cambodians asked Americans about the body powder they used to keep dry in the summer, a product they
were unfamiliar with. Mexicans asked Cambodians to buy them a skin-whiten-
ing facial cream available only in Asian stores and also sold Cambodians gold
rings with an unusual "diamond" cross-hatching that made shiny reflections.
Phea's American friend talked with her about sex and men—Phea's first discus-
sion of these subjects with an American woman. Their English lessons included
"forbidden" words not covered in English-as-a-second-language classes. The
female bonds at the warehouse, in addition to the ethnic diversity, created a

workplace culture that led Phea to understand her experience as a Cambodian refugee in the United States as one of integration rather than conflict and inequality, even though the work itself was economically disadvantaged.

Conclusion

Work is among the most important features of the new lives Indochinese refugees create in the United States. Because they lack education, must take care of family members, or are in poor health, many refugees do not seek work. Others receive public assistance because they cannot find jobs or have too many children to support on a minimum-wage job that does not provide health insurance. Even when they do locate employment, many refugees earn low wages that leave them in or just above poverty. Refugees from the middle class fare better, but they often experience downward mobility because they never reenter the prestigious occupations they had in their homeland. These problems alone make conflict and inequality central to the experience of Indochinese refugees in the United States.

Yet work in the American economy has many cultural consequences for refugees—a point missed by the ethnic-resilience model that conceives of immigrant and refugee adaptation primarily as a search for occupational and income attainment. For some Vietnamese, many Cambodians and Laotians, and almost all Hmong, the transition from work in agriculture or fishing to work in factories and service jobs is a profound shock. Many feel that they have less economic independence in the United States than in their homelands, and that money is too central to the American way of life. This cultural change in the meaning of work is painful for the refugees. But it cannot be attributed to the conflict between migrants and natives, non-European and European Americans, depicted by the ethnic-resilience model. Rather, it results from moving from a preindustrial to an industrial economy—an experience shared by many European immigrants during the nineteenth and early twentieth centuries.

Not only does work occur in a cultural context, but culture can influence a refugee's choice of work. When Vietnamese women select a job, they do so in ways that are consistent with their roles as wives and mothers within Vietnamese culture, not simply for monetary gain. Workplaces are also among the most important arenas in which refugees encounter American culture. As the Cambodian lathe worker in suburban Chicago exemplifies, refugees blend elements of American culture with their native culture. Far from resisting assimilation at all costs, Indochinese refugees recognize the contributions that other cultures can make to their own. This ability to integrate diverse cultures began in Southeast Asia, where Chinese, Indian, and French influences have been absorbed by the indigenous cultures for hundreds of years. The ethnic-resilience model's rejection of the "melting-pot" ideology in the U.S. context risks ignoring the process of cultural fusion that has occurred in other parts of the world and that immigrants and refugees bring to the United States.

Workplaces also are sites for constructing social identities. Whether refugees work in skilled white-collar jobs, as did the Cambodian nurse, or unskilled blue-collar jobs, as did the Cambodian warehouse worker, determines many aspects of their integration into American society. As expected by the ethnic-resilience model, the Cambodian nurse developed a strong ethnic minority identity because she primarily interacted with whites on the job and came to view assimilation as largely a myth. An ethnically diverse but gender-homogeneous workplace, however, also contributed to the formation of an ethnic identity for the Cambodian warehouse worker. A sense of cultural distinctiveness arises not only from conflict with a dominant group but also through positive interaction with different ethnic groups each contributing a distinct worldview and material goods. Working among women immigrants from Mexico and the Middle East, as well as native-born white and Chicana women, led that Cambodian warehouse worker to an identity based on shared differences.

nine

Conclusion

Refugees have an experience with political oppression and violence, flight rather than departure, and exile instead of access to the homeland. The Indochinese refugee experience began during the era of European decolonization and continued through the cold war between the United States and the former Soviet Union. When Vietnam was partitioned into a Communist North and pro-West South in 1954, the United States helped France transport more than 800,000 refugees to South Vietnam. It then supplied aid to these refugees, further deepening American involvement in the country and ultimately paving the way for military intervention. The United States supported the South Vietnamese policy of relocating peasants to fortified villages during the early 1960s. Then, between 1965 and 1968, the U.S. Army used violence to induce peasant migration to government-controlled areas. In Laos the United States became responsible for evacuating allied ethnic groups, like the Hmong, and lowland Laotians who fled American bombing aimed at depriving Communist forces of a support base. In Cambodia massive American bombing forced rural populations to move to the comparative safety of cities. The people of Vietnam, Laos, and Cambodia experienced uprooting within their homeland before any of them engaged in international migration.

The ending of the war marked the beginning of the first mass movement from mainland Southeast Asia despite the extensive migration history from neighboring Asian countries like India and China. Following the collapse of pro-American regimes in 1975, the United States transported 125,000 Vietnamese to safety, many of whom had worked for the South Vietnamese or American government. Into the 1980s, individuals associated with pro-American governments and the U.S. military were subject to persecution by the new Communist regimes in Vietnam, Laos, and Cambodia. But these actions alone, while inhumane, would not have been sufficient to generate the more than 2 million refugees who ultimately fled to adjacent countries in Southeast Asia. In Vietnam and Laos repressive economic policies, a totalitarian political system, and persecution of ethnic minorities provided the motivations for mass flight. In Cambodia the refugee crisis was caused by Khmer Rouge genocide and then famine and war following the Vietnamese invasion. Refugees from Vietnam, Laos, and Cambodia account for about one-half of all political migrants permanently resettled in the West between 1975 and 1990 and are the largest population of political migrants in the United States.

Indochinese refugees are distinguished from immigrants and other refugees by their historical relationship to the United States. Once they arrive, however, they confront what countless newcomers before them have endured: an adaptation process involving community formation, relations with natives, increasing political involvement, changing familial roles, and the struggle for economic advancement. According to the oldest perspective on immigrant and refugee adaptation, the adaptation process is characterized by gradual integration as newcomers adopt the culture of the host society. This assimilation model focuses on how foreigners become like natives. A more recent perspective views the adaptation process as a conflict among groups of unequal power and privilege that reinforces ethnic differences. For this ethnic-resilience model, the result is pluralism as newcomers rally within their ethnic communities for protection and collective advancement. After two decades of migration and settlement, it is evident that Indochinese refugees in the United States do not exhibit as much integration and cultural transformation as the assimilation model suggests. Still, neither does their experience reveal as much pluralism and conflict as the ethnic-resilience model would lead one to expect.

Refugees from Vietnam, Laos, and Cambodia do not fit the assimilation model because they arrive with a unique relationship to the United States. The fact that the United States contributed to the conditions that led to their flight gives Indochinese refugees a historical distinctiveness that will remain long after their initial cultural differences have been modified by the birth of new generations in the United States. Indochinese refugees also reject the assimilation model's simplified choice between preserving homeland traditions or accepting those in the United States. Rather than transplanting traditions, they re-create communal institutions that are an amalgamation of both cultures.

The new pluralism in American cities further belies the integrationist assumptions of the assimilation model. Indochinese refugees and their descendants are as likely to interact on a daily basis with African Americans, Hispanics, and Asians as they are with whites of European ancestry. The assimilation model presumes the existence of a core culture, which is difficult to discern within contemporary urban diversity.

Integration also is more likely to occur when immigrants and refugees approach the new society as individuals. Yet Indochinese refugees belong to families, communities, and other social networks. This collective adaptation reinforces the refugees' ethnicity because they maintain these networks not simply for cultural preservation but because family and community are means for solving problems raised by migration and resettlement.

Finally, some of the refugees have experienced severe antagonism from natives. Most of them perceive extensive prejudice and discrimination. The assimilation model assumes that American society is open to newcomers if they are willing to integrate. Yet racism inevitably reinforces pluralism by encouraging the refugees to recognize their ethnic distinctiveness.

For all of the pluralism and conflict experienced by refugees from Vietnam, Laos, and Cambodia, there is still more integration and cultural transformation than portrayed by the ethnic-resilience model. This model correctly points to immigrant and refugee communities as vital sources of support in the adaptation process. Yet Indochinese communities are also sites for intense conflict about the pace and direction of the adaptation process.

Conversely, the model overemphasizes the conflict between natives and migrants as the definitive feature of the adaptation process. Where this conflict does warrant attention, the model does not distinguish the different forms of antagonism between native whites and the newcomers compared with that involving ethnic minorities like African Americans.

Nor can the adaptation of Indochinese refugees be primarily characterized as a struggle for occupational and income attainment, as suggested by the ethnic-resilience model. This emphasis neglects the noneconomic areas of adaptation related to the family and gender. Jobs also are more than incomes because workplace cultures can foster integration even when the work is poorly paid. Indeed, Indochinese refugees do not seek to maintain their ethnicity at all costs. Instead, they blend aspects of American culture that they find of value with elements of their native culture that they deem worth preserving.

Lastly, the formation of ethnic communities among Indochinese refugees is not solely a defensive move to ward off the hardships imposed by the larger society. Refugees' desire to maintain their ethnicity is one motive for community formation. But the resulting pluralism is very much influenced by local urban conditions. Cities vary in the opportunities they present for settlement and community formation, and thus pluralism is partly the result of changing social and economic conditions at the neighborhood level.

For Indochinese refugees, the most accurate description of the adaptation process is one that acknowledges the tension between integration and pluralism. Pluralism is a central theme in their experience in the United States because of the international context of migration and the transnational quality of communal institutions; collective rather than individual adaptation; and new urban diversity added to traditional racial conflict. But the adaptation process cannot be reduced to newcomers versus natives. The refugees contend among themselves for resources and authority; they combine traits from the homeland and host society, particularly in noneconomic areas of social life; and they form communities very much constrained by local urban conditions.

As the adaptation of refugees from Vietnam, Laos, and Cambodia makes apparent, adjustment to a new society involves a dynamic polarization between pluralism and integration. The refugees recognize the reality, even necessity, of difference and diversity in a society where conflict is more often the rule than cooperation. At the same time, they accept the inevitability, even desirability, of change and of becoming someone new.

Appendix A. Historical, Demographic, and Cultural Characteristics of Vietnam, Laos, and Cambodia*

	Vietnam	Laos	Cambodia
First kingdom	A.D. 938	A.D. 1707	ca. A.D. 100
Ethnic groups (%)	Vietnamese (85)	Lao (50)	Khmer (85)
	Chinese	Hmong	Chinese
	Montagnards	Mien	Vietnamese
	Cambodians	Lao Theung	Cham (Muslims)
		Tai Dam	
Religions	Buddhism	Buddhism	Buddhism
	Taoism	Animism	
	Confucianism		
	Christianity		
	Caodaism		
Population (1, 000s)	66, 200	4, 139	8, 246
Rural (%)	80	81	88
Capital	Hanoi	Vientiane	Phnom Penh

*Vietnam is officially known as the Socialist Republic of Vietnam. Laos is officially known as the Lao People's Democratic Republic.
Sources: Center for Applied Linguistics 1981; Europa Publications 1994; United Nations 1993

Appendix B. Demographic, Social, and Economic Characteristics of Vietnamese, Laotians, Cambodians, and Hmong in the United States, 1990 (in percent unless otherwise indicated)

	Total U.S. population	Vietnamese	Laotian	Cambodian	Hmong
DEMOGRAPHICS					
Number	248,709, 873	614,547	149,014	147,411	90,082
Female	51	47	48	52	49
Top four states	California (12)	California (46)	California (39)	California (46)	California (52)
	New York (7)	Texas (11)	Texas (6)	Massachusetts (10)	Minnesota (19)
	Texas (7)	Virginia (3)	Minnesota (4)	Washington (8)	Wisconsin (18)
	Florida (5)	Washington (3)	Washington (4)	Texas (4)	Colorado (1)
NATIVITY					
Foreign-born	8	80	79	81	65
Foreign-born now U.S. citizens	40	42	17	17	9
Median age foreign-born	37	30	26	26	22
Median age native-born	33	8	5	5	5
LANGUAGE					
Other than English	14	94	97	96	97
English spoken not "very well"	6	61	68	70	76
Linguistically isolated	3	42	52	55	60

	Total U.S. population	Vietnamese	Laotian	Cambodian	Hmong
FAMILY					
Type					
Married couple	80	72	82	69	82
Female-headed with children under 18 years	16	10	9	21	11
Households with other kin present	5	22	19	21	19
Number of children born per woman	2.1	2.7	3.6	3.5	6.2
Children under 18 years living with two parents	73	77	83	71	86
Families with three or more workers	13	21	19	21	7
EDUCATION					
Eighth grade and less	10	20	45	51	61
High school diploma	30	18	19	12	11
Bachelor's degree	13	13	4	4	3
EMPLOYMENT					
Occupation					
Operator, laborer	15	21	44	30	32
Service	13	15	15	18	20
Technical, sales	32	30	15	23	19
Managerial, professional	26	18	5	10	13
Self-employed	7	6	2	4	1
Unemployed	6	8	9	10	18
INCOME					
Household					
Median ($1,000s)	30.0	29.8	23.0	18.8	14.3
With public assistance	8	25	20	51	67
Family					
Per capita ($1,000s)	14.4	9.0	5.6	5.1	2.7
Below poverty level	10	24	32	42	62
HOUSING					
Owner-occupied	64	43	28	23	13
VETERANS U.S. ARMED FORCES					
Men (number)	Comparison not	5, 968	1, 057	650	1, 093
Women (number)	meaningful	634	76	51	63

Source: U.S. Department of Commerce 1993

Chronology

1627	French influence in Vietnam begins when a missionary adapts Vietnamese language to Roman alphabet.
1787	French military intervene in Vietnamese politics.
1820	First American, a sea captain, lands in Vietnam.
1861	French forces capture Saigon.
1863	French influence extends into Cambodia.
1887	France creates Union of Indochina.
1918	The Vietnamese people have first contact with American soldiers when the French government "loans" the U.S. Army Vietnamese workers (they are recruited from colony owing to a labor shortage in France during World War I).
1940	Japanese troops occupy Indochina during World War II.
1940s	First Indochinese arrive in the United States as immigrants.
1945	France seeks return of its colonies in Indochina.
1946	Start of First Indochina War (France against the Vietminh seeking independence).
1953	Cambodia and Laos gain independence.
1954	Vietnam gains independence and is partitioned into a Communist North and a pro-West South; the United States helps France evacuate 800,000 refugees from the North to the South.
1957	Beginning of Communist insurgency in South Vietnam.
1959	First American soldier killed in South Vietnam; Special Forces contact the Hmong and other highland groups in Laos.
1962	Large-scale deployment of American military advisors in South Vietnam.
1964	Naval skirmish off the coast of North Vietnam leads U.S. Congress to grant President Johnson military power to intervene in Southeast Asia.

1965   Arrival of American combat troops in South Vietnam signals beginning of the Second Indochina War.

1968   Number of American troops in South Vietnam peaks.

1970   Prince Sihanouk of Cambodia is deposed by pro-American general.

1973   Paris Peace Agreement ends American military involvement in South Vietnam.

1975   North Vietnamese Army captures Saigon; Khmer Rouge guerrillas capture Phnom Penh; Royalist government flees from Laos; 125,000 Vietnamese and 5,000 Cambodian refugees are transported to the United States.

1978   Vietnam invades Cambodia; Vietnamese persecution of ethnic Chinese starts exodus by sea, dubbed "the boat people" by the media.

1979   China invades Vietnam; number of boat people peak at 200,000 and refugee arrivals to Thailand by land peak at 180,000; fighting between Vietnam, Cambodia, and China diminishes, ending the Third Indochina War.

1980   More than 166,000 Indochinese refugees arrive in the United States, the peak year for their migration; U.S. Congress passes the Refugee Act of 1980, the first law to codify an apolitical definition of refugee and the responsibility of the federal government to assist refugee resettlement.

1984   Median household income of the Vietnamese who arrived in 1975 equals that of Americans.

1987   U.S. Congress passes Amerasian Homing Act, granting all Amerasians in Vietnam the right to emigrate to the United States.

1989   Gunman kills five and wounds 30 Cambodian and Vietnamese children in a Stockton, California, school yard.

1991   Indochinese refugee population in the United States passes 1 million.

Works Cited

AAP. 1990. "Vietnamese Congress in America Continues Push for Freedom." *Asian American Press*, 31 August.

———. 1992. "Asian Wins Landmark Foreign Accent Bias Case in Washington State." *Asian American Press*, 7 February.

ABCN. 1990. "The Sincere Sacrifice of Nguyen Kim Bang." *Asian Business and Community News* 8, no. 12:25–26.

———. 1992a. "World Conference of Free Vietnamese Appeals to World on Vietnam." *Asian Business and Community News* 10, no. 6:13–14.

———. 1992b. "Minnesota: Tempco Bias Case Goes to Trial." *Asian Business and Community News* 10, no. 3:13–14.

Abhay, Krisna, Anna M. Portz, and Ly K. Tran. 1991. *Leadership and Management: A Comparative Study of Mutual Assistance Associations*. Washington, D.C.: Indochina Resource Action Center.

ACVA. 1982. "Impacted Areas." Letter sent to the U.S. Department of Health and Human Services, 24 November 1982. New York: American Council of Voluntary Agencies.

Adler, Shelley R. 1991. "Sudden Unexpected Nocturnal Death Syndrome among Hmong Immigrants: Examining the Role of the 'Nightmare.'" *Journal of American Folklore* 104, no. 411:54–71.

Alba, Richard D. 1990. *Ethnic Identity: The Transformation of White America*. New Haven, Conn.: Yale University Press.

Aldrich, Howard E., and Roger Waldinger. 1990. "Ethnicity and Entrepreneurship." *Annual Review of Sociology* 16:111–35.

Allen, Rebecca, and Harry H. Hiller. 1985. "The Social Organization of Migration: An Analysis of the Uprooting and Flight of Vietnamese Refugees." *International Migration* 4:439–51.

Anderson, Dave. 1984. "Hmong Leaders Are Seeking to Prevent Opium Arrests." *Minneapolis Star and Tribune*, 20 April. *Newsbank*, Social Relations, microfiche 24, grids D2–3.

Angeloff, Sam. 1967. "As Ky Bolsters His Rule, an American 'Ark' Sealifts a Village." In *Nation Building in Vietnam*, edited by the Agency for International Development, 17–18. Washington, D.C.: Agency for International Development.

Arax, Mark. 1993. "The Child Brides of California." *Los Angeles Times*, 4 May. *Newsbank*, Social Relations, microfiche 41, grids B1–5.

Archdeacon, Thomas J. 1983. *Becoming American: An Ethnic History*. New York: Free Press.

Aronson, Leonard. 1973. "Uptown Doesn't Fit Plan." *Today*, 24 January.

Bach, Robert L., and Rita Carroll-Seguin. 1986. "Labor Force Participation, Household Composition and Sponsorship among Southeast Asian Refugees." *International Migration Review* 20, no. 2:381–404.

Baer, Florence E. 1982. "'Give Me . . . Your Huddled Masses': Anti-Vietnamese Refugee Lore and the 'Image of Limited Good.'" *Western Folklore* October, 275–91.

Baizerman, Michael, and Glenn Hendricks. 1988. *A Study of Southeast Asian Youth in the Twin Cities of Minneapolis and St. Paul, Minnesota*. Washington, D.C.: U.S. Office of Refugee Resettlement.

Banister, Judith. 1985. *The Population of Vietnam*. International Population Reports Series P-95, no. 77. Washington, D.C.: U.S. Department of Commerce.

Barnet, Richard. 1983. *The Alliance*. New York: Simon & Schuster.

Becker, Elizabeth. 1986. *When the War Was Over: Cambodia's Revolution and the Voices of Its People*. New York: Touchstone Books.

Benson, Janet E. 1990. "Households, Migration, and Community Context." *Urban Anthropology and Studies of Cultural Systems and World Economic Development* 19 (Spring–Summer):9–29.

Bernier, Linda. 1977. "The Vietnamese Strangers in a Strange Land." *Los Angeles Herald Examiner*, 19 August. *Newsbank*, Social Relations, microfiche 50, grids A12–14.

Bishop, Katherine. 1989a. "18th-Century Law Snares Vietnamese Fishermen." *New York Times*, 26 November.

———. 1989b. "USA's Culinary Rule: Hot Dogs Yes, Dogs No." *New York Times*, 5 October.

Blaufarb, Douglas. 1977. *The Counterinsurgency Era*. New York: Free Press.

Bliatout, Bruce T. 1993. "Hmong Death Customs: Traditional and Acculturated." In *Ethnic Variations in Dying, Death, and Grief: Diversity in Universality*, edited by Donald. P. Irish, Kathleen F. Lundquist, and Vivian J. Nelsen, 79–100. Washington, D.C.: Taylor & Francis.

Bonacich, Edna. 1972. "A Theory of Middleman Minorities." *American Sociological Review* 38, no. 5:583–94.

Bonacich, Edna, and John Modell. 1980. *The Economic Basis of Ethnic Solidarity: Small Business in the Japanese-American Community*. Berkeley: University of California Press.

Brune, Tom, and Eduardo Comacho. 1983. *Race and Poverty in Chicago*. Chicago: Community Renewal Society.

Bui, Diana. 1983. "The Indochinese Mutual Assistance Associations." In *Bridging Cultures: Southeast Asian Refugees in America*, edited by the Asian American Community Mental Health Training Center, 167–80. Los Angeles: Asian American Community Mental Health Training Center.

Cain, Bruce, and Roderick Kiewiet. 1986. "California's Coming Minority Majority." *Public Opinion*, February–March, 50–52.

Calkins, Royal, and Denice A. Rios. 1989. "Refugee Leader Fuels a Futile Dream." *Fresno Bee*, 23 July. *Newsbank*, Social Relations, microfiche 52, grids C3–8.

Caplan, Nathan, John K. Whitmore, and Marcella H. Choy. 1989. *The Boat People and Achievement in America: A Study of Family Life, Hard Work, and Cultural Values*. Ann Arbor: University of Michigan Press.

Cardinaux, Alfred L. 1959. "Commentary: Alfred L. Cardinaux on Father Harnett." In *Vietnam: The First Five Years*, edited by Richard Lindholm, 87–92. East Lansing: Michigan State University.

Carlos, Jess. 1984. "Argyle Strip Sees New Life." *Sunday Star*, 29 January.

Center for Applied Linguistics. 1981. *The People and Cultures of Cambodia, Laos, and Vietnam*. Washington, D.C.: Center for Applied Linguistics.

Chalmers, David M. 1981. *Hooded Americanism: The History of the Ku Klux Klan*. New York: Franklin Watts.

Chan, Sucheng, ed. 1994. *Hmong Means Free: Life in Laos and America*. Philadelphia: Temple University Press.

Chanda, Nayan. 1982. "Economic Changes in Laos, 1975–1980." In *Contemporary Laos: Studies in the Politics and Society of the Lao People's Democratic Republic*, edited by Martin Stuart-Fox, 116–28. St. Lucia: University of Queensland Press.

———. 1986. *Brother Enemy: The War after the War*. New York: Macmillan.

Chapelier, Georges, and Josyane Van Maderghem. 1971. "Plain of Jars, Social Change under Five Years of Pathet Lao Administration." *Asia Quarterly* 1:75, no. 1.

Chase, Richard A. 1990. *Minority Elders in Minnesota*. St. Paul: Wilder Research Center.

Chicago Local Community Fact Book: Chicago Metropolitan Area, 1960. 1963. Chicago: Chicago Community Inventory, University of Chicago.

Chicago Reader. 1977. "Reader's Digest of Neighborhood News." *Chicago Reader*, 21 October.

Chicago Tribune. 1989. "Dog-Eating Divides West Coast." *Chicago Tribune*, 9 October.

Clancy, John F. 1979. "Ill-Housed, Ill-Clothed and Grateful." *Philadelphia Inquirer*, 18 November. *Newsbank*, Social Relations, microfiche 67, grids B6–7.

Coakley, Tom. 1982. "Refugees Criticize Program." *Denver Post*, 16 May. *Newsbank*, Social Relations, microfiche 25, grids E14–F1.

Cutler, Irving. 1982. *Chicago: City at Mid-Continent*. Dubuque: Kendall/Hunt Publishing.

Deinard, Amos S., and Timothy Dunnigan. 1986. "Hmong Health Care: Reflections on a Six-Year Experience." *International Migration Review* 21, no. 3: 857–65.

De Meth, Jerry. 1976. "Things Getting Better in Uptown." *Sun Times*, 5 December.

Denver Post. 1985. "Stranger in a Strange Land." *Denver Post*, 27 January. *Newsbank*, Social Relations, microfiche 7, grids G6–10.

Desbarats, Jacqueline. 1985. "Indochinese Resettlement in the United States." *Annals of the Association of American Geographers* 75, no. 4:522–38.

Doerner, William R. 1985. "Asians: To America with Skills." *Time*, 8 July, 42–44.

D'Oro, Rachel, Dina Cowan, Nancy Chin, G. M. Bush, and Sophie Yarborough. 1994. "Families Mourn Loved Ones Lost to Violence." *Long Beach Press-Telegram*, 17 July.

Dunnigan, Timothy, Miles McNall, and Jeylan T. Mortimer. 1993. "The Problem of Metaphorical Nonequivalence in Cross-Cultural Survey Research: Comparing the Mental Health Statuses of Hmong Refugee and General Population Adolescents." *Journal of Cross-Cultural Psychology* 24, no. 3:344–65.

Dunwoody, Ellen. 1982. "Battering in Indochinese Refugee Families." *Response*, September–October, 1–2.

Europa Publications. 1994. *Europa World Year Book 1994.* London: Europa Publications.

Felsman, J. Kirk, Mark C. Johnson, Frederick T. L. Leong, and Irene C. Felsman. 1989. *Vietnamese Amerasians: Practical Implications of Current Research.* Washington, D.C.: U.S. Office of Refugee Resettlement.

Fitzgerald, Frances. 1973a. *Fire in the Lake: The Vietnamese and the Americans in Vietnam.* New York: Vintage Books.

———. 1973b. "The Struggle and the War: The Maze of Vietnamese Politics." In *Southeast Asia: The Politics of National Integration*, edited by John McAlister, Jr., 542–61. New York: Random House.

Franken, Mark. 1981. *Review of Fact Finding Mission to Texas Gulf Coast and Recommendations.* Unpublished Interoffice Memorandum. Washington, D.C.: U.S. Catholic Conference.

Freeman, James A. 1989. *Hearts of Sorrow: Vietnamese-American Lives.* Stanford, Calif.: Stanford University Press.

Fremstad, Lee. 1981. "Vietnam War May Live among Refugees in U.S." *Sacramento Bee*, 16 August. *Newsbank*, Social Relations, microfiche 48, grids A12–14.

Fuchs, Lawrence H. 1990. *The American Kaleidoscope: Race, Ethnicity, and the Civic Culture.* Hanover, N.H.: University Press of New England.

Gallup Poll. 1990. "Groups Not Wanted as Neighbors." In *The Gallup Poll: Public Opinion 1989*, 63–79. Wilmington, Del.: Scholarly Resources.

Gans, Herbert J. 1962. *The Urban Villagers: Group and Class in the Life of Italian-Americans.* New York: Free Press.

———. 1979. "Symbolic Ethnicity: The Future of Ethnic Groups in America." *Ethnic and Racial Studies* 2, no. 1:1–19.

Glazer, Nathan, and Daniel P. Moynihan. 1963. *Beyond the Melting Pot: The Negroes, Puerto Ricans, Jews, Italians, and Irish of New York City.* Cambridge, Mass.: MIT Press.

Gold, Steven J. 1989. "Differential Adjustment among New Immigrant Family Members." *Journal of Contemporary Ethnography* 17, no. 4:408–34.

———. 1992. *Refugee Communities: A Comparative Field Study.* Newbury Park, Calif.: Sage.

Gold, Steven J., and Nazli Kibria. 1993. "Vietnamese Refugees and Blocked Mobility." *Asian and Pacific Migration Journal* 2, no. 1:27–56.

Goldstein, Beth L. 1986. "Resolving Sexual Assault: Hmong and the American Legal System." In *The Hmong in Transition*, edited by Glenn L. Hendricks, Bruce T. Downing, and Amos S. Deinard, 135–43. New York: Center for Migration Studies.

———. 1989. "In Search of Survival: The Education and Integration of Hmong Refugee Girls." *Journal of Ethnic Studies* 16, no. 2: 1–27.

Goldstein, Ira, and William L. Yancey. 1988. "Neighborhood Disputes and Intergroup Tension Events in Philadelphia: 1986–1988." In *The State of Intergroup Harmony—1988*, edited by the Philadelphia Commission on Human Relations, 43–62. Philadelphia: Philadelphia Commission on Human Relations.

Gordon, Linda. 1987. "Southeast Asian Refugee Migration to the United States." In *Pacific Bridges: The New Immigration from Asia and the Pacific Islands,* edited by James T. Fawcett and Benjamin V. Carino, 153–74. Staten Island, N.Y.: Center for Migration Studies.

Gordon, Milton. 1964. *Assimilation in American Life: The Role of Race, Religion, and National Origins*. New York: Oxford University Press.

Gozdziak, Elzbieta. 1988. *Older Refugees in the United States: From Dignity to Despair*. Washington, D.C.: Refugee Policy Group.

Greenberg, Nikki F. 1985. "Starting Over." *Newsweek*, 15 April.

Haines, David W. 1980. "Mismatch in the Resettlement Process: The Vietnamese Family versus the American Housing Market." *Journal of Refugee Resettlement* 1, no. 1:15–19.

———. 1986. "Vietnamese Refugee Women in the U.S. Labor Force: Continuity or Change?" In *International Migration: The Female Experience*, edited by Rita J. Simon and Caroline B. Brettell, 62–75. Totowa, N.J.: Rowman and Allenheld.

———. 1988. "Kinship in Vietnamese Refugee Resettlement: A Review of the U.S. Experience." *Journal of Comparative Family Studies* 19, no. 1:1–17.

———. 1989. "Introduction." In *Refugees as Immigrants: Cambodians, Laotians, and Vietnamese in America*, edited by David W. Haines, 1–23. Totowa, N.J.: Rowman & Littlefield.

Haines, David W., ed. 1985. *Refugees in the United States: A Reference Book*. Westport, Conn.: Greenwood Press.

Haldane, David. 1989. "Dog: Two Refugees Face Trial." *Los Angeles Times*, 13 March. *Newsbank*, Social Relations, microfiche 17, grids A5–6.

Hammond, Ruth. 1989. "Rumors of War." *Twin Cities Reader*, 25–31 October.

———. 1993. "Lost in Translation: For Immigrants in Court, Bad Interpreters Rig the Jury." *Washington Post*, 24 October.

Hanners, David. 1982. "Klan Patrols Day for Viet Shrimpers." *Dallas Morning News*, 23 May. *Newsbank*, Social Relations, microfiche 25, grids A3–5.

Harles, John C. 1993. *Politics in the Lifeboat: Immigrants and the American Democratic Order*. Boulder, Colo.: Westview Press.

Hayslip, Le Ly, with Jay Wurts. 1989. *When Heaven and Earth Changed Places: A Vietnamese Woman's Journey from War to Peace*. New York: Doubleday.

Hein, Jeremy. 1992. *States and International Migrants: The Incorporation of Indochinese Refugees in the United States and France*. Boulder, Colo.: Westview Press.

———. 1993a. "International Migrants or Welfare Clients: The Selection of a Master Status for Indochinese Refugees by American Voluntary Agencies." *Journal of Sociology and Social Work* 20, no. 1:115–30.

———. 1993b. "Refugees, Immigrants, and the State." *Annual Review of Sociology* 19:43–59.

———. 1994. "From Migrant to Minority: Hmong Refugees and the Social Construction of Identity in the United States." *Sociological Inquiry* 64, no. 3: 281–306.

Henkin, Alan B., and Carole A. Singleton. 1992. "Looking Forward: Indochinese Refugee Expectations for Post-Resettlement Change." *International Review of Modern Sociology* 22 (Autumn):45–56.

Herring, George D. 1986. *America's Longest War*. New York: Knopf.

Hickey, Gerald C. 1964. *Village in Vietnam*. New Haven, Conn.: Yale University Press.

Hill, Sidney. 1985. "Vietnamese, Socialists a Volatile Mix." *San Jose Mercury News*, 26 May. *Newsbank*, Social Relations, microfiche 28, grids D4–5.

Hirschman, Charles. 1983. "America's Melting Pot Reconsidered." *Annual Review of Sociology* 9: 397–423.

Hoang, Mai. 1992. "Asian American Republicans in Houston." *Asian Business and Community News* 10, no. 8: 17.

Horton, Tom. 1981. "Trial Begins in Viet Suit against Texas Klan." *Baltimore Sun*, 12 May. *Newsbank*, Social Relations, microfiche 27, grids A14–15.

Hume, Ellen. 1985. "Vietnam's Legacy: Indochinese Adapt Quickly in U.S., Using Survival Skills." *Wall Street Journal*, 21 March.

IRAC. 1986. *Indochinese Community Leadership Convention*. Washington, D.C.: Indochinese Resource Action Center.

Institute for Asian Studies. 1988. *Thailand: A First Asylum Country for Indochinese Refugees*. Bangkok: Institute for Asian Studies, Chulalongkorn University.

Ivins, Molly. 1979a. "Killing Sharpens Texas Feud on Vietnamese Fishing." *New York Times*, 9 August.

———. 1979b. "Vietnamese and Chicanos Clashing in Denver Barrio." *New York Times*, 24 August.

Jackson, Karl D. 1989. "The Ideology of Total Revolution." In *Cambodia, 1975–1978: Rendezvous with Death*, edited by Karl D. Jackson, 37–78. Princeton, N.J.: Princeton University Press.

Jackson, Larry. 1969. "The Vietnamese Revolution and the Montagnards." *Asian Survey* 19, no. 5: 313–30.

Jacobson, Lester. 1975. "Uptown's Future Is Bright, Residents Say." *Uptown News*, 22 April.

Japanese American Citizens League. 1985. Documents on racially motivated anti-Asian incidents and events, 1981–1985. Personal communication with the author. San Francisco: Japanese American Citizens League.

Jasso, Guillermina, and Mark R. Rosenzweig. 1990. *The New Chosen People: Immigrants in the United States*. New York: Russell Sage Foundation.

Jensen, Leif I. 1988. "Patterns of Immigration and Public Assistance Utilization, 1970–1980." *International Migration Review* 23, no. 1:51–83.

Judicature. 1988. "The Changing Face of America: How Will Demographic Trends Affect the Courts?" *Judicature* 72, no. 2:125–33.

Jumper, Roy. 1957. "Mandarin Bureaucracy and Politics in South Vietnam." *Pacific Affairs* 30, no. 1:47–58.

Kalergis, Mary M. 1989. *Home of the Brave: Contemporary American Immigrants*. New York: E. P. Dutton.

Kane, Maury. 1987. "Hidden Pain of Refugees." *Stockton Record*, 1 February. *Newsbank*, Social Relations, microfiche 10, grids D6–7.

Karnow, Stanley. 1983. *Vietnam: A History*. New York: Penguin Books.

Kasarda, John. 1989. "Urban Industrial Transition and the Underclass." *Annals of the American Academy of Political and Social Science* 501:26–47.

Kaufman, Marc. 1984a. "Hmong Talk of Exodus from Phila." *Philadelphia Inquirer*, 7 September. *Newsbank*, Social Relations, microfiche 66, grids B9–10

———. 1984b. "U.S. Moves on Rights for Hmong." *Philadelphia Inquirer*, 8 September. *Newsbank*, Social Relations, microfiche 66, grid B11.

———. 1984c. "Anti-Asian Attacks Cited in Logan." *Philadelphia Inquirer*, 11 September. *Newsbank*, Social Relations, microfiche 63, grids B10–11.

———. 1984d. "At the Mercy of America." *Philadelphia Inquirer*, 21 October. *Newsbank*, Social Relations, microfiche 81, grids B13–14, C1–5.

Kelly, Gail P. 1977. *From Vietnam to America: A Chronicle of the Vietnamese Immigration to the United States*. Boulder, Colo.: Westview Press.

Khoa, Le Xuan, and Diana D. Bui. 1985. "Southeast Asian Mutual Assistance Associations: An Approach for Community Development." In *Southeast Asian Mental Health: Treatment, Prevention, Services, Training, and Research*, edited by T. C. Owan, 209–24. Washington, D.C.: National Institute of Mental Health.

Kiang, Peter N. 1990. "Southeast Asian Parent Empowerment: The Challenge of Changing Demographics in Lowell, Masschusetts." *Vietnam Generation* 2, no. 3:5–15.

Kibria, Nazli. 1989. "Patterns of Vietnamese Refugee Women's Wagework in the U.S." *Ethnic Groups* 7, no. 2:297–323.

———. 1990. "Power, Patriarchy, and Gender: Conflict in the Vietnamese Immigrant Community." *Gender and Society* 4, no. 1:9–24.

———. 1993. *Family Tightrope: The Changing Lives of Vietnamese Americans*. Princeton: Princeton University Press.

Kim, Young Y. 1989. "Personal, Social, and Economic Adaptation: 1975–1979 Arrivals in Illinois." In *Refugees as Immigrants: Cambodians, Laotians, and Vietnamese in America*, edited by D. W. Haines, 86–104. Totowa, N.J.: Rowman & Littlefield.

King, Wayne. 1982. "U.S. Vietnamese Rally for Resistance." *New York Times*, 3 June.

Kinnard, Douglas. 1977. *The War Managers*. Hanover, N.H.: University Press of New England.

Kinzer, Stephen. 1992. "Vietnamese, Easy Target, Fear Ouster by Germany." *New York Times*, 6 December.

Klein, Michael. 1990. "Hmong Protest in Support of Rebels." *Eau Claire Leader–Telegram*, 2 February.

Komer, Robert. 1986. *Bureaucracy at War*. Boulder, Colo.: Westview Press.

Kurtzman, Laura. 1990. "Cultural Clash Has Bittersweet End; Boy Will Stay Cripple." *San Jose Mercury News*, 21 December. *Newsbank*, Social Relations, microfiche 84, grid C10.

Kurtzman, Laura, and Ken McLaughlin. 1990. "Fiery, Fatal Promise." *San Jose Mercury News*, 21 November. *Newsbank*, Social Relations, microfiche 84, grid F1.

Lafont, Pierre-Bernard. 1982. "Buddhism in Contemporary Laos." In *Contemporary Laos: Studies in the Politics and Society of the Lao People's Democratic Republic*, edited by Martin Stuart-Fox, 148–62. St. Lucia: University of Queensland Press.

Lai, Eric. 1992. "Humanitarian Project in Communist Laos Sparks Protest." *Asian American Press*, 11 September.

Lamphere, Louise, ed. 1992. *Structuring Diversity: Ethnographic Perspectives on the New Immigration*. Chicago: University of Chicago Press.

Lane, Dale, and Dennis Rockstroh. 1987. "Vietnamese Protest of Hayden Speech at SJCC Heats Up." *San Jose Mercury News*, 3 June. *Newsbank*, Social Relations, microfiche 44, grids D2–3.

Lang, Perry, and Evelyn Hsu. 1982. "Troubled Hill at Hunters Point." *San Francisco Chronicle*, 2 July. *Newsbank*, Social Relations, microfiche 34, grids F6–7.

Lawyers Committee for Human Rights. 1989. *Refuge Denied: Problems of Vietnamese and Cambodians in Thailand and the Admission of Indochinese Refugees into the United States*. New York: Lawyers Committee for Human Rights.

Leader–Telegram. 1990. "Student Fearful after Racial Attack." *Eau Claire Leader–Telegram*, 14 May.

Ledgerwood, Judy. 1990. "Portrait of a Conflict: Exploring Changing Khmer-American Social and Political Relationships." *Journal of Refugee Studies* 3, no. 2: 135–54.

Lee, Gary Y. 1982. "Minority Policies and the Hmong." In *Contemporary Laos: Studies in the Politics and Society of the Lao People's Democratic Republic*, edited by Martin Stuart-Fox, 199–219. St. Lucia: University of Queensland Press.

Lemoine, Jacques, and Christine Mougne. 1983. "Why Has Death Stalked the Refugees?" *Natural History*, November, 6–19.

Lewis, Glenn. 1981. "Uneasy Peace Predicted as Shrimping Season Nears." *Houston Post*, 14 May. *Newsbank*, Social Relations, microfiche 31, grids G9–10.

Lewy, Guenter. 1978. *America in Vietnam*. New York: Oxford University Press.

Light, Ivan. 1972. *Ethnic Enterprise in America: Business and Welfare among Chinese, Japanese, and Blacks*. Berkeley: University of California Press.

Lindholm, Richard. 1959. "American Aid and Its Financial Impact." In *Vietnam: The First Five Years*, edited by Richard Lindholm, 317–23. East Lansing: Michigan State University.

Long, Lynellyn D. 1993. *Ban Vinai: The Refugee Camp*. New York: Columbia University Press.

Lovell, Madeline L., Thuango Tran, and Chi D. Nguyen. 1987. "Refugee Women: Lives in Transition." *International Social Work* 30:317–25.

Luong, Bui V. 1959. "The Role of Friendly Nations." In *Vietnam: The First Five Years*, edited by Richard Lindholm, 48–53. East Lansing: Michigan State University.

Luu, Van. 1989. "The Hardships of Escape for Vietnamese Women." In *Making Waves: An Anthology of Writings by and about Asian-American Women*, edited by Asian Women United of California, 60–72. Boston: Beacon Press.

Lyman, Thomas A. 1990. "Proverbs and Parables in Mong Njua (Green Miao)." *Zeitschrift des Deutschen Morgenländischen Gesellschaft* 140, no. 2:326–42.

Mangan, Andy. 1982. "Klansmen Find Waters Rough in Quest to Woo Fishermen." *Austin American-Statesman*, 11 June. *Newsbank*, Social Relations, microfiche 29, grids D4–5.

Marr, David. 1972. "The Rise and Fall of 'Counterinsurgency': 1961–1964." In *The Pentagon Papers (Senator Gravel Edition), Volume 5. Critical Essays*, edited by Noam Chomsky and Howard Zinn, 202–10. Boston: Beacon Press.

Massey, Douglas S. 1981. "Dimensions of the New Immigration to the United States and the Prospects for Assimilation." *Annual Review of Sociology* 7: 57–85.

Matsuoka, Jon K., and Donald H. Ryujin. 1989–90. "Vietnamese Refugees: An Analysis of Contemporary Adjustment Issues." *Journal of International Applied Social Sciences* 14, no. 1:23–45.

Maxwell, Neil. 1979. "U.S. Is Entering a Civil Rights Conflict in Texas Town That Involves Vietnamese." *Wall Street Journal*, 10 August.

Mayotte, Judy A. 1992. *Disposable People? The Plight of Refugees*. Maryknoll, N.Y.: Orbis Books.

McCoy, Alfred W. 1972. *The Politics of Heroin in Southeast Asia*. New York: Harper & Row.

McLaughlin, Ken, and Laura Kurtzman. 1990. "Bang Plagued by Personal and Political Woes." *San Jose Mercury News*, 22 November. *Newsbank*, Social Relations, microfiche 84, grids D13–14.

Miller, Merle. 1980. *Lyndon, an Oral Biography*. New York: G. P. Putnam.

Milloy, Ross. 1980. "Vietnam Fallout in a Texas Town." *New York Times Magazine*, 6 April.

Min, Pyong G. 1987. "Factors Contributing to Ethnic Business: A Comprehensive Synthesis." *International Journal of Comparative Sociology* 28, nos. 3–4:173–93.

Miner, Michael, and Sam Washington. 1971. "The Promise of Progress." *Chicago Sun Times*, 25 March.

Mitchell, Roger. 1987. "The Will to Believe and Anti-Refugee Rumors." *Midwestern Folklore* 13, no. 1:5–15.

Mortland, Carol A., and Judy Ledgerwood. 1987. "Refugee Resource Acquistion: The Invisible Communication System." In *Cross-Cultural Adaptation: Current Approaches*, edited by Young Y. Kim and William B. Gudykunst, 286–306. Newbury Park, Calif.: Sage.

Muir, Karen L. S. 1988. *The Strongest Part of the Family: A Study of Lao Refugee Women in Columbus, Ohio*. New York: AMS Press.

Munger, Ronald G. 1986. "Sleep Disturbances and Sudden Death of Hmong Refugees: A Report on Fieldwork Conducted in the Ban Vinai Refugee Camp." In *The Hmong in Transition*, edited by Glann L. Hendricks, Bruce T. Downing, and Amos S. Deinard, 379–98. New York: Center for Migration Studies.

Nee, Victor, and Jimy Sanders. 1985. "The Road to Parity: Determinants of the Socioeconomic Achievements of Asian Americans." *Ethnic and Racial Studies* 8, no. 1: 75–93.

New York Times. 1981. "Videotapes of Klan Leader Shown at Shrimper Hearing." *New York Times*, 13 May.

———. 1985. "Vietnamese Reviving a Chicago Slum." *New York Times*, 2 January.

———. 1986. "Vietnamese Group in Church Dispute." *New York Times*, 26 December.

———. 1989. "Of Citizens, and Poachers." *New York Times*, 5 October.

Ngo, Hai V. 1991. "Postwar Vietnam: Political Economy." In *Coming to Terms: Indochina, the United States, and the War*, edited by Douglas Allen and Ngo V. Long, 65–88. Boulder, Colo.: Westview Press.

Ngor, Haing, with Roger Warner. 1987. *A Cambodian Odyssey*. New York: Macmillan.

Nguyen, Duc Q. 1988. "California's Southeast Asians Enter the Political Arena." *Refugee Reports*, 9, no. 11:10–12.

Nguyen, Liem T., and Alan B. Henkin. 1982. "Vietnamese Refugees in the United States: Adaptation and Transitional Status." *Journal of Ethnic Studies* 9, no. 4:101–16.

Nguyen, Nga A., and Harold L. Williams. 1989. "Transition from East to West: Vietnamese Adolescents and Their Parents." *Journal of the American Academy of Child and Adolescent Psychiatry* 28, no. 4:505–15.

Nguyen, Van C. 1983. *Vietnam under Communism, 1975–1982*. Stanford, Calif.: Hoover Institution Press.

Nguyen, Van H. 1993. "Southeast Asian Refugee Resettlement in the United States: A Socioeconomic Analysis." In *American Mosaic: Selected Readings in America's Multicultural Heritage*, edited by Young I. Song and Eugene C. Kim, 215–36. Englewood Cliffs, N.J.: Prentice-Hall.

Nichols, J. Bruce. 1988. *The Uneasy Alliance: Religion, Refugee Work, and U.S. Foreign Policy*. New York: Oxford University Press.

Nordland, Rod. 1983. "Promised Land Is Eluding Many Southeast Asians Here." *Philadelphia Inquirer*, 28 March. *Newsbank*, Social Relations, microfiche 11, grids B14, C1–3.

O'Conner, Lily C. 1992. "Vietnamese Win Discrimination Case against DoD; Others May Have a Claim." *Asian Business and Community News* 10, no. 5:17.

Oliver, Myrna. 1988. "Immigrant Crimes: Cultural Defense—a Legal Tactic." *Los Angeles Times*, 15 July.

Olney, Douglas. 1986. "Population Trends." In *The Hmong in Transition*, edited by Glenn L. Hendricks, Bruce T. Downing, and Amos S. Deinard, 179–83. New York: Center for Migration Studies.

Osborne, Milton. 1980. "The Indochinese Refugees: Cause and Effects." *International Affairs* 56, no. 1:37–53.

Park, Robert E. 1950. *Race and Culture*. Glencoe, Ill.: Free Press.

———. 1967 [1914]. "Racial Assimilation in Secondary Groups." In *Robert E. Park on Social Control and Collective Behavior*, edited by Ralph H. Turner, 114–32. Chicago: University of Chicago Press.

Pentagon Papers (Senator Gravel Edition). 1971. *The Defense Department: History of U.S. Decision Making on Vietnam*. Boston: Beacon Press.

Perlmann, Joel. 1988. *Ethnic Differences: Schooling and Social Structure among the Irish, Italians, Jews and Blacks in an American City, 1880–1935*. New York: Cambridge University Press.

Peters, Heather A. 1988. *A Study of Southeast Asian Youth in Philadelphia: A Final Report*. Washington, D.C.: U.S. Office of Refugee Resettlement.

Pfeffer, Max J. 1994. "Low-Wage Employment and Ghetto Poverty: A Comparison of African-American and Cambodian Day-Haul Farm Workers in Philadelphia." *Social Problems* 41, no. 1:9–29.

Philadelphia Commission on Human Relations. n.d. *Asians and Their Neighbors: A Public Investigatory Hearing*. Philadelphia: Philadelphia Commission on Human Relations.

Ponchaud, François. 1989. "Social Change in the Vortex of Revolution." In *Cambodia, 1975–1978: Rendezvous with Death*, edited by Karl D. Jackson, 151–78. Princeton, N.J.: Princeton University Press.

Portes, Alejandro. 1984. "The Rise of Ethnicity: Determinants of Ethnic Perceptions among Cuban Exiles in Miami." *American Sociological Review* 49, no. 3:383–97.

———. 1990. "From South of the Border: Hispanic Minorities in the United States." In *Immigration Reconsidered*, edited by Virginia Yans-McLaughlin, 160–86. New York: Oxford University Press.

Portes, Alejandro, and Robert L. Bach. 1985. *Latin Journey: Cuban and Mexican Immigrants in the United States*. Berkeley: University of California Press.

Portes, Alejandro, and Robert D. Manning. 1986. "The Immigrant Enclave: Theory and Empirical Examples." In *Competitive Ethnic Relations*, edited by Susan Olzak and Joanne Nagel, 47–68. Orlando, Fla.: Academic Press.

Portes, Alejandro, and Rubén G. Rumbaut. 1990. *Immigrant America: A Portrait*. Berkeley: University of California Press.

Pulaski, Alex, and Anne Dudley. 1992. "Would Ban on Animal Killings Infringe on Religious Beliefs?" *Fresno Bee*, 1 April. *Newsbank*, Social Relations, microfiche 36, grids E14–F1.

Ragas, Wade R. 1980. "Housing the Refugees: Impact and Partial Solutions to the Housing Shortages." *Journal of Refugee Resettlement* 1, no. 1:40–48.

Refugee Reports. 1986a. "Statistical Issue." *Refugee Reports* 7, no. 12:3–14.

———. 1986b. "Refugees Learn to Flex Political Muscle." *Refugee Reports* 7, no. 11:1–7.

———. 1986c. "Refugees Help Rebuild Chicago Neighborhood." *Refugee Reports* 7, no. 5:8–10.

———. 1987. "Elderly Southeast Asian Refugees: Still Strangers in a Strange Land." *Refugee Reports* 8, no.5:1–9.

———. 1988. "Cambodia: Peace at Last or the Return of Pol Pot." *Refugee Reports* 9, no. 7:1–8.

———. 1989. "Update." *Refugee Reports* 10, no. 2:11.

———. 1993a. "Statistical Issue." *Refugee Reports* 14, no. 12:5–13.

———. 1993b. "121,000 Refugee Admissions Planed for FY 94: Administration Concedes Its Plan Is 'Not Bold.'" *Refugee Reports* 14, no. 9:1–8.

———. 1994. "CANDO: Volunteers from U.S. Help Cambodians Shape New Future." *Refugee Reports* 15, no. 5:12–14.

Reider, Jonathan. 1985. *Canarsie: The Jews and Italians of Brooklyn against Liberalism*. Cambridge: Harvard University Press.

Reinhold, Robert. 1989. "After Shooting, Horror but Few Answers." *New York Times*, 19 January.

Rick, Kathryn, and John Forward. 1992. "Acculturation and Perceived Intergenerational Differences among Hmong Youth." *Journal of Cross-Cultural Psychology* 23, no. 1:85–94.

Roberts, Alden E. 1988. "Racism Sent and Received: Americans and Vietnamese View One Another." In *Race and Ethnic Relations*, vol. 5, edited by C. Marret and C. Leggon, 75–97. Greenwich, Conn.: JAI Press.

Rockstroh, Dennis. 1987a. "From San Jose, They Plot Vietnam's Rebirth." *San Jose Mercury News*, 7 April. *Newsbank*, Social Relations, microfiche 34, grids C4–5.

———. 1987b. "Viets Ordered from Church." *San Jose Mercury News*, 6 March. *Newsbank*, Social Relations, microfiche 29, grids F7–8.

Rogge, J. R., 1985. "The Indo-Chinese Dispora: Where Have All the Refugees Gone?" *The Canadian Geographer* 29, no. 1:65–72.

Rolnick, Sharon. 1990. "Reducing Teenage Childbearing in the Hmong Community: First Year Results." *Vietnam Generation* 2, no. 3:53–61.

Roper Report. 1982. "Immigrant Group Has Been a Good/Bad Thing for the Country." *Roper Report* 82–84. Storrs, Conn.: Roper Center for Public Opinion, University of Connecticut.

Rose, Peter I., ed. 1993. "Interminority Affairs in the U.S.: Pluralism at the Crossroads." *Annals of the American Academy of Political and Social Science* 530 (complete issue).

Ruefle, William, William H. Ross, and Diane Mandell. 1992. "Attitudes toward Southeast Asian Immigrants in a Wisconsin Community." *International Migration Review* 26, no. 3:877–98.

Ruiz, Hiram A. 1993. "The Montagnards: A Resettlement Challenge." *Refugee Reports* 14, no. 9:12–13.

Rumbaut, Rubén G. 1989. "The Structure of Refuge: Southeast Asian Refugees in the United States, 1975–1985." *International Review of Comparative Public Policy* 1:97–129.

Rumbaut, Rubén G., and Kenji Ima. 1988. *The Adaptation of Southeast Asian Refugee Youth: A Comparative Study*. Washington, D.C.: U.S. Office of Refugee Resettlement.

Rutledge, Paul J. 1990. "Boon Vongsurith." *Journal of Refugee Studies* 3, no. 4: 365–69.

St. Paul Pioneer Press. 1993a. "Wausau Vote Is Deplored by Teachers." *St. Paul Pioneer Press*, 17 December.

———. 1993b. "Woman Fined for Housing Bias against Hmong." *St. Paul Pioneer Press*, 25 February.

Salisbury, Ann. 1976. "U.S. Is Not What They Expected." *Los Angeles Herald Examiner*, 24 May. *Newsbank*, Social Relations, microfiche 26, grids D6–7.

Sanders, Jimy, and Victor Nee. 1987. "Limits of Ethnic Solidarity in the Enclave Economy." *American Sociological Review* 52, no. 6:745–73.

Schell, Jonathan. 1988. *The Real War: The Classic Reporting of the Vietnam War*. New York: Pantheon Books.

Schmickle, Sharon. 1983. "Officials Grapple with Folk Use of Opium by Hmongs [*sic*] in State." *Minneapolis Star and Tribune*, 23 August. *Newsbank*, Social Relations, microfiche 39, grid G11.

Scott, George M., Jr. 1988. "To Catch or Not to Catch a Thief: A Case of Bride Theft among the Lao Hmong Refugees in Southern California." *Ethnic Groups* 7, no. 2:137–51.

———. 1990. "Hmong Aspirations for a Separatist State in Laos: The Effects of the Indo-China War." In *Secessionist Movements in Comparative Perspective*, edited by Ralph R. Premdas, S. W. R. de A. Samarasinghe, and Alan B. Anderson, 111–25. New York: St. Martin's Press.

Sege, Irene. 1993. "Suicide or Sacrifice." *Boston Globe*, 15 July. *Newsbank*, Social Relations, microfiche 61, grids B8–13.

Shawcross, William. 1977. *Side-Show: Kissinger, Nixon and the Destruction of Cambodia*. New York: Pocket Books.

Sherman, Spencer. 1986. "When Cultures Collide." *California Lawyer* 6 (January):32–36.

Sheybani, Malek-Mithra. 1987. "Cultural Defense: One Person's Culture Is Another's Crime." *Loyola of Los Angeles International and Comparative Law Annual* 9 (Summer):751–83.

Silvers, Amy R. 1992. "Culture Clash: Hmong Duel Stuns Two Worlds." *Milwaukee Journal*, 14 February. *Newsbank*, Social Relations, microfiche 8, grids B7–8.

Simon, Rita J. 1983. "Refugee Families' Adjustment and Aspirations: A Comparison of Soviet Jewish and Vietnamese Immigrants." *Ethnic and Racial Studies* 6, no. 4: 492–504.

———. 1986. "Refugee Women and Their Daughters: A Comparison of Soviet, Vietnamese, and Native-Born American Families." In *Refugee Mental Health in Resettlement Countries*, edited by Carolyn L. Williams and Joseph Westermeyer, 157–72. Washington, D.C.: Hemisphere Publishing.

Sleeper, Jim. 1990. *The Closest of Strangers: Liberalism and the Politics of Race in New York*. New York: W. W. Norton.

Solovitch, Sara. 1984. "Outbursts Mark Hearing on Asians." *Philadelphia Inquirer*, 28 October. *Newsbank*, Social Relations, microfiche 81, grid C6.

Southern Poverty Law Center. 1981a. "The Klan Attacks Immigrant Fishermen in Galvaston Bay." *Klanwatch Intelligence Report*, May.

———. 1981b. "Judge Orders End to Klan Harassment of Vietnamese in Texas." *Klanwatch Intelligence Report*, June.

Stark, Dorothy. 1972. "Residents Want Their Pride Back." *Today*, 2 April.

Starr, Paul D. 1981. "Troubled Waters: Vietnamese Fisherfolk on America's Gulf Coast." *International Migration Review* 15, no. 1:226–38.

Starr, Paul D., and Alden E. Roberts. 1981. "Attitudes toward Indochinese Refugees." *Journal of Refugee Resettlement* 1, no. 4:51–66.

———. 1982. "Attitudes Toward New Americans: Perceptions of Indo-Chinese in Nine Cities." In *Research in Race and Ethnic Relations*, vol. 3, edited by C. Marret and C. Leggon, 165–86. Greenwich, Conn.: JAI Press.

Stein, Barry N. 1979. "Occupational Adjustment of Refugees: The Vietnamese in the United States." *International Migration Review* 13, no. 1:25–45.

Steinberg, Jim. 1989. "Political Violence Spotlights Fresno Vietnamese." *Fresno Bee*, 27 August. *Newsbank*, Social Relations, microfiche 79, grids D14, E1.

Steinberg, Stephen. 1989. *The Ethnic Myth: Race, Ethnicity, and Class in America*. Boston: Beacon Press.

Story, Mary, and Linda J. Harris. 1988. "Food Preferences, Beliefs, and Practices of Southeast Asian Refugee Adolescents." *Journal of School Health* 58, no. 7:273–76.

———. 1989. "Food Habits and Dietary Change of Southeast Asian Refugee Families Living in the United States." *Journal of the American Dietetic Association* 89, no. 6:800–803.

Strand, Paul J. 1984. "Employment Predictors among Indochinese Refugees." *International Migration Review* 28, no. 1:50–64.

Strand, Paul J., and Woodrow Jones, Jr. 1985. *Indochinese Refugees in America: Problems of Adaptation and Assimilation*. Durham, N.C.: Duke University Press.

Sullivan, Marianna. 1978. *France's Vietnam Policy: A Study of French-American Relations*. Westport, Conn.: Greenview Press.

Sutter, Valerie O. 1990. *The Indochinese Refugee Dilemma*. Baton Rouge: Louisiana State University Press.

Sutton, William W., Martha Woodall, and Edward Colimore. 1984. "Council: No Probe of Attacks." *Philadelphia Inquirer*, 4 September. *Newsbank*, Social Relations, microfiche 63, grid B12.

Sweeney, Paul. 1982. "Tolerance in a Texas Town." *Texas Observer*, 17 September.

Taft, Julia, David North, and David Ford. 1980. *Refugee Resettlement in the U.S.* Washington, D.C.: New Transcentury Foundation.

Takaki, Ronald. 1993. *A Different Mirror: A History of Multicultural America*. Boston: Little, Brown.

Tang, John, and Thomas P. O'Brien. 1990. "Correlates of Vocational Success in Refugee Work Adaptation." *Journal of Applied Social Psychology* 20, no. 17: 1444–52.

Tenhula, John. 1991. *Voices from Southeast Asia: The Refugee Experience in the United States*. New York: Holmes & Meier.

Thomas, W. I., and Florian Znaniecki. 1927. *The Polish Peasant in Europe and America*, vols. 3–5. New York: Alfred A. Knopf.

Tien, Liang, and Denny Hunthausen. 1990. "The Vietnamese Amerasian Resettlement Experience: From Initial Application to the First Six Months in the United States." *Vietnam Generation* 2, no. 3:16–30.

Tilly, Charles. 1990. "Transplanted Networks." In *Immigration Reconsidered*, edited by Virginia Yans-McLaughlin, 79–95. New York: Oxford University Press.

Tobin, Joseph J., and Joan Friedman. 1983. "Spirits, Shamans, and Nightmare Death: Survivor Stress in a Hmong Refugee." *American Journal of Orthopsychiatry* 53, no. 3:439–48.

Tollefson, James W. 1989. *Alien Winds: The Reeducation of America's Indochinese Refugees*. New York: Praeger.

Tran, Thanh V. 1988. "Sex Differences in English Language Acculturation and Learning Strategies among Adults Aged 40 and over in the United States." *Sex Roles* 19, nos. 11–12:747–58.

———. 1990. "Language Acculturation among Older Vietnamese Refugee Adults." *Gerontologist* 30, no. 1:94–99.

———. 1992. "Adjustment among Different Age and Ethnic Groups of Indochinese in the United States." *Gerontologist* 32, no. 4:508–18.

United Nations. 1993. *Statistical Yearbook: Thirty-Eighth Issue*. New York: United Nations.

U.S. Catholic Conference. 1985. *In Our Fathers' Land: Vietnamese Amerasians in the United States*. Washington, D.C.: U.S. Catholic Conference.

U.S. Commission on Civil Rights. 1987. *Recent Activities against Citizens and Residents of Asian Descent*. Washington, D.C.: U.S. Commission on Civil Rights.

———. 1990. *Civil Rights Issues Facing Asian Americans in the 1990s*. Washington, D.C.: U.S. Commission on Civil Rights.

U.S. Committee for Refugees. 1988. *World Refugee Survey*. Washington, D.C.: U.S. Committee for Refugees.

———. 1993. *World Refugee Survey*. Washington, D.C.: U.S. Committee for Refugees.

U.S. Community Relations Service. 1985–90. *Summary Table 5.A. Special Interest New Alerts*. Personal communication with the author. Washington, D.C.: U.S. Department of Justice.

U.S. Department of Commerce. 1980a. *1980 Census of Population. Texas. General Social and Economic Characteristics*. Washington, D.C.: U.S. Department of Commerce.

———. 1980b. *1980 Census of Population and Housing. Census Tracts for Philadelphia SMSA*. Washington, D.C.: U.S. Department of Commerce.

———. 1991. "Race and Hispanic Origin." *1990 Census Profile No. 2*. Washington, D.C.: U.S. Department of Commerce.

———. 1993. *1990 Census of Population: Asians and Pacific Islanders in the United States*. Washington, D.C.: U.S. Department of Commerce.

U.S. Department of Health and Human Services (DHHS). 1983. "Refugee Resettlement Program: Placement Policy." *Federal Register* 239 (12 December):55,300–302.

U.S. Department of State. 1954. "Evacuating Refugees from North Viet-Nam." *Department of State Bulletin* 790:241.

———. 1955. "Exodus: Report on a Voluntary Mass Flight to Freedom Viet-Nam, 1954." *Department of State Bulletin* 815:222–29.

———. 1982a. *Foreign Relations of the United States, 1952–1954*. Vol. 13, *Indochina*. Washington, D.C.: U.S. Department of State.

———. 1982b. *Foreign Relations of the United States, 1955–1957*. Vol. 1, *Vietnam*. Washington, D.C.: U.S. Department of State.

U.S. General Accounting Office (GAO). 1983. *Greater Emphasis on Early Employment and Better Monitoring Needed in Refugee Resettlement Program.* Washington, D.C.: U.S. General Accounting Office.

U.S. Operations Mission to Vietnam. 1962. *Annual Report.* Saigon: U.S. Operations Mission to Vietnam.

U.S. Office of Refugee Resettlement (ORR). 1984, 1987, 1988, 1989, 1991, 1992, 1993. *Report to the Congress: Refugee Resettlement Program* [annual report]. Washington, D.C.: U.S. Office of Refugee Resettlement.

U.S. Senate. 1965. *Refugee Problems in South Vietnam and Laos.* Judiciary Subcommittee to Investigate Problems Concerning Refugees and Escapees. 13 July–30 September.

———. 1967. *Civilian Casualty, Social Welfare, and Refugee Problems in South Vietnam.* Judiciary Subcommittee to Investigate Problems Concerning Refugees and Escapees. 10 May–16 October.

———. 1968. *Refugee and Civilian War Casualty Problems in South Vietnam.* Judiciary Subcommittee to Investigate Problems Concerning Refugees and Escapees. 9 May.

———. 1969. *Civilian Casualty, Social Welfare, and Refugee Problems in South Vietnam. Part II.* Judiciary Subcommittee to Investigate Problems concerning Refugees and Escapees. 24 and 25 June.

———. 1970a. *Refugee and Civilian War Casualty Problems in Indochina: A Staff Report.* Judiciary Subcommittee to Investigate Problems concerning Refugees and Escapees. 28 September.

———. 1970b. *Refugee and Civilian War Casualty Problems in Laos and Cambodia.* Judiciary Subcommittee to Investigate Problems concerning Refugees and Escapees. May.

———. 1972a. *Problems of War Victims in Indochina.* Judiciary Subcommittee to Investigate Problems concerning Refugees and Escapees. 8 May.

———. 1972b. *War Victims in Indochina: Reports Prepared for the Subcommittee to Investigate Problems concerning Refugees and Escapees by the General Accounting Office.* Judiciary Subcommittee to Investigate Problems concerning Refugees and Escapees. 23 May.

———. 1973a. *Relief and Rehabilitation of War Victims in Indochina. Part I: Crisis in Cambodia.* Judiciary Subcommittee to Investigate Problems concerning Refugees and Escapees. April.

———. 1973b. *Relief and Rehabilitation of War Victims in Indochina. Part III: North Vietnam and Laos.* Judiciary Subcommittee to Investigate Problems concerning Refugees and Escapees. 31 July.

———. 1984. *Vietnamese Currency Transfer Legislation.* Subcommittee on Financial Institutions, Committee on Banking, Housing, and Urban Affairs. 20 June.

Van Praag, Nicholas. 1985. "Refugee Fishermen on the Gulf Coast." *Refugees* December, 13–15.

Vega, William A., and Rubén G. Rumbaut. 1991. "Ethnic Minorities and Mental Health." *Annual Review of Sociology* 17:351–83.

Wain, Barry. 1981. *The Refused: The Agony of the Indochina Refugees.* New York: Simon & Schuster.

Waldinger, Roger. 1992. "Immigration and Urban Change." *Annual Review of Sociology* 15:211–32.

Waldron, Candace. 1987. *Health Issues for Cambodian Women: Needs Assessment Summary*. Boston: Massachusetts Department of Public Health.

Walter, Ingrid. 1981. "One Year after Arrival: The Adjustment of Indochinese Women in the United States (1979–1980)." *International Migration* 1–2:129–52.

Washburn, Gary. 1973. "Uptown Seen as Possible Extension of Newtown." *Chicago Tribune*, 17 June.

Waters, Mary. 1990. *Ethnic Options: Choosing Identities in America*. Berkeley: University of California Press.

Welaratna, Usha. 1993. *Beyond the Killing Fields: Voices of Nine Cambodian Survivors in America*. Stanford, Calif.: Stanford University Press.

Westermeyer, Joseph. 1982. *Poppies, Pipes, and People: Opium and Its Use in Laos*. Berkeley: University of California Press.

Wiesner, Louis A. 1988. *Victims and Survivors: Displaced Persons and Other War Victims in Viet-Nam, 1954–1975*. New York: Greenwood Press.

Wilkinson, Tracy, and David Reyes. 1989. "Shooting of Writer Underscores Tensions among Vietnamese in the U.S." *Los Angeles Times*, 27 August. *Newsbank*, Social Relations, microfiche 63, grids C9–11.

Wilson, Kenneth, and W. Allen Martin. 1982. "Ethnic Enclaves: A Comparison of the Cuban and Black Economies in Miami." *American Journal of Sociology* 87, no. 1:135–60.

Wilson, Kenneth, and Alejandro Portes. 1980. "Immigrant Enclaves: An Analysis of the Labor Market Experiences of Cubans in Miami." *American Journal of Sociology* 86, no. 2:295–319.

Wilson, Terry. 1988. "Judge Tells Tribesmen to Study U.S." *Chicago Tribune*, 30 June.

Wilson, William J. 1987. *The Truly Disadvantaged: The Inner City, the Underclass, and Public Policy*. Chicago: University of Chicago Press.

Wilstach, Nancy. 1976. "One Year Later: Culture Shock, Loneliness." *Montgomery Advertiser*, 25 April. *Newsbank*, Social Relations, microfiche 17, grids E10–11.

Wines, Michael. 1990. "French Said to Spy on U.S. Computer Companies." *New York Times*, 18 November.

Wurfel, David. 1967. "The Saigon Political Elite: Focus on Four Cabinets." *Asian Survey* 17, no. 8:527–39.

Yang, Mao. 1990. "The Education of Hmong Women." *Vietnam Generation* 2, no. 3:62–87.

Ziner, Karen L. 1990. "Judge Rules Autopsy on Hmong Violated 1st Amendment Rights." *Providence Journal-Bulletin*, 13 January. *Newsbank*, Social Relations, microfiche 1, grid B4.

———. 1993. "A Prayer for Democracy, Peace." *Providence Journal-Bulletin*, 22 May. *Newsbank*, Social Relations, microfiche 41, grids A13–14.

Zolberg, Aristide R., Astri Suhrke, and Sergio Aguayo. 1989. *Escape from Violence: Conflict and the Refugee Crisis in the Developing World*. New York: Oxford University Press.

Bibliographic Essay

The literature on Indochinese refugees is not as developed as one would expect given their length of time in the United States and the considerable public and governmental interest in their migration and adaptation. Most research is on the Vietnamese. There is a growing literature on the Hmong but very little on Cambodians and even less on Laotians. There are more statistical analyses of refugee employment rates and public assistance use than any other form of research.

The most current research on Indochinese refugees can often be found in the journals *International Migration Review* and *Journal of Refugee Studies*. The *Social Science Index* is the most accessible reference work for locating journal articles on the Indochinese and other refugees. Two institutes have taken the lead in collecting published material on Indochinese refugees: the Southeast Asian Refugee Studies Project at the University of Minnesota (Minneapolis) and the Southeast Asian Resource Action Center (Washington, D.C.).

Scholarly publications lag at least a year or more behind current developments—a particular problem in the case of the ever-changing situation for refugees. *Refugee Reports* is a monthly newsletter published by the U.S. Committee for Refugees (Washington, D.C.). It covers the latest international and domestic events involving refugees and is especially valuable for its statistical information and policy analysis. *Newsbank* is a microfiche collection of articles from more than 500 local newspapers in which one can locate the most current news stories on Vietnamese, Laotians, Hmong, and Cambodians in the United States, particularly articles on cultural events and community relations.

Two annual reports issued by the federal government are highly informative and can be easily ordered. The U.S. Office of Refugee Resettlement publishes *Report to the Congress: Refugee Resettlement Program*. It covers policy developments and provides statistics on refugee arrivals as well as basic information on their adaptation, such as state of residence, employment, and public assistance use. The U.S. Bureau for Refugee Programs publishes *World Refugee Report*, a country-by-country summary of refugee flight, temporary asylum, and permanent resettlement throughout the globe.

A complete understanding of Indochinese refugees must begin with the conditions that led to their flight. The Vietnam War and related U.S. military intervention in Cambodia and Laos has generated a huge literature. Beginning readers will find Karnow (1983) both comprehensive and accessible. Wiesner

(1988) provides specific coverage of the refugees created during the war. On conditions following the collapse of pro-American governments in 1975, see Becker (1986) for Cambodia, Nguyen (1983) for Vietnam, and the chapters in *Contemporary Laos* (see the citation under Chanda [1982]) for Laos.

Two memoirs covering this period are particularly good at conveying the lived events for those who were not there. Ngor (1987) portrays the destruction of Cambodian society and culture under the Khmer Rouge, as do the oral histories in Welaratna (1993). Hayslip (1989) describes her life in both rural and urban South Vietnam during the war, as well as her marriage to an American soldier. The culture and wartime experiences of the Hmong in Laos are available in a collection of oral histories recorded by friends and relatives of the Hmong who relate their stories (Chan 1994).

The dramatic flight from Vietnam, Laos, and Cambodia during the late 1970s and early 1980s is captured by Wain (1981), while a more scholarly examination of the refugee crisis in the region can be found in Sutter (1990). Conditions for the refugees while waiting in Southeast Asia for resettlement or repatriation is covered by Long (1993), Nichols (1988), and Tollefson (1989). A survey of the literature on refugees in general is presented by Hein (1993b).

The adaptation of Indochinese refugees in the United States is a very complex topic owing to the multiple dimensions of adjustment (e.g., work and family) and group differences (e.g., the Vietnamese compared with the Hmong). Fortunately, there is an increasing number of oral histories from Indochinese refugees concerning their lives in the United States. These should be consulted before reading the scholarly literature on the topic, particularly by those lacking firsthand contact with the people they wish to learn about. Tenhula (1991) provides coverage of all the refugee groups from Southeast Asia in their own words. A linked series of oral histories by Vietnamese refugees describing their war experiences, flight, and resettlement in the United States is available from Freeman (1989). The hardship of resettlement for Cambodians and the Hmong can also be gleaned from Welaratna (1993) and Chan (1994). Although specifically about politics, the interview data presented by Harles (1993) reveals much about the Laotian refugees' perceptions of the United States in contrast to their homeland.

With respect to the literature produced by social scientists, a useful starting point is the reference work by Haines (1985). The arrival and initial adaptation of the first-wave Vietnamese is best documented by Kelly (1977). The refugees' settlement patterns and internal migration within the United States is analyzed by Desbarats (1985). With respect to the refugees' employment and earnings, the major works are Bach and Carroll-Seguin (1986); Caplan et al. (1989); and Strand and Jones (1985). Rumbaut (1989) examines the effect of special assistance programs for refugees on their employment and use of public assistance. More attention is now being paid to the family and kinship (Haines 1988; Simon 1986), gender roles (Kibria 1993; Muir 1988), and community formation (Gold 1992). See Hein (1992) for an analysis of U.S. resettlement policy, its difference from that in France, and its impact on the refugees' social networks and communities. Ruefle et al. (1992), Roberts (1988), and Starr and Roberts (1982) analyze Americans' views of the refugees. Although relying exclusively on statistical analyses, the anthology by Haines (1989) is the single best coverage of Indochinese refugee adaptation in the United States.

Index

Domino effect, and foreign policy, 12
D'Oro, Rachel, 70
Dudley, Anne, 110
Duke, David, 78
Dulles, John Foster, 12
Dunnigan, Timothy, 9, 107
Dunwoody, Ellen, 119

Eastern European refugees, 13
Economic factors: adaptation process and, 8; Asian businesses in Chicago's Uptown neighborhood and, 54, 58, 67; competition with Indochinese refugees and, 69, 90; employment opportunities for Indochinese refugees and, 135, 142; ethnic enclave thesis and, 5; exploitation among ethnic communities and, 8; fishing vessels and Texas Gulf Coast incidents and, 75–76, 77–79; French colonial period in Southeast Asia and, 11; Korean immigrant businesses and, 82–83; as motive for migration from homeland, 37–38, 41; mutual assistance associations (MAAs) and, 94, 95; postwar conditions in South Vietnam and, 26; women refugees and, 118
Economic Opportunity Act of 1964, 17
Education: Amerasian youths and, 124; antirefugee attitudes related to, 73; assimilation model and, 7; early marriage and, 126; emphasis in refugee families on, 122, 127; Hmong youths and, 124; Indochinese refugees in Philadelphia and, 88–90; job training programs and, 138–49; mothers' level of education and work experience and, 127; refugee political participation regarding, 104
Eisenhower, Dwight D., 13, 15, 19
Elections, refugee participation in, 105
Employment, 134–51; adjustment patterns by months of residence and, 137–38; antirefugee attitudes and, 73, 74, 91; comparison of previous and current occupations in, 138, 139; conflicts in marriage over, 120; cultural factors affecting, 134, 150; discrimination in, 92, 105–6; English proficiency and, 137–38;

ethnic-resilience model and, 8, 134, 150, 154; expectations of youths regarding, 124, 126; Indochinese refugees in Philadelphia and, 69, 81–87, 88, 91; levels of urbanization and economic modernization affecting, 138–40; mutual assistance associations (MAAs) and, 95, 146, 149; resettlement after Thai camps and expectation of refugees regarding, 43–44; sponsoring agency and, 76; women refugees and, 118–19, 140–41
English proficiency, and employment, 137–38
Equal Employment Opportunity Commission, 105
Ethnic Chinese refugees: fictive kinship among, 132; mutual assistance associations (MAAs) for, 54; in Vietnam, 27, 35, 48, 58
Ethnic enclave thesis, 5
Ethnicity: adaptation and, 4; assimilation model and, 4; ethnic-resilience model and concept of, 8–9; refugees' desire to maintain, 154; U.S. culture and influence of, 7
Ethnic minorities: assimilation model and urban presence of, 50–51. *See also specific groups*
Ethnic-resilience model: collective dimension of adaptation and, 7, 112, 132; concept of ethnicity used in, 8–9; conflict in refugee communities and, 4, 8, 111; diversity in ethnic communities and, 8, 90–91, 153; Indochinese refugees and reconsideration of, 7–9, 153–54; local urban conditions and, 9; overview of theory of, 4–5; political interests and participation and, 92; racial conflict and, 90–91; work experience and economic achievement in, 8, 134, 150, 154
Europa Publications, 155
European refugees, 1, 5, 71, 101
Family and kinship, 112–33; adaptation process and, 112, 132; age seniority and, 112, 127–28; Amerasian youths adaptation and, 123–24; assimilation model and, 3–4, 112; Cambodian refugees and, 23, 113–16, 144–45; changing relationships

The Author

Jeremy Hein is associate professor of sociology at the University of Wisconsin–Eau Claire. He received his B.A. from Hampshire College in 1983 and his M.A. and Ph.D. from Northwestern University, the latter in 1989. Specializing in international migration, racial and ethnic minorities, and comparative historical sociology, he has received funding for his research from the National Science Foundation and the Centre National de la Recherche Scientifique. He is the author of *States and International Migrants* (1992), which compares the origins of American and French resettlement policies and their impact on Indochinese refugees.

The Editor

Thomas J. Archdeacon is professor of history at the University of Wisconsin-Madison, where he has been a member of the faculty since 1972. A native of New York City, he earned his doctorate from Columbia University under the direction of Richard B. Morris. His first book, *New York City, 1664–1710: Conquest and Change* (1976), examines relations between Dutch and English residents of that community during the late seventeenth and early eighteenth centuries. Building on that work, he has increasingly concentrated his research and teaching on topics related to immigration and ethnic-group relations. In 1983 he published *Becoming American: An Ethnic History.*